Trauma Informed Classrooms

Trauma Informed Classrooms

What We Say and Do Matters

Edited by

Katia González and Rhoda Frumkin

BRILL

LEIDEN | BOSTON

Cover illustration: Photograph by Lexi Zang

All chapters in this book have undergone peer review.

Library of Congress Cataloging-in-Publication Data

Names: Gonzalez, Katia, 1973- editor. | Frumkin, Rhoda, 1949- editor.
Title: Trauma informed classrooms : what we say and do matters / Edited by Katia González and Rhoda Frumkin.
Description: Leiden ; Boston : Brill, [2021] | Includes bibliographical references and index.
Identifiers: LCCN 2021021502 (print) | LCCN 2021021503 (ebook) | ISBN 9789004465343 (paperback) | ISBN 9789004465350 (hardback) | ISBN 9789004465367 (ebook)
Subjects: LCSH: Affective education. | Psychic trauma in children. | Psychic trauma in adolescence. | Classroom environment. | Teacher-student relationships.
Classification: LCC LB1072 .T73 2021 (print) | LCC LB1072 (ebook) | DDC 370.15/34--dc23
LC record available at https://lccn.loc.gov/2021021502
LC ebook record available at https://lccn.loc.gov/2021021503

Typeface for the Latin, Greek, and Cyrillic scripts: "Brill". See and download: brill.com/brill-typeface.

ISBN 978-90-04-46534-3 (paperback)
ISBN 978-90-04-46535-0 (hardback)
ISBN 978-90-04-46536-7 (e-book)

Copyright 2021 by Koninklijke Brill NV, Leiden, The Netherlands.
Koninklijke Brill NV incorporates the imprints Brill, Brill Nijhoff, Brill Hotei, Brill Schöningh, Brill Fink, Brill mentis, Vandenhoeck & Ruprecht, Böhlau Verlag and V&R Unipress.
All rights reserved. No part of this publication may be reproduced, translated, stored in a retrieval system, or transmitted in any form or by any means, electronic, mechanical, photocopying, recording or otherwise, without prior written permission from the publisher. Requests for re-use and/or translations must be addressed to Koninklijke Brill NV via brill.com or copyright.com.

This book is printed on acid-free paper and produced in a sustainable manner.

Contents

Preface VII
Acknowledgments XIII
List of Figures and Tables XIV
Notes on Contributors XV
Reflections: Exercises XX

1 Trauma-Informed Early Childhood Classrooms: A Balanced Approach to Fuel Resilience in the Child and Teacher 1
　Helen Mele Robinson and Loreta Andersen

2 The Tiniest Tears: Grief and Loss in Childhood 26
　Carolyn Oglio-Taverner

3 Techniques for Creating Trauma-Sensitive Learning Environments for Children 59
　Jennifer Lauria

4 Mindfulness in the Trauma Informed Classroom: Using Yoga and Meditation to Infuse Classrooms with Coping Skills, Resilience, Self-Expression, and Safety 94
　Deryn A. Susman

5 The Fine Arts and Teaching Efficacy: Creativity and Decision-Making 117
　Kathleen M. Palladino

6 The Impact of Social Support on First Year Teacher Development 149
　Eman Metwally

7 Collaboration across Disciplines to Treat Children Exposed to Adverse Childhood Experiences 169
　Karen Prihoda

8 A Call for Trauma-Informed Understanding at Colleges and Universities 205
　Ange Concepcion and Kevin Nadolski

9 Trauma-Informed Classrooms: An Empathic Approach 226
   Vanessa Smith-Washington and Edna Aurelus

Index 241

Preface

The topic of trauma-informed classrooms is an important one. Now more than ever, schools are seeing an increase of students exposed to stressors (what may be considered toxic stressors) and ways it impacts students' learning and development. Trauma is often defined as "… any event that is experienced by an individual as physically or emotionally harmful because the individual perceives his life or the life of someone he loves as threatened. Traumatic events include: community violence, domestic violence, sex trafficking, serious medical illness, natural disasters, neglect, physical abuse, displacement and refugee trauma, school violence, sexual abuse, terrorism, loss of a loved one/traumatic grief, psychological maltreatment" (Pickens & Tschopp, 2017, p. 1).

The ability of educators to provide a nurturing environment to support students' cognitive, social-emotional, and physical well-being can impact not only the classroom as a learning space but may also have a long lasting effect on children and families. In addition, educators are seeking ways to not only support students during traumatic events but also provide an environment and skills to help students manage stressors related to trauma.

There is a concentrated effort in schools to target students' overall mental health by focusing on ways in which individualized and group experiences, together with specific partnerships and support systems, could impact learning and growth. Many educators are seeking ways to not only become better informed on this topic but also gain specific knowledge and skills to create safe and nurturing learning spaces. The need for educators to consider students' developmental stages and individual needs as they search for appropriate resources is paramount. Attention to culturally responsive practices and ways in which intercultural connections are established are important factors impacting ways in which educators can support the individual and group needs of families and students.

This book provides readers with the opportunity to explore how trauma impacts students' cognition and overall growth, the meaning of trauma-informed classrooms and how to create nurturing spaces, ways in which different stakeholders can collaborate in the development of spaces that are supportive, and a special section on how stressors in the classroom can be minimized to support overall well-being in students. In addition, many of the chapters related to common stressors in communities and schools are included, along with chapters targeting ways in which specific strategies can be implemented in classrooms to minimize triggers. Although most of the book specifically focuses on younger grades and students, a chapter is included related to ways in which higher education can nurture and support students in college campuses.

As chapters were being finalized for inclusion into this book, the world, as we knew it, was forever changed. Covid 19 invaded our spaces, and forced all of us to maintain social distance, be mindful of the many ways our actions could impact the welfare of those we know and care about, and be especially conscious, supportive and thoughtful of those we did not know. Covid 19 created a change of society's norms and familiar structures and added many challenges to our daily lives. The need for much needed routines to create a sense of normalcy became essential as we all came together to address this new challenge. This situation is clearly one that is unprecedented.

For educators, Covid 19 created new stressors that may have not been present before, both personally and professionally. Educators in Pre K -12 settings had to quickly create effective partnerships with families, similar to a co-teaching experience, considering how to translate evidence- based classroom practices to an online environment.

In addition, educators had to make decisions on ways to create online classroom spaces that met the various needs of students while creating community in a time of great distress.

Pitts (2020) explained how, as a teacher, feeling "… helpless during this time" did not create feelings of being "…helpless as a teacher" (#1). As Pitts (2020) so eloquently discussed, "…the ending of the physical gathering of our classes does not mean that we cannot still teach critically in critical times" (#6). This new challenge opened the door for further reflection related to barriers that may impact schooling for many, issues of equity and equality, and the very important role of teachers' own well- being and need of support.

Educators became resourceful agents of change, guiding and supporting many students and families while establishing and reinforcing relationships with colleagues as they engaged in a new "working normal." While providing a safe environment for students was crucial, so too it was crucial for educators to develop within that environment the systems that will help students gain the skills and dispositions that will enable them to grow into resilient individuals.

Educators took on an action-oriented stance to put into place structures to enable students to feel supported during these times. The home setting began to serve a dual purpose, as teachers and families became increasingly aware how during these times, it was necessary to also consider the mindset that they and the children needed in order to make this situation successful. The belief that "all of us are in this together" plus a feeling of positivity – a "yes, we can!" attitude – combined to create a willingness to communicate and interact in ways that enable us to move forward.

For students, the adults in their lives became instrumental forces representing and leading the way of this "new normal" and these collaborative practices between all stakeholders could only help. The "new normal" may have looked different on the surface (i.e. masks) but what didn't change was the need for learners to feel safe and supported with educators and family members nurturing their socio-emotional growth in positive ways.

Sometimes, it seems that children/students are the wisest among us. They look for the "sunny side" in their environment and strive to hold onto it. These mini-philosophers envision their surroundings from a bright perspective that makes possible a future filled with a belief that all will soon be well.

In the words of nine-year-old Lexi:

> If there was positivity in the world, everyone would be happy. The world will be a better place. If there was not that much positivity in the world, it would break the bonds between everything and nothing. Being with my family, having fun, creating things, these are my happy things.

Continue on to read and see the creative products that express what Lexi felt when Covid first started.

Poetry by Lexi Zang (2020)

Different Sides
"The light was there. I saw it once, I blinked again and it was gone."

My Sides
"Hope in the light, it was there, bigger than square."

Color in the air
"Color here, color there, color everywhere. I can see it brighter than the sun as it beats down on me, as if we are one."

Feelings
"I have many feelings and so do you. I've got many feelings and we can prove they are true."

I am me
"Me is me. They are they. We all are. Everyone is their own self."

Different days
"We can be ourselves. We can be us. We can be amazing, that's just us."

Flash flash, dash dash
"Flash flash, dash dash. I see it flying in the wind. It never talks only screams of joy come out within."

Chapters Reflections

Some of the authors utilized first person to convey personal experiences and reflections.

Chapter 1
In the first chapter, "Trauma Informed Early Childhood Classrooms: A Balanced Approach to Fuel Resilience in the Child and Teachers," the authors, Helen Robinson and Loreta Andersen begin with the various definition of trauma, ways in which a balanced approach can facilitate the development of nurturing spaces while taking into account the stages of child development. The authors also explore ways in which primary and secondary stressors could impact various stakeholders.

Chapter 2
Carolyn Oglio-Taverner, the author of "The Tiniest Tears: Grief and Loss in Childhood," reminds readers that children, like adults, experience feelings of grief. It is important to allow them to grieve in their own way. When bereaved children are given the opportunity to express their grief in accordance with their own levels of understanding and to be part of events such as memorials and funerals, they are able to remember and celebrate the life of their loved one who is deceased. By listening to grieving children and acknowledging that they, too, are mourners, we communicate to them that they are not alone.

Chapter 3
In "Techniques for Creating Trauma-Sensitive Learning Environments for Children," Jennifer Lauria points to mindfulness methods and a growth mindset approach as effective social-emotional (SEL) supports to promote both healing and self-empowerment in students who have experienced trauma. She introduces a range of techniques that can be used effectively by educators in the classroom and also by caregivers at home. An added focus on wellness for educators and a recommendation for expanded curricula in teacher education programs to prepare future educators to effectively use SEL supports rounds out this timely chapter.

Chapter 4
In "Mindfulness in the Trauma-Informed Classroom," Deryn Sussman calls our attention to the alarming notion that, for American students, stress levels are

at an all-time high. These responses to stress, whether due to environmental factors from home or resulting from school-based stressors, interfere with students' socialization skills as well as with meaningful learning. Some educators have noted that the integration of philosophies and practices of yoga has proven beneficial for assisting students in developing increased resilience and decreased stress and anxiety. Additionally, the focus of yoga on the present moment can help students who have experienced past trauma remain focused on "the now." The chapter concludes with a sampling of yoga techniques, including both traditional practices and author-developed scripts – each adaptable to a range of age groups.

Chapter 5
In "The Fine Arts and Teaching Efficacy: Creativity and Decision Making," Kathellen Palladino discusses ways in which teachers' background in the fine arts may impact their pedagogy and ways in which they address the needs of students exposed to or experiencing trauma. Kathleen provides readers with an opportunity to consider ways in which the fine arts could "guide practices" and the selection of evidence based strategies.

Chapter 6
In "The Impact of Social Supports on First Year Teacher Development," Eman Metwally addresses ways in which mentorship and school support systems could impact the experiences of a first year teacher. Eman, through a reflective lens, explores ways in which the concept of mentorship may not be a "one size fits all" approach and how teachers may need individualized mentorship with different mentors to address various aspects of professional development. This chapter is particularly important at a time in which educators are taken on different roles to meet the various needs of students and families.

Chapter 7
In "Collaboration Across Disciplines to Treat Childhood Exposed to Adverse Childhood Experiences (ACEs)," Karen Phiroda pinpoints the need to research what may impact close collaboration between educators, medical professionals, and social workers to collaborate in providing action plans for students exposed to ACEs. Karen provides insights from these experts on ways they see collaboration happening and some of the barriers that may impact partnerships.

Chapter 8
In "A Call for Trauma-Informed Understanding in Colleges and Universities," Angelica Concepcion and Kevin Nadolski explore the need for higher education to focus on ways to best support Generation Z students who have been

exposed to or have experienced trauma. Connecting theory to practice, the authors provided examples on various ways college campuses can systematically create support systems for students.

Chapter 9

In "Trauma-Informed Classrooms: An Empathic Approach," Vannessa Smith-Washington and Edna Aurelis provide readers with insights into their own perspectives related to the ways in which empathy plays a major role in both their professions. Whether we are considering the teaching or health profession, empathy is discussed as crucial for enabling practitioners to interact successfully with a range of other individuals. The authors draw upon insights from the literature, together with their own personal reflections, to shed light on this matter.

References

Pickens, I. B., & Tschopp, N. (2017). *Trauma-informed classrooms*. National Council of Juvenile and Family Court Judges. https://www.ncjfcj.org/sites/default/files/NCJFCJ_SJP_Trauma_Informed_Classrooms_Final.pdf

Pitts, J. (2020, May 15). Teaching as activism, teaching as care. *Teaching Tolerance*. https://www.tolerance.org/magazine/teaching-as-activism-teaching-as-care

Wissman, K. K., & Wiseman, A. M. (2011). "That's my worst nightmare": Poetry and trauma in the middle school classroom. *Pedagogies: An International Journal, 6*(3), 234–249. doi:10.1080/1554480X.2011.579051

Acknowledgments

Thanks to our families, friends, students, and colleagues for always providing ongoing feedback and engaging in important discussions related to the profession. A big appreciation to Ted, Mia, Ma, Harvey, and Suzanne for their love and support.

Special thanks and love to Lexi Zang for the insightful poems and for the cover.

Figures and Tables

Figures

1.1 The ACE study pyramid.   4
1.2 Association between ACEs and negative outcomes.   5
4.1 Have students write positive attributes of their best selves to reference throughout the school day.   110
4.2 On an inhale, bring the hands into a heart position. On an exhale, close the hands into fists.   114
4.3 Trace the box with your finger, while following the labeled breathing pattern.   115
6.1 Pedagogical and emotional support for new teachers.   164
7.1 Effects of ACEs on a child (blue: short-term effects; orange: challenges to collaboration; red: long-term effects).   196

Tables

3.1 Mindfulness resources and beginning techniques for educators.   66
3.2 Children's literature on mindfulness, meditation, and social and emotional learning elements.   70
3.3 Recommended works of children's literature for exploring growth mindsets.   81
5.1 Background of participants.   135
5.2 Reflection on fine art strategies observed during the study.   136
5.3 An analysis of common themes among lesson plans collected.   138
5.4 An analysis of common themes among open-ended surveys given.   139
6.1 Dispositions.   158
6.2 Mentorship.   160
6.3 Experience.   161
7.1 Impacts of ACEs social-emotional and physical health.   184
7.2 Collaboration of experts.   187
7.3 Interventions.   191
8.1 Institution profiles.   216
8.2 Offices represented on BIT/CARE teams at five institutions.   217

Notes on Contributors

Loreta Andersen
(Ed.D.) has a doctorate in Instructional Leadership from St. John's University, Queens, New York. She has worked as an early childhood educator in both private and public schools and as an adjunct assistant professor in the School of Education, Department of Curriculum and Instruction at the City University of New York–College of Staten Island. Dr. Andersen's research focuses on developing positive social leadership skills in early childhood students within multi-cultural urban school settings. She is highly interested in understanding and developing empathy and emotional resilience in young children. Dr. Loreta Andersen continues to share her knowledge though presentations and workshops at conferences and symposiums.

Edna Aurelus
is an Assistant Professor and alumna at Wagner College. Dr. Aurelus has a Doctorate in Advanced Nursing Practice from Arizona State University and a post-doctorate degree in Psychiatric Mental Health Nurse Practitioner. Dr. Aurelus is dually board certified from the American Nurses Credentialing Center (ANCC) as a Family Nurse Practitioner and Psychiatric Mental Health Nurse Practitioner.

Dr. Aurelus' extensive experience in psychiatry includes the old St. Vincent Hospital known now as Richmond University Medical Center (RUMC), South Beach Psychiatric Center, Banner Behavioral Health Hospital and Perryville Prison, the only state female prison in Arizona. She is currently the Lead Professor for the psychiatric nursing course at Wagner. She is the author of multiple peer-reviewed articles. Dr. Aurelus adopts the concept of psychological safety and empathy in her classroom to encourage students to participate in class discussion without any fear. She is aware of how stressful and traumatic experiences can be affect learning. She is very vocal for women empowerment through education and social justice, which is one of the many reasons she started her own foundation in her native country in 2014 called EVS Smile Foundation.

Ange Concepcion
is the Assistant Dean of Campus Life at Wagner College, located on Staten Island, NY. She has been a college student affairs administrator for nearly a decade, working primarily in housing & residential life and student conduct. Her research interests include sexual assault prevention, Title IX, change management, leadership development, and Catholic higher education leadership.

Ange received her B.S. in Physics from Loyola University Chicago, M.S.Ed. in Higher Education Administration & Policy from Northwestern University, and a Ph.D. in Administration and Supervision, Church and Non-Public School Leadership from Fordham University.

Rhoda Frumkin
(Ed.D.) received her doctorate from Rutgers University in New Jersey. She is Professor and Director of Student Teaching and Professional Field Experiences of the Education Department at Wagner College in New York. Her expertise is in literacy learning and special education. Her research interests include culturally responsive practices and intercultural partnerships and the impact of literacy learning in students and families.

Katia González
(Ed.D.) received her doctorate from Columbia University-Teachers College in New York. She is Professor and Chair of the Education Department at Wagner College in New York and serves as Director of Graduate Education Programs. Her expertise is in early childhood special education, curriculum development and culturally responsive practices in teacher education. Her research interests include the role of intercultural communication and culturally responsive practices in schools, strategies and techniques to enhance and measure critical thinking, and the impact of community and family in inclusive education.

Jennifer Lauria
(Ed.D.) recently completed her 18th year as a Professor of Education, departmental administrator, and community-engaged scholar at Wagner College in New York City. Prior to her tenure at Wagner College, Dr. Lauria taught diverse Pre K-5 student populations at P.S. 22 in the New York City public school system for 9 years. Currently, she has embarked on a new professional chapter as an educational entrepreneur working as an educational consultant, innovative learning specialist, and Chief Executive Officer of her newly founded consultancy firm, Dr. Jennifer Lauria, LLC. In her new roles, she provides educational leadership, professional development, and instructional support to district and school building leaders, faculty, students, and families. Selected areas of expertise include: leadership, teacher education, innovative pedagogy, curriculum development, educational technologies, program evaluation, health and wellness for educators, cultivating respectful learning environments, and mindfulness methods as SEL supports.

Eman Metwally
is a Learning Specialist at Staten Island Academy in New York. Ms Metwally holds a dual Bachelors degree in English and General/Special Childhood Education

and has completed her Master's Degree at Wagner College in Early Childhood and Special Education. Ms Metwally's passion is closely collaborating with families and students to engage in intercultural connections. Ms Metwally has participated in field experiences in the tri-state area, and has been a part of many afterschool programs dedicated to student advancement and success. In addition, Ms Metwally has traveled to Barcelona Spain, to experience first hand the importance of different modalities of learning and culturally responsive practices. Her thesis titled "The Impact of Social Support on First Year Teacher Development: A Case Study," examined the role of support systems and mentorship and its impact on a teacher's first year experience. Her passion lies in creating an innovative and supportive environment, for both teachers and students, to thrive and find their potential.

Fr. Kevin Nadolski
(OSFS) is a priest with the Oblates of St. Francis de Sales and was born and raised in Philadelphia, PA. A graduate of Temple University, Catholic University of America, and DeSales School of Theology, Fr. Nadolski holds degrees in journalism, theology, and education administration. He also holds a Ph.D. from Fordham University in Administration and Supervision, Church and Non-Public School Leadership.

Fr. Nadolski has worked as a teacher and principal in Catholic high schools and also served as vocation director, director of the seminary, director of development and communications, and assistant provincial for the Oblates in Wilmington, DE. He presently serves at DeSales University as Vice President for Mission and Assistant Professor of Education.

Carolyn Oglio-Taverner
is currently the Director of the Wagner College Early Childhood Center. She holds a Master's degree in Developmental Psychopathology from Columbia University, Teachers' College and a Ph.D. in Developmental Psychology from the Graduate Center, City University of New York. Along with her position as Director, she is also an Adjunct Professor of Psychology at Wagner College, teaching courses in Child Psychology and Death and Dying, and a founding member of Emma's Place, Staten Island Grief Center, a not-for-profit agency which offers free counselling services to children and families who have suffered losses in their lives.

Kathleen M. Palladino
is a graduate from Wagner College (B.A. '18 and M.S.Ed. '19) and holds an M.S.Ed. in Early Childhood Education/Special Education and a B.A. in Childhood Education 1–6/Special Education 1–6 and Spanish. She is currently a

nursery school teacher at St. Patrick Catholic Academy in Bay Ridge, Brooklyn. As an educator, she is dedicated to incorporating the arts into classroom life and to creating safe, nurturing environments that allow each child to flourish individually and as a group.

Karen Prihoda
is currently a middle school special education teacher in Staten Island, New York She holds a Bachelor's degree in Childhood Education, Special Education and Spanish and a Master's degree in Early Childhood Education and Special Education from Wagner College in New York. Along with her teaching position, she also works with a non-profit in Trenton, New Jersey to provide summer camp and after school activities for children in low income neighborhoods.

Helen Mele Robinson
(Ph.D.) has her doctorate in Language, Literacy and Learning from Fordham University. As a tenured assistant professor with twenty plus years in higher education she has taught foundational courses, curriculum courses and guided pre-service teachers in their fieldwork. Dr. Robinson has shared her knowledge and presented at regional, national and international conferences. Dr. Robinson's research and publications focus on an array of topics including preparing culturally responsive pre-service teachers, exploring the influence of technology on young children, as well as the current chapter examining the impact of trauma on the young child.

Vannessa Smith-Washington
is an Assistant Professor of Education at Wagner College in New York. Dr. Smith-Washington holds a Master's Degree in Reading Education (K-12) from CUNY Queens College, a Masters' in School Leadership from Long Island University, Brooklyn Campus and a Doctorate in School Leadership and Curriculum Instruction from the University of Phoenix.

Dr. Smith-Washington's passion is to mentor, train and supervise pre-service and novice teachers. She is permanently New York City and New York State certified in Special Education (K-12), Reading Education and School/District Leadership. She has worked closely with teachers, clinicians, school supervisors, administrators and parents and is a strong advocate for children and continues her research in teacher resiliency and mentorship.

Deryn A. Susman
is a 2019 graduate from Wagner College's Undergraduate Education Department, after studying theater and childhood education. During her final year at Wagner, Susman focused her studies around bringing mindfulness and Yoga to

the classrooms she worked in, culminating in a written thesis on this matter. To help with the research process, Susman enrolled in the Breathe for Change 200-Hour Yoga Instructor Certification: a program intended to teach educators how to inform their teaching practices with a Yoga practice. Susman has completed extensive research on trauma informed teaching and Yoga practices, in addition to a 20-Hour Trauma Informed Yoga Certification with Feet on the Ground in 2020. Susman is now a first grade teacher with Achievement First, and working towards a Masters in the Art of Teaching at Relay College. Susman has a very active instagram page related to her pedagogical practices @MissDeryn.

Reflections: Exercises

Below are scenarios that are based on actual situations. Read each scenario and consider the circumstances provided. Respond to each question or prompt. Include a rationale for each response. We encourage you to reflect on these scenarios before and after reading the chapters for further reflection.

Scenario #1

The following is the reflection of a classroom teacher who just found out that her school is closing due to the pandemic:

> The school is closing down; today will be our last day at the school because of major health concerns. We just heard that when we leave for the day, we should take with us whatever we will need to continue teaching our classes from home. Workshops will be provided to help us to transition from face-to-face instruction to a completely virtual format.
>
> My first response is concern for my students. How do they feel right now? This change is so abrupt. How will they adjust to this change to online learning?
>
> My next response feels really selfish. How will I handle this? I've just gotten used to teaching my own class – without a cooperating teacher with whom I can co-plan. There is no student teaching supervisor with whom to meet to discuss next steps, and no colleagues to meet for lunch and a chat about how best to teach the next math unit.
>
> I'm worried, and feel stressed.

Questions for discussion:
1. My students will not be returning to school tomorrow. They just found out about this, and they look confused and unsure about what will happen next. What can I do and say RIGHT NOW to support them?
2. I have a great relationship with my students. I am so glad that I get along well with their families. How can I keep up these connections with my students and their families? I am not at all certain that I can keep positive relationships going and teach effectively online. I am feeling a lot of doubt about my abilities, and am worried that I can't do it all. Now what?

REFLECTIONS: EXERCISES　　　　　　　　　　　　　　　　　　　　　　　　XXI

Scenario #2

One of the students in your freshman learning community seems to be having some difficulty in adjusting to the college environment. He has been absent repeatedly and has missed handing in several assignments. He seldom contributes to class discussions, and you have noticed that he walks out alone when class is over. You are wondering what steps you should take, if any, to support this student.

Questions for discussion:
1. Discuss factors that may be contributing to this student's difficulty in adjusting to college.
2. Discuss the kinds of supports that colleges and universities often have in place at the beginning of the first year to help students to make a smooth transition from high school to college.
3. You know that your college sends out a form after the first six weeks of classes for faculty to use for reporting any concerns about specific students. You are wondering whether you should report your concerns now, wait two more weeks to receive the form and then report your concerns, whether you should speak with this student, or whether you should not intervene at all. Discuss your rationale for the choice you make as well as any choice you reject.

Scenario #3

Below is the written text of an interview between Mr. Z, a classroom teacher of a 3rd and 4th grade self-contained special education 12:1:1 class – 12 students, one teacher, and one paraprofessional – in a public school in New York City, and Mr. X, a graduate student. Mr. X developed the interview questions, and Mr. Z responded shortly after the school was closed as a result of the pandemic. After the school closure, the students received all instruction in a virtual format.

1. *How have you and your students adjusted to this new reality of virtual teaching and learning? What does your virtual classroom look like, and how have administrators stepped in to support their teachers and students?*

It took about 3-4 weeks before all of the students had devices and Wi-Fi. At first, it was very overwhelming for the students and myself because the expectations were not clear. We rolled it out within two days and it was not seamless.

There was a lot of connection by phone at first. We would check on the students and families to see if they were safe. We would then inquire about the process to receive a device, and direct them to resources so that they could attain one. It is now week 12 and everyone has figured out how to log on and access assignments. Some of the students are inconsistent in completing assignments and the quality of the work is inconsistent as well. Some students will write paragraphs using the tools and resources given, while others may say, "hi," or post an expletive on the stream. We use Google Classroom and it reminds me of Blackboard for college students. This is troublesome for students who have issues following directions, reading and doing their work independently. There is a Google Meets option that is used to encourage discussion and to check in with the students and families. We were directed not to mimic the school day in regards to having 50-minute periods of teaching one after the other. My administration has been extremely understanding and supportive during this time. They had realistic goals and gave us extended time to get things in order. They supplied multiple resources for lesson ideas and allowed us to share resources with each other. They were available at all times via email, phone, or chat. They encouraged us to invite them into Google Meets so that they could participate. They called families that we had trouble contacting and they also met with us weekly to give updates and review protocols. They gave us the autonomy to set up our classrooms as we wished and then provided feedback from that point.

2. *What kind of techniques are you using to establish a positive virtual learning environment and how are you able to maintain student engagement and motivation during these trying times?*

We (my paras and myself) offer feedback to every assignment and comment made by each student. It is a challenge because students don't really respond back as they would in class and they rarely make comments to each other. When we notice that a student is having trouble we will call home to either walk them through the issue, or reiterate content. There are a lot of social emotional learning assignments in addition to academic assignments. This is a traumatic time for students, families, and teachers, so it is necessary to present an outlet for them to express their feelings and have us address them. The school provides Google Meets sessions for parents to speak to a social worker weekly about different issues such as grief, adjustment, and time management. Compliments and phone calls with praise have been a way that we engage and motivate students. We also post photos and videos of us from class to convey that this is a continuation of the learning we did in school and not an end to the school year.

3. *What kind of assessment tools or techniques are you utilizing in your virtual classroom?*

Each assignment is reviewed and feedback is given by the teacher. Numerical grades do not bear as much of an importance at this time. Giving a student a 53 may discourage them from logging on and trying since this is a new concept. Feedback, however, commends the student for what they did well and then provides viable next steps to improve. The DOE is not assigning numerical grades this semester. The third marking period will be graded as "S" for "Satisfactory" or "N" for "Needs Improvement." The average for the school year will be written as "Meets Grade Level Standards" or "Needs Improvement." Since this was a new system, grades are not valued as much as noted errors and ways to fix those deficits.

4. *As a 3rd and 4th grade special education 12:1:1 self-contained classroom teacher, how have you been able to teach responsively and differentiate instruction to meet students' IEP goals? What kind of additional challenges have you found yourself facing during this new process of remote teaching working with students with special needs?*

I have assigned different tasks based on the reading levels of the students. The math content allows for students to begin at the same level prior to remote learning. There are many visuals posted, videos for auditory learning, and some class projects that allow students to use manipulatives and tactile materials to create a project. It was a struggle to reach each goal of each student because they are not in front of me in the classroom. Their level of independence and attention span is minimal. I am not there to give verbal prompts or redirect them to the correct entry point. Some students are clearly getting help from someone at home. I see this as valuable, but some parents and siblings don't understand how to scaffold and release control so that the work is authentically their own. Some students use Google to find answers and paste what Siri states. Monitoring their working habits is a struggle. OT goals are hard for those providers because you need to be in-person to do physical activities. The OT has posted videos of exercises, yoga, and meditations which I've posted on my class wall. It is hard to encourage students to meet their goals when they type a few words and then log off.

5. *There has been much controversy surrounding Governor Cuomo's recent remarks regarding his mission to "reimagine education" with Bill Gates, focusing on the further implementation of technology in teaching practices. After this experience of teaching virtually during the pandemic, would you consider yourself a*

promoter of virtual instruction? Should New York City revolutionize the education system?

I believe the pandemic has allowed teachers and students alike to become very familiar with using technology as a learning tool. I would support a blended learning experience where Google Classroom and other modalities are used to support what is done in the physical classroom. It can in no way replace the system of learning that takes place between a teacher and his or her class in a physical environment. When students have an array of issues to be met (e.g. academic, emotional and social), those needs cannot be met behind a computer screen or over the phone. Besides academic progress, teachers and students form a bond that encourages them to persevere and meet demands. This is an asset that can only be developed in person in a physical setting. Students need human contact, social interaction, and time to express themselves to teachers and their peers. New York City should use this stepping stone as a way to encourage students and teachers to be more technologically savvy. Since most students and teachers were given devices that allow for online learning, they should be able to keep them so that half the battle is won right there. After everyone has an equal technological playing field, the revolution can take place. There has to be a brick and mortar setting where real relationships can develop. Students need a place to go to besides their homes or rooms. They need to make friends and bond with teachers. I think the DOE can utilize technology more often, but as a supplement to the school setting, not a replacement.

Reflections from Mr. X, a graduate student:

Mr. Z continues to inspire me through his highly effective teaching practices as well as his answers to our interview. This interview really opened my eyes to the real-world struggles teachers can face without warning and with the expectation of finding ways to keep students engaged in a virtual environment. I was relieved to hear that through all the struggles of the initial confusion due to the pandemic, Mr. Z's school community were able to collaborate and reach out to parents and guardians of students to ensure everyone's safety, as well as having an education action plan in place. It seems like the administrators really "stepped up to the plate," so I give credit to Mr. Z and the wonderful staff at the school for a job well done. I was also relieved to read that the typical grading system has been eliminated, allowing for both teachers and students to emphasize true learning rather than focusing on students being able to meet a particular numerical grade. I was especially interested in Mr. Z's answer to #3, since it is hard enough to teach a classroom of students virtually, and yet Mr. Z has the challenge of teaching students with individualized special needs in a remote way. Although I think Mr. Z has done a great job of adapting and managing each students' progress to meet their IEP goals, I do think that there will need to be some additional resources for teachers who work in special education to have more of an impact on their students during a remote teaching experience. I wholeheartedly agree with Mr. Z's answer to question #5. Even before the pandemic, there has been a technological revolution occurring in our world, and our reliance on technology is only going to increase in all aspects, including education. In many ways, the pandemic has forced an educational revolution, and that's not necessarily such a bad thing. As Mr. Z touched upon, every student should have access to technological resources, however, technology will never be able to replace the benefits of physical instruction, for learning content and for social development. A hybrid or blended learning experience could be the future of New York City education, and I think both Mr. Z and I would both fully support it.

Questions for discussion:
1. Do you agree with Mr. Z's opinion that a hybrid or blended experience "could be the future of New York City education?" Why or why not?
2. Do you think that a "hybrid or blended experience" is the best option for students with special needs? Why or why not?
3. How can Mr. Z help his students to maintain engagement and sustain attention during the virtual lessons?
4. A paraprofessional is assigned to this class. How can the paraprofessional provide support to increase engagement and learning opportunities for the students?

CHAPTER 1

Trauma-Informed Early Childhood Classrooms
A Balanced Approach to Fuel Resilience in the Child and Teacher

Helen Mele Robinson and Loreta Andersen

Abstract

This chapter explores understanding different types of trauma students may have experienced or are experiencing and the impact such trauma has on the developing child. Details are presented about several research studies which focus on childhood abuse, neglect, and home/community challenges and how such adverse childhood experiences affect the behaviors of children within educational settings. How students exhibit challenging behaviors in the classroom or school setting resulting from trauma is considered. The need for an effective developmentally appropriate, balanced approach to fuel resilience using a dynamic process within and between individuals and their environment is addressed in depth. In the early childhood classroom setting, teachers are informed about how to utilize trauma-informed strategies to be able to provide a trusting, safe classroom environment which allows children to thrive. The effects of secondary traumatic stress on teachers/caregivers due to prolonged exposure from nurturing, caring, and supporting their traumatized students is also discussed. Suggestions and approaches based on research are given to offer teachers ways to provide themselves with self-care that promote resilience and a pathway for success in their quest as educators.

Keywords

early childhood – trauma informed – resilience – adversity – pedagogy – support – child development

1 Understanding Trauma in the Developing Child

To begin to discuss the issue of trauma-informed classrooms, an understanding of the meaning of what trauma is needs to be considered. Trauma is a response to a negative external event or series of events which exceeds the child's regular coping skills (McInerney & McKlindon, 2019). A young child witnessing an event that threatens the life or physical security of a loved one can also be traumatic, as their sense of safety depends on the perceived safety of their parents and caregivers (Lieberman & Van Horn, 2009; National Child Traumatic Stress Network Schools Committee [NCTSNSC], 2019). The definition of trauma that focuses on young children describes the experience of and highlights the factors that influence the perception of trauma and focuses on developmental facets of young children (Center of Early Childhood Mental Health Consultation, 2019). Traumatic experiences may include neglect, physical and sexual abuse, bullying, community-based violence, extreme poverty, the loss of a parent or primary caretaker, or natural disasters (Felitti et al., 1998). Traumatic experiences can impact brain development and behavior inside and outside of the classroom (McInerney & McKlindon, 2019).

A traumatic event is an incident that causes physical, emotional, spiritual, or psychological harm (Cafasso, 2016). There are three classifications for trauma: acute trauma, chronic trauma and crossover trauma. Type I or acute trauma is a traumatic event that happens one time, consisting of events such as a car accident, death of a loved one, or being the victim of a crime or a natural disaster. An acute trauma response has also been referred to as Post Traumatic Stress Disorder (Center for Early Childhood Mental Health Consultation, 2019). Type II or chronic trauma is repetitive trauma which occurs over an extended period (Statman-Weil & Sorrels, 2018; Poag, 2018). Chronic trauma can occur when an individual experiences multiple traumatic incident such as abuse and neglect, or having cancer or being in a natural disaster (NCTSNS, 2008; Oklahoma Department of Mental Health & Substance Abuse Services, 2014). Another aspect of Type II trauma is complex trauma which is like chronic trauma but occurs earlier in life, from birth to age 6, and is often perpetrated by a caregiver or other trusted individual (NCTSNS, 2008). Chronic and complex trauma include traumatic experiences such as child abuse, neglect, emotional abuse, physical abuse, or witnessing domestic violence, and could also be caused by exposure to community violence or war (Statman-Weil & Sorrels, 2018; Poag, 2018). Type III trauma is known as Crossover Trauma and is the result of a single event that is traumatic enough to produce a long-lasting impact. This includes experiences such as a school shooting with mass casualties, car accident with fatalities, or refugee relocation (Crisis Prevention Institute [CPI], 2017).

2   Adverse Childhood Experiences

Research of how trauma experienced during childhood could impact an adult's well-being initially began with a survey administered by Dr. Vincent Felitti in

1985 (Stevens, 2012). In an effort to understand why patients were dropping out of his obesity program, he asked a list of questions. One question he asked a female patient had an unexpected response: "What age were you when you became sexually active? The patient tearfully responded, "It was when I was four years old, with my father" (Stevens, 2012, para. 10). This response and pivotal experience began Dr. Felitti's twenty-five-year journey to understand the connection between childhood trauma and subsequent mental and physical health problems of adults. Dr. Felitti began working with medical epidemiologist Dr. Robert Anda and the Centers for Disease Control (CDC) to conduct a groundbreaking study that focused on childhood abuse, neglect and household challenges and the impact on later-life. This longitudinal study included over 17,000 Health Maintenance Organization members from Southern California receiving physical exams and completing confidential surveys regarding their childhood experiences and current health status and behaviors. The study focused on adverse experiences that occurred in childhood (Stevens, 2012).

According to the CDC (2019), Adverse Childhood Experiences, or ACEs, are potentially traumatic events that occur in childhood from 0–17 years. ACE traumatic events include experiencing abuse, neglect, or violence, witnessing violence in the home, or having a family member attempt or die by suicide. Stressors in the home environment that can undermine a child's sense of safety, stability, and bonding include growing up in a household with substance abuse, mental health problems, or instability (CDC, 2019). The ACE Study revealed that "adverse experiences in childhood were very common, even in the white middle-class, and that these experiences are linked to every major chronic illness and social problem that the United States grapples with – and spends billions of dollars on" (Stevens, 2012, para. 7).

For the Adverse Childhood Experiences Study questionnaire, study participants responded to questions in three categories concerning aspects of child abuse, household challenges, and neglect. Participants were given a score of "1" for each negative experience to which they responded "Yes. A participant's score had a cumulative effect on health and overall life experiences" (Herbert, Peterson, & Dunsmore, 2019, p. 4). As noted in Figure 1.1, the study results indicated that as the number of ACEs increases, so does the possibility of negative outcomes of risky health behaviors, chronic health conditions, low quality of life potential, and early death (CDC, 2019). The ACE Study (CDC, 2019) results revealed that ACEs influence health and well-being throughout an individual's lifespan.

The ACE Study (CDC, 2019) findings suggest that adverse childhood experiences are major risk factors for the leading causes of illness, disability and death as well as poor quality of life in the United States. An adult who has experienced childhood trauma, in particular chronic trauma and complex trauma,

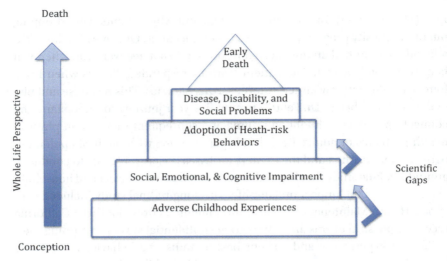

FIGURE 1.1   The ACE study pyramid

has a far greater chance of experiencing issues with mental illness or substance abuse, are less likely to complete their education or be gainfully employed, and are more likely to have physical health problems than their non-abused peer (Putnam, 2006). Figure 1.2 represents the array of health and social problems that have been documented to have a causal relationship to ACE Score Risk Factors. This includes anxiety, depression, smoking, obesity, alcohol abuse, alcoholism, illegal drug use, IV drug abuse, suicide attempts, intimate partner violence, hallucinations, teen and unintended pregnancies, spontaneous abortion, or fetal death (Anda, n.d.). Understanding that these health and social issues are a consequence of ACEs, and reducing ACEs will significantly improve the health of the general population in the United States (CDC, 2019).

As presented in the 2011/2012 National Survey of Children's Health, in the United States approximately 35 million children, ages 0–17, have been exposed to one or more adverse childhood experiences. In 2015, the CDC estimated that cases of substantiated child maltreatment would generate consequences that cost the United States $428 billion (Committee on Oversight and Reform, 2019). A proactive perspective for these staggering figures is currently being reviewed by the House of Representatives Committee on Oversight and Reform (2019). In his hearing testimony, Pennsylvania House of Representatives Committee member Frank Keller declared that childhood trauma is preventable and treatable; the effects of traumatic experiences can be identified, the damage can be healed, and children who have experienced trauma can become thriving and productive adults. The committee is seeking additional federal funding to enable the development of a whole-child comprehensive approach for

FIGURE 1.2   Association between ACEs and negative outcomes

identifying, treating and preventing childhood trauma ("Identifying, preventing, and treating childhood trauma …," 2019).

The existence of ACEs in a child's environment will not definitively result in a child experiencing negative health and quality of life outcomes. The impact of positive influences and environmental factors need to be present to ameliorate and prevent the many possible negative health and life outcomes (CDC, 2019). Lessons learned from the ACE study offer implications for improving educational practices to provide students with the tools for resilience in the face of adversity and a culture of trauma-sensitive schools (Herbert et al., 2019, p. 4).

3   A Balanced Approach in the Early Childhood Classroom

To victims, trauma is not an event that happened in the past; the experience leaves an imprint on the mind, brain, and body. This imprint has consequences for how an individual manages to survive in the present (van der Kolk, 2014, p. 21). When schools understand the educational impact of trauma, they can make trauma sensitivity a regular part of how a school operates. This helps provide a safe, supportive environment where students can make positive connections with adults and peers (Massachusetts Advocates for Children and Harvard Law School, n.d.). A school can support all children to feel safe physically, intellectually, emotionally and socially, which are the four major domains of child development (Massachusetts Advocates for Children and Harvard Law School, n.d.; Davidson, 2019). The acronym for the physical, intellectual, emotional, and social developmental areas is P.I.E.S. The physical development of a child addresses body awareness, small motor skills and large motor skills. Intellectually, the cognitive development of a child focuses on the mind and brain with abilities such as creative thinking skills, language and literacy, problem solving, and following directions. The emotional development of a child includes identifying and expressing feelings, a positive self-concept, and understanding the feelings of others. Social development comprises skills such as sharing, cooperation, social interaction with others, following appropriate behaviors, and turn-taking. In an early childhood school setting, the four domain areas of development need to be supported equally (Graybill, 2105).

To reflect on the topic of P.I.E.S. and a teacher offering a balanced curriculum, think about your own school experience. For example, how did your high school science teacher meet your P.I.E.S. areas of development? When planning to teach, do you think your high school science teacher gave attention to your development beyond your cognitive growth? Did your teacher create an environment that equally supported your physical, intellectual, emotional, and social development? In an early childhood classroom environment, a teacher creating a balanced learning experience would equally support a child's P.I.E.S. development. Academic subjects would be incorporated for 25% of daily planning. The teacher would allow time during the school day to physically move around (25%) and to engage with other students socially (25%), and opportunities would be planned for children to express their emotions (25%) through art activities, songs during Circle Time, and talking with the teacher. Early childhood educators addressing all areas of a child's development have students primed to succeed in school.

The National Association for the Education of Young Children (NAEYC, 2009) advocates providing educational opportunities for all four domain areas; this can be achieved by providing developmentally appropriate practice (DAP) in the classroom setting. DAP is an approach to teaching that is grounded in research on how young children develop and learn, acknowledging what is individually appropriate, and culturally important, for each child. As stated in the NAEYC DAP Position Statement (2009), all the domains of development and learning – physical, intellectual, emotional, and social – are important and closely interrelated. A child's development and learning in one domain influences and is influenced by what transpires in other domains. This base of knowledge documents the interrelatedness of the developmental domains and the importance of a comprehensive curriculum for a child's well-being and success. Teachers are an integral factor in promoting young children's optimal learning and development, and can do so by offering a high-quality DAP experience for all children (NAEYC, 2009).

Trauma can undermine a child's ability to learn, create healthy attachments, be able to form supportive relationships, and follow classroom expectations (NCTSSNSC, 2008; NAEYC, 2009). The exposure of young children to traumatic situations and the resulting life-long consequences underscore the need for effective, developmentally appropriate interventions that address complex trauma (Holmes, Levy, Smith, Pinne, & Neese, 2014). Teachers understanding how to meet the needs of children who have experienced trauma can enable students to thrive in educational settings (Dorado & Zakrzewski, 2013).

4 Trauma in the Classroom

Recent research (Bethel, Carle, Hudziak, Gombojav, Powers, Wade, & Braverman, 2017) indicates that at least 46.3% of children in America's schools today have experienced, or are experiencing, toxic trauma due to repetitive ACEs within their homes or communities. These youngsters may be either witnessing or are victims of repetitive crime, violence, and/or abuse in their everyday lives. This problem affects not only middle school, junior high, and high school students. Pupils as young as three and four years of age have been, or are being, exposed to frequent traumatic events, such as domestic and community violence (Finkelhor, Turner, Ormond, & Hamby, 2009; Schwartz, & Proctor, 2000). In fact, data collected from a 2003 to 2004 nationwide study across 40 states revealed that the prekindergarten expulsion rate was 3.2 times the rate for K-12 students among youths exhibiting problem behaviors in classrooms.

Children with ACEs may display behaviors that are not considered the norm in general education classrooms. Kicking, hitting, spitting, and/or throwing things at teachers, staff, and classmates are just some of the behaviors that may be presented by youngsters who are victims of adverse experiences within their homes and/or communities (Lieberman, Chu, Van Horn, & Harris, 2011). These children may also retreat within themselves, refusing to do classwork and instead preferring to hide under tables or inside closets, still calling negative attention to themselves and leaving the teacher and the rest of the class confounded with how to handle such situations. Such behavior causes ongoing disturbances within the classroom, with instructional minutes exchanged for time used to calm a child in crisis, usually until the next disruption occurs (Holmes et al., 2015).

Although this troublesome conduct is currently increasing in the early grades (Bethel et al., 2017), the presence of unacceptable behavior has been occurring for decades. There have been several studies (Kim & Cicchetti, 2003; Shonk, & Cicchetti, 2001; Hoffman-Plotkin & Twentyman, 1984) conducted over the past

30 years that highlight the relationship between consistent traumatic events and the risk for academic and behavioral issues. One such study (Darwish, Esquivel, Houtz, & Alfonso, 2001) focused on the social skills of pre-school children during free play. For three months, teachers and therapists watched and recorded the social interactions of 30 preschoolers playing together. Although all the participants came from the same socioeconomic backgrounds, fifteen of the children had a variety of maltreatment experiences prior to the study. Significant differences in social skills were noted between the children who had experienced adverse childhood events and those who did not. Those children with histories of neglect and/or abuse displayed great difficulty with self-control during play and were weak in interpersonal social skills.

The results of a similar study conducted in 2010 by Milot, Ehtier, St-Laurent, and Povost, added additional empirical support to the impact of traumatic experiences on maltreated pre-school children. Using two different questionnaires designed to measure the relationship between manifestation of trauma symptoms and classroom behavior issues in young children (the Trauma Symptom Checklist for Young Children and the Child Behavior Checklist 1 ½–5 years Teacher Report Form), the researchers gathered data about the children's internalizing and externalizing behaviors from answers provided by teachers of the pre-kindergarteners. Two global scales generated from the teachers' responses were then tested for a possible mediating effect of trauma symptoms on the behavior of the pre-school children. The outcomes supported the idea that trauma-related symptoms result from maltreatment as an adverse childhood experience and such an ACE may affect psychosocial development leading to maladjusted classroom behaviors (Milot, Ehtier, St-Laurent, & Povost, 2010).

The effects of maltreatment of young children on academic maladjustment was another focus of research conducted to determine whether young children who were abused or neglected were more at risk for academic problems (Shonk & Cicchetti, 2001). After obtaining teachers' evaluations, school records, and camp counselors' ratings of 229 socioeconomically disadvantaged children (ages 5–12 years), 146 of whom had been mistreated, the researchers discovered that the abused children exhibited multiple forms of academic risks. The adverse childhood experiences appeared to interfere with the children's cognitive abilities, thus placing these children more in danger of academic failure. Along with the academic problems, an increase in behavioral dysfunction was also noted (Shonk & Cicchetti, 2001).

Although mental health issues in schools are usually overseen by counselors and psychologists, it is becoming more prevalent for classroom teachers to be responsible for most behavioral interventions (Franklin et al., 2012). This is primarily due to the shortage of mental health care providers available (Murphy, 2016). It is estimated that one counselor may serve up to 465 students in one school. The numerous caseloads are so overwhelming, there is no counseling time available for the mounting numbers of crises in the early grades. Thus, the majority of behavior problems in pre-kindergarten, kindergarten, first, and second grade must be addressed by the classroom teachers. However, in most general education classrooms, the teachers have not received any training in how to help children with ACEs who may act negatively toward authority figures and/or peers (Murphey & Sacks, 2019). In fact, responses obtained from teachers during semi-structured interviews about the teachers' experiences working with students who had histories of trauma revealed that the teachers did not feel they had the knowledge needed to support such students nor manage them properly (Alisic, 2012). Instead of the classroom being utilized for positive engaging lessons, the environment may instead become disruptive, with general education teachers forced to direct attention and energy to maintaining order (Murphey & Sacks, 2019). Depending on educators to act as therapists or mental health providers is not only unfair to the teacher, but also runs the risk of escalating a crisis event due to possible triggers that may cause re-traumatization reactions from the disruptive student (Carello & Butler, 2014). Teachers who resort to yelling or punitive measures to stop dysregulated behaviors may actually lead students with histories of trauma to be reminded of past personal trauma that can cause these students to react with even more stress (Pickens & Tschopp, 2017).

Unfortunately, for years schools have dealt with children in crisis modes by addressing the overt behavior. Removal of the disruptive child from the classroom, in-school and out-of-school suspensions, and even permanent expulsions have been the usual responses to restoring calm for the teacher and classroom (Gilliam, 2005). The underlying root cause of the disruptive child's behavior is rarely or never investigated. It is only recently that educators have become aware that children presenting with problem negative behaviors may not be acting in purposeful defiant ways, but instead be displaying such anti-social behaviors because these children are suffering from impaired self-regulation systems and compromised social-emotional skills (Courtois, 2008). In fact, many times children who are labeled as *learning disabled* or *mentally challenged* may be victims of complex traumatic experiences. This unhealthy trauma affects the children's brains, leading to impaired cognitive function and poor social-emotional skills (Wright, 2014).

5   Getting to the Root Causes of Problem Behaviors in the Classroom

Schools and educators often work with children who have experienced trauma, but teachers may not always be able to identify who these students are. Teachers need to be aware of reminders, also known as triggers, that could cause retraumatization. A situation, attitude or expression, or certain environments can trigger a response that replicates the loss of power, control, or safety, much like the dynamics of the original trauma (Zgoda, Hizel, & Hizel, 2019). The trigger could be the sights, sounds, or smells present in the classroom, like the way a teacher might stand assertively with arms crossed, the way a classmate excitedly reacts vocally during playtime, or the aroma from a small group cooking activity. These actions may present strong cues from past negative experiences. Retraumatization is a conscious or unconscious reminder of past trauma that results in a re-experiencing of the initial traumatic event (Zgoda et al., 2019). Interactions happening in the classroom between children or between the teacher and a student could result in a student reacting to the trigger and being retraumatized, causing a behavioral response of fight, flight, or freeze (Pickens & Tschopp, 2017; Blaustein & Kinniburgh, 2010).

Responding to danger is at times necessary for survival. If you were being chased by a tiger, it would be prudent to take flight and flee, but in a classroom in the United States children do not have to run from tigers. A child's reaction to real or perceived danger in the classroom setting might arouse a flight response. A child might literally run away from an encounter or situation that provokes an overwhelming emotional response the child cannot handle. Their behavior might appear to be defiant, but it is for self-protection. In a situation where a child feels they are being overpowered or have no control, a child might appear to be irritated, angry, hyperactive or hypervigilant. A fight response might be generated in this kind of scenario, and they might act violently towards others or even themselves (Blaustein & Kinniburgh, 2010; Alexander, 2019). Dissociation or a freeze response is a strategy a child might choose when they believe fight or flight are not an option (Manitoba Trauma Information & Education Center, 2013). In the freeze response, a child views the impending danger as being inescapable. The student wants to disappear from what they perceive to be a confrontation, but may take no action, as if they were to stay still the identified threat might go away.

Children living in dysfunctional households filled with violent episodes or abusive relationships may be so preoccupied with their own continued existence that such thoughts interfere with a child's ability to think coherently (Cook, Spinazzola, Ford, Lanktree, Blaustein, & Cloitre, 2005). For example, a child who is abused by a parent or caretaker, or who witnesses repetitive abuse of other family members in the home, may live in constant fear of the possibility that the scary event may take place again at any time. This fear causes the child to be in a constant survival mode and unable to focus on learning anything academic. The main goal in such a child's life becomes to learn how to protect oneself and stay alive (Cook et al., 2005; Courtois, 2008).

Recent research (Holmes et al., 2015) in school discipline is grounded in the neuroscience of attachment, which emphasizes the significance of relationships (Schore, 2001). Children who have or are growing up in dysfunctional households, and/or live in communities plagued by violent crimes, may not have developed strong healthy attachments to primary caregivers and thus may possess little to no social/emotional skills (Arvidson, Kinniburg, Howard, Spinazzola, Strothers, Evans, et al., 2011). School and classroom environments may be perceived as more threats to these youngsters' survival, thereby impairing such children's ability to function academically and socially as successfully as the rest of their peers (Carello & Butler, 2014). In addition to limited or non-existent positive social emotional skills, the multiple adverse events experienced by the youngsters interfere with their executive function abilities, such as logic, reasoning, and/or problem-solving skills (Holt, Finkelhor, & Kantor, 2007). Whenever a child's conscious mind is overtaken by powerful negative emotions, the young person's ability to think and make good decisions becomes impeded. Instead, the brain relies on automatic survival responses – fight, flight, or freeze (van der Kolk, 2005). This type of primitive thinking interferes with school success (McEwen, 2000).

Overactive stress responses due to adverse childhood experiences in certain youths' lives are the likely causes of most negative behavior in the classroom (Lieberman, Chu, Van Horn, & Harris, 2011). Due to unnecessary hypervigilance, a student with multiple ACEs may be so threatened by having no control over the environment that aggressive or non-compliant behaviors may surface in the classroom as a means of survival for that student. What the teacher perceives as *disruptive behavior* from a *defiant student* may be that pupil's only way of coping with fear and loss of control. Unfortunately, when such a student is removed from the classroom or suspended from school for a period of time, the student experiences additional adversity due to lack of connection to classmates and feelings of isolation (Follette & Vijay, 2008).

With limited human resources and little or no training in management of mental health issues, educators resort to using ubiquitous discipline strategies that just provide temporary resolutions. Any such tactics that do not recognize the emotional safety of the already traumatized students may indeed provoke more long-term anti-social behaviors. For those youngsters who need secure trust in order to build strong positive relationships which are essential for success in school and life (Carello & Butler, 2014; Jimenenz, Wade, Lin, Morrow, & Reichman, 2016), classrooms must become *trauma-informed* (Holmes et al., 2015).

6 Becoming Trauma-Informed

As educators become more aware of the connection between adverse childhood experiences and the potential for disruptive behavior in the classroom, they can then treat students displaying such dysregulation by using *trauma-informed strategies* (Pickens & Tschopp, 2017). For example, instead of yelling at a child in crisis mode, the teacher can maintain a calm atmosphere while attempting to build a connection with the youngster. Once children begin to feel safe and connected with a trusted adult, then they can learn to understand and regulate their emotions (Dombo & Sabatino, 2019). Instead of resorting to old punitive discipline strategies for controlling purposes, teachers can employ approaches that help the students learn how to manage their own behavior in positive ways (Pickens & Tschopp, 2017). Additionally, teachers can work with very young children by fostering resiliency through building strong trusting attachments with the students. This strategy especially helps those youngsters who have never had a healthy attachment with their primary caregiver. The teachers can also help their students to learn how to self-regulate by modeling positive coping skills. Furthermore, educators can provide multiple opportunities for students to experience success doing different tasks in order to build the child's sense of self-confidence. These strategies, based on the Attachment, Regulation, and Competency framework (ARC) developed by Blaustein and Kinniburg (2010), have all proven to be highly successful when used to treat traumatic stress in students.

Other effective trauma-informed interventions, such as the Head Start Trauma Smart (HSTS), can be used with preschool children to decrease the stress of chronic trauma and to foster age-appropriate social and cognitive development (Holmes, Levy, Smith, Pinne, & Neese, 2005). The Head Start Trauma Smart (HSTS) integrates three existing evidence-informed modalities: the ARC, Trauma-Focused Cognitive Behavioral Therapy (TF-CBT), and Early Childhood Mental Health Consultation, The ARC is based on building positive attachment, developing self-regulation, and acknowledging competency. Trauma-Focused Cognitive Behavioral Therapy (TF-CBT), consists of a set of trauma-specific components such as parenting skills, relaxation skills, trauma narration and processing, and enhancing safety. Early Childhood Mental Health Consultation usually involves a mental health clinician working within a pre-school setting to decrease problem behavior and promote socio-emotional development through facilitating changes in teacher behavior and the classroom environment. By integrating all three of these modalities, the HSTS intervention provides another way for complex trauma in young children to be successfully addressed within the children's classroom. Some schools have even introduced therapy dogs into the building (McKibben, 2018). These dogs are specially trained to work with children and provide comfort to those caring for the animal. The canines have proven to change children's moods from sad to happy, which is essential to promoting a calm and welcoming classroom atmosphere.

Another successful calming intervention is the use of mindfulness, which teaches students that they can block out stressful stimuli using special breathing exercises. Children as young as kindergarten age are now being taught how to recognize their own feelings and the feelings of others and how to deal with those feelings by taking different types of breaths in order to remain calm during moments of conflict. Using this strategy, students have been able to not only help themselves, but also are able to promote peace in their classrooms (Montgomery, Van Driel, & Vandendriessche, 2019). Some teachers have also added safe spaces into their classrooms where students can go if they need to calm down. Within these quiet spaces, there may be art supplies enabling children to draw about what may be upsetting them. Other teachers have incorporated the use of aromatherapy based on the calming effect some all-natural essential oils have when diffused into the surrounding air (Johnson, 2018).

Whatever trauma-informed strategies educators choose to use with their students, it is imperative that the students' emotional safety be the priority. Teachers should never attempt to teach about trauma as doing so may put the students at the risk of retraumatization (Carello & Butler, 2014). It is better to proceed with compassion and responsibility when working with the students, utilizing developmentally appropriate practices with young children. Providing a consistently safe environment filled with trusted adults, complete with predictable outcomes, encouraged by supportive friends who value and respect one another, and knowing how to self-regulate emotions are the factors that lay the foundation for trauma-informed classrooms.

7   Secondary Traumatic Stress

It is not unusual for teachers to develop a secondary stress disorder as a byproduct of working with traumatized students. Being exposed to troubling behaviors every day in the classroom can leave the educators feeling physically, intellectually, emotionally, and socially drained. If this type of stress is not addressed, it can lead to problems that interfere with personal life (Bowers, 2014). Many adults who work with individuals experiencing traumatic events may develop their own symptoms of stress. A teacher trying to manage the child in crisis also must manage his/her own emotions. If the teacher suppresses his/her feelings, *secondary traumatic stress* may set in (Figley, 1995; Pryce, Shackelford & Pryce, 2007).

Teachers who develop this type of stress may present with symptoms such as poor concentration, sleep disturbances, appetite changes, increased heart rate, and may harbor feelings of hopelessness, isolation, being anxious, and/or become overwhelmed with anger, sadness, and/or helplessness (Figley, 1995). Such symptoms occur as a result of the empathic strain and general exhaustion the teachers suffer from dealing with children in distress every day. Even though teachers may learn and apply certain strategies to help manage children who exhibit symptoms of toxic trauma, these educators may not realize how the daily stressors take a toll on their own lives. As the teachers face working with traumatized children while at the same time attempting to engage the rest of the class in academic learning, such a situation may very well contribute to underlying physical, mental, emotional, and social health problems (Borntrager, Caringi, van den Pol, Crosby, O'Connell, Trautman, & McDonald, 2012). The toll of daily emotional drain stemming from caring for children who exhibit negative behaviors due to ACEs has been found to affect teachers lives both inside and outside of the classroom (Borntrager et al., 2012; Hydon, Wong, Langley, Stein, & Kataoka, 2015).

Ordinary secondary stress in the education field can result from a variety of job stressors, such as school quality reviews, curriculum demands, an arduous administrator, standardized test scores used for teacher evaluation purposes, and/or benchmark deadlines. Secondary *traumatic* stress experienced by teachers is a specific response to becoming stressed out from sharing the trauma story and resulting dysregulated behavior of a student who has been or is currently a victim of adverse childhood experiences. The educator unknowingly takes on the emotions of the child as the teacher learns about the child's underlying trauma (Pryce, Shackelford, & Pryce, 2007). The constant exposure to the child in stress is emotionally draining. If this secondary stress is not addressed and the teacher is not taught ways to cope with it, the stress will lead to physical exhaustion, known as *compassion fatigue* (Figley, 1995). Untreated, eventually this can lead to teacher burnout causing the teacher to leave the job.

Results from research indicated that school staff reported very high levels of secondary traumatic stress (Borntrager et al., 2012). Using the Secondary Traumatic Stress Scale developed by Bride, Robinson, Yegidis, and Figley (2004), the researchers questioned 300 participants gathered from personnel across six public schools in a variety of communities in northwestern USA. Each member of the study had to respond to a 17-item self-report using a 5-point Likert scale measure designed to assess difficulties at the workplace ranging from *never* to *very often*. Approximately 75% of the sample showed high scores in areas indicative of symptoms of high stress. The outcome of this study suggested that public school employees may be exposed to excessive levels of direct and secondary trauma at the workplace more often than thought.

In studying why some teachers are more stressed than others, McCarthy (2019) found that the most stressed teachers were the ones who believe the demands at work exceeded their available resources for help. Furthermore, the stressed teachers reported in a survey that managing student behavior was the top stressor on the list of many other issues. As teachers go above and beyond to try to empathize with the students who have a history of trauma, the educators' health becomes at risk. Constant work, no breaks, being isolated in the classroom away from colleagues, and no support from administration can be personally overwhelming and further complicates the situation if the teachers themselves have their own personal unresolved histories of trauma. These can get triggered when the teacher interacts with students who have or are experiencing adverse childhood experiences. Without any training in how to manage the traumatized child's behavior, compounded by the educator's own possibly erroneous coping mechanisms, the trauma situation in the classroom may not be correctly addressed. This makes the classroom even more physically and psychologically unsafe for everyone.

This problem of secondary traumatic stress and compassion fatigue is not necessarily restricted to educational settings. In fact, several studies have been conducted over time regarding how such stress affects specialists in mental health professions. A review of 32 research studies focusing on common correlates and predictors of compassion fatigue in mental health professionals conducted by Turgoose and Maddox (2017) yielded important information about the negative effects of working in psychologically distressing environments. The review emphasized that several psychosocial factors, such as empathy and histories of past personal trauma present in professionals who work with trauma-stressed clients, were predictors of compassion fatigue in the mental health workers. Those workers who were highly empathetic with the clients suffering from traumatic stress, and who themselves may have experienced personal distressing events, were more likely to develop symptoms of secondary traumatic stress leading to compassion fatigue. Such revelations are significant for everyone working with individuals of all ages who may have been or are currently experiencing adverse events in their lives, whether in the field of mental health or the field of education. Since there may be no way of initially knowing whether professionals may be predisposed to secondary traumatic stress, it is therefore highly important to take the well-being of these specialists into account before engaging them in constant encounters with trauma victims (Turgoose & Maddox, 2017).

As time goes on, the risk factors associated with secondary traumatic stress may begin to interfere with the professional's ability to carry out their daily work obligations. Often, teachers end up leaving their jobs due to the negative effect of secondary traumatic stress (Larwood, & Paje, 2004). Many teachers are just not prepared to handle the behaviors of students who are experiencing stress. Feelings of incompetence due to lack of preparation in dealing with traumatic stress, along with lack of a support team, can cause many educators to leave the teaching profession. For teachers to remain mentally healthy and retain the enormous energy needed for teaching all students, it is necessary to address any possible secondary traumatic stress they may be experiencing and obtain continuous support as they face daily classroom challenges (Barlet & Steber, 2019).

8   Managing Secondary Stress

Since research demonstrates that the issue of secondary traumatic stress is prevalent and a definite cause of poor health among teachers who work with traumatized students, it is imperative that care be taken to preserve the educators' well-being. It appears that several means to address this vicarious stress are beginning to be recognized based on recent findings. For example, a study conducted by Caringi, Stanick, Trautman et al. (2015) investigated which factors lessened stress in school personnel. Qualitative methods were utilized to develop a broader understanding of how educators experience secondary traumatic stress in public school settings. Although the outcomes suggest that trauma experiences of students deeply impacted teachers' interest in remaining in the profession, it was also discovered that educators cited colleagues and family members as important areas of support for dealing with work-related stresses. Such results suggest that efforts to promote the health and well-being of educators by having support systems in place may be very helpful for those educators who must deal with secondary traumatic stress. Furthermore, evidence from the Turgoose and Maddox study (2017) indicated that factors such as practicing mindfulness also helped to protect professionals from developing secondary traumatic stress. Breathing techniques that promoted relaxation were conducive to the teachers' ability to remain calm amid stressful situations. Other methods that proved to be helpful with secondary stress reduction were exercising regularly, getting adequate sleep, and practicing other self-awareness activities, such as yoga (Pickens & Tschopp, 2017).

Learning to be aware and caring for one's own health needs must become a priority among every educator. The NCTSN (2008) offers several tips to teachers who may be in danger of developing secondary traumatic stress. It is suggested that educators first be aware of specific signs of the effects of such trauma, such as experiencing increased impatience with students, difficulty planning, decreased concentration, feeling numb, intrusive thoughts, and/or having dreams about the students' trauma (NCTSN, 2008). It is also important that teachers avoid becoming isolated in the classroom; instead, having a team of colleagues for support keeps the educators connected and strong. Additionally, taking time to care for oneself by eating well, exercising, and engaging in fun activities can help to alleviate current stress and prevent the occurrence of any future secondary traumatic stress (NCTSN, 2008).

Just as the adults benefit from connecting with others and keeping calm, it is helpful to model positive social/emotional learning for all the children in the classroom. Research shows that most of the negative behavior displayed by the ACE children is a result of their fear of loss of control. Such children may feel threatened in the classroom because they have not learned to interact positively with others. They need to feel safe and supported. Safety can be felt through connections with people who have a calm and focused presence. Teachers can help these children and help themselves by establishing and maintaining a calm classroom environment that radiates trust and consistency. As teachers practice mindful regulation strategies, they can teach these techniques to their students through the process of co-regulation. Coaching these children in ways to calm themselves and manage their emotions, along with giving the children a chance to make positive choices, can help the students to feel safe and reduce the level of stress for everyone in the classroom (Pickens & Tschopp, 2017).

It is vital that teachers and their students acquire different constructive ways of coping with workplace stress. Alleviating and preventing the impact of secondary traumatic stress should be a foremost concern of every organizational leader. While educators learn to adopt lifestyles and work habits that help them prevent or reduce adverse stress effects, organizations need to utilize a variety of prevention strategies and assist staff with efforts to remain healthy. Based on a report by Bell, Kulkami, and Dalton (2003), it is strongly suggested that organizations consider creating a culture that normalizes the effects of working with trauma survivors. Schools that recognize and are prepared to support teachers affected by traumatic stress and students affected by trauma are trauma-informed schools. Such schools provide hope for the entire school community by having strategies in place that promote wellness, maintain positive environments, and protect the wellbeing of everyone involved. This is essential for achieving an effective organization filled with successful teachers and students. Encouraging discussions among colleagues, providing resources related to trauma available to all staff, having accessible counselors and social workers, ensuring a safe work environment, and adopting policies that promote and support staff self-care are just a few of the ways recommended to make secondary traumatic stress at the worksite manageable (Bell, Kulkami, & Dalton, 2003).

9 Lessons Learned

In the 1980s, the concept of cultural competence emerged in the healthcare field and was later applied to educational settings (Tustin, 2019). Cultural competence refers to behaviors, attitudes, and beliefs that allow a specialist to effectively engage with people whose cultural beliefs are different than their own. It is required for doctors and nurses to understand a patient's culture in order to be able to offer treatment (Tustin, 2019). In one example, although nurses are required to touch patients to manage care, in the Orthodox Jewish culture any kind of touch between a man and woman who are not married to each other is prohibited (Yellon & Gurion, 2016). A female nurse needs to understand this religious principle when providing care for a Jewish male patient.

In the healthcare field, cultural awareness involves self-examination with in-depth exploration of one's cultural and professional background (Neese, 2017). As in the healthcare field, a prerequisite for cultural competence is a teacher being self-reflective and gaining an awareness of their own cultural identity. For teachers, being culturally competent is integral for curriculum planning and for efficacious interactions with children, parents, and school staff. An understanding of the elements that comprise their own cultural mosaic allows for recognition and appreciation for the differences among students and their families who are dissimilar from the teacher's own culture (National Education Association, 2019; Chao & Moon, 2005).

Much like cultural competence began in the medical setting, lessons learned from trauma-informed care in healthcare settings are now influencing the practices of teachers in the school setting. Understanding the trauma students have experienced or are experiencing begins with a teacher's self-reflection of trauma the educator has experienced. As teacher Candance Hines reflected, "When I was in elementary school, I was often bullied because of my brown skin … being a Black teacher allows me to see my students as they are. I connect with them and interpret the cultural differences" (2018, #1 and #2).

How can a teacher provide a classroom environment that enables students who have experienced trauma to thrive? One possible approach that began in the healthcare field and can be utilized in educational environments is the concept of *changing perceptions, changing care* (CPI, 2017). When a teacher observes a child misbehaving or behaving inappropriately, instead of thinking: what is wrong with this child? The teacher can reflect on: what happened to this child (Brodovsky & Kiernan, 2017)?

Schools have an important role to play in providing stability and a safe space for children and connecting them to caring adults. In addition to serving as a link to supportive services, schools can adapt curricula and behavioral interventions to better meet the educational needs of students who have experienced trauma (McInerney & McKlindon, n.d.). To be able to foster student growth, the aim of a trauma-informed classroom is to infuse an understanding of the impact of trauma and adverse life experiences on students and promote a physically and psychologically safe environment (Pickens & Tschopp, 2017). Being a trauma-informed or trauma-sensitive school means being informed and sensitive to trauma, but also as providing a protected, secure and understanding school environment for students with a primary goal of acknowledging triggers and preventing retraumatization (McInerney & McKlindon, n.d.). Teachers providing a trusting, safe classroom environment allow children to spend less time in survival response mode and more time being able to play and learn (Brodovsky & Kiernan, 2017).

References

Alexander, J. (2019). *Building trauma-sensitive schools: Your guide to creating safe, supportive learning environments for all students.* Paul H. Brookes Publishing Co., Inc.

Alisic, E. (2012). Teachers' perspectives on providing support to children after trauma: A qualitative study. *School Psychology Quarterly, 27*(1), 51–59.

Anda, R. (n.d.). *The adverse childhood experiences study: Child abuse and public health.* https://www.preventchildabuse.org/images/docs/anda_wht_ppr.pdf

Arvidson, J., Kinniburg, K., Howard, K., Spinazzola, J., Stronthers, H., Evans, M., Andres, B., Cohen, C., & Blaustein, M. (2011). Treatment of complex trauma in young children: Developmental and cultural consideration in application of the ARC intervention model. *Journal of Child and Adolescent Trauma, 4*, 34–51.

Baldry, A. C. (2003). Bullying in schools and exposure to domestic violence. *Child Abuse & Neglect, 27*, 713–732.

Barlett, J. D., & Steber, K. (2019, May 9). *Child trends.* https://www.childtrends.org/publications/how-to-implement-trauma-informed-care-to-build-resilience-to-childhood-trauma

Bell, H., Kulkami, S., & Dalton, L. (2003). Organizational prevention of vicarious trauma. *Families in Society: The Journal of Contemporary Human Services, 84*, 463–470.

Bethell, C. D., Carle, A., Hudziak, J., Gombojav, N., Powers, K., Wade, R., & Braverman, P. (2017). Frameworks and measurement methods to assess adverse childhood experiences of children and families: Toward approaches to promote child well-being in policy and practice. *Academic Pediatric Association, 17*, 51–69. https://www.academicpedsjnl.net/article/S1876-2859(17)30324-8/pdf

Better Brains for Babies. (2019). *Child development principles*. Georgia Department of Human Services. http://www.bbbgeorgia.org/childDevelopment.php

Birdwell, J. (2009, July 23). Upcoming summit focuses on economic benefits of early childhood development. *Oklahoma Gazette*, para. 6. http://www.okgazette.com/oklahoma/article-4137-upcoming-summit-focuses-on-economic-benefits-of-early-childhood-development.html

Blaustein, M. E., & Kinniburgh, K. M. (2010). *Treating traumatic stress in children and adolescents: How to foster resilience through attachment, self-regulation, and competency*. Guilford Press.

Borntrager, C., Caringi, J. C., van den Pol, R., Crosby, L., O'Connell, K., Trautman, A., & McDonald, M. (2012) Secondary traumatic stress in school personnel. *Advances in School Mental Health Promotion, 5*(1), 38–50. doi:10.1080/1754730X.2012.664862

Bowers, T. (2004). Stress, teaching and teacher health. *Education 3–13. International Journal of Primary, Elementary and Early Years Education, 32*, 73–80.

Bride, B., Robinson, M., Yegidis, B., & Figley, C. (2004). Development and validation of the Secondary Traumatic Stress Scale. *Research on Social Work Practice, 14*, 27–35.

Brodovsky, B., & Kiernan, K. (2017). *How to talk to children about flight, fight and freeze*. https://makingsenseoftrauma.com/wp-content/uploads/2016/02/How-to-Talk-to-Children-about-Freeze-Flight-and-Fight.pdf

Cafasso, J. (2016, January 28). *Traumatic events*. https://www.healthline.com/health/traumatic-events

Carello, J., & Butler, L. D. (2014). Potentially perilous pedagogies: Teaching trauma is not the same as trauma-informed teaching. *Journal of Trauma & Dissociation, 15*, 153–168.

Caringi, J., Stanick, C., Trautman, A., Crosby, L., Devlin, M., & Adams, S. (2015). Secondary traumatic stress in public school teachers: Contributing and mitigating factors. *Advances in School Mental Health Promotion, 8*(4), 244–256. doi:10.1080/1754730X.2015. 1080123

Center for Early Childhood Mental Health Consultation. (2019). *Defining trauma*. https://www.ecmhc.org/tutorials/trauma/mod1_1.html

Centers for Disease Control and Prevention. (2019, April). *About adverse childhood experiences*. https://www.cdc.gov/violenceprevention/childabuseandneglect/acestudy/aboutace.html

Chao, G. T., & Moon, H. (2005, November). The cultural mosaic: A metatheory for understanding the complexity of culture. *Journal of Applied Psychology, 90*(6), 1128–1140. doi:10.1037/0021-9010.90.6.1128

Child and Adolescent Health Measurement Initiative. (2013). *Overview of adverse child and adolescent health measurement initiative experiences among US children.* Data Resource Center, supported by Cooperative Agreement 1-U59-MC06980-01 from the U.S. Department of Health and Human Services, Health Resources and Services Administration (HRSA), Maternal and Child Health Bureau (MCHB). https://www.childhealthdata.org/docs/drc/aces-data-brief_version-1-0.pdf?Status=Master

Cook, A., Spinazzola, J., Ford, J., Lanktree, C., Blaustein, M., Cloitre, M., et al. (2005). Complex trauma in children and adolescents. *Psychiatric Annals, 35*(5), 390–398.

Courtois, C. A. (2008). Complex trauma, complex reactions: Assessment and treatment. *Psychological Trauma: Theory, Research, Practice, and Policy, S*(1), 86–100. doi:10.1037/1942-9681.s.1.86

Crisis Prevention Institute. (2017). *Trauma informed care resources guide.* https://www.crisisprevention.com/CPI/media/Media/download/PDF_TICRG.pdf?_gl=1*1b0jkme*_gcl_aw*RoNMLjE1NzQxMDQ1NzAuQ2owSoNRaUFuOG51QlJDekFSSXNBSmNkSWZNcXFjMU9DdzZLektGdUZtXoFZdoVRWHVrZmtxU3BhYkdjdVk4TzBzNURJdmY4eUZIYU03MGFBZ1FoRUFMMd193YoI

Darwish, D., Esquivel, G. B., Houtz, J. C., & Alfonso, V. C. (2001). Play and social skills in maltreated and non-maltreated preschoolers during peer interactions. *Child Abuse & Neglect, 25*(1), 13–31.

Davidson, M. (n.d.). *PIES a child's development.* https://slideplayer.com/slide/9819884/

DeMatteo, M. (2019, March 19). *7 surprising classroom triggers for kids who experienced trauma (and how to avoid them): Create a trauma-sensitive classroom.* We Are Teachers. https://www.weareteachers.com/classroom-trauma-triggers/

Dombo, E. A., & Sabatino, C. A. (2019). Trauma care in school. *American Educator, 43*(2), 18–21.

Dorado, J., & Zakrzewski, V. (2013, October 23). *How to help a traumatized child in the classroom.* The Greater Good Science Center at the University of California, Berkeley. https://greatergood.berkeley.edu/article/item/the_silent_epidemic_in_our_classrooms

Figley, C. (1995). *Compassion fatigue: Coping with secondary traumatic stress disorder in those who treat the traumatized.* Brunner-Routledge.

Felitti, V., Anda, R., Nordenberg, D., Williamson, D., Spitz, A., Edwards, V., Koss, M., & Marks, J. (1998). Relationship of childhood abuse and household dysfunction to many of the leading causes of death in adults: The Adverse Childhood Experiences (ACE) study. *American Journal of Preventive Medicine, 14*, 4.

Finkelhor, D., Turner, H., Ormond, R., & Hamby, S. (2009). Violence, abuse, and crime exposure in a national sample of children and youth. *Pediatrics, 124*, 1411–1423.

Flannery, M. (2019, July 10). *Inside a trauma informed classroom.* http://neatoday.org/2019/07/10/inside-a-trauma-informed-classroom/

Flook, L., Goldberg, S. B., Pinger, L., Bonus, K., & Davidson, R. J. (2013). Mindfulness for teachers: A pilot study to assess effects on stress, burnout and teaching efficacy. *Mind, Brain and Education, 7*(3), 10.

Follette, V., & Vijay, A. (2008). Retraumatization. In G. Reyes, J. Elhai, & J. D. Ford (Eds.), *Encyclopedia of psychological trauma* (pp. 586–589). John Wiley & Sons.

Ford, J. D. (2011). Assessing child and adolescent complex traumatic stress reactions. *Journal of Child and Adolescent Trauma, 4*(3), 217–232.

Franklin, C. G. S., Kim, J. S., Ryan, T. N., Kelly, M. S., & Montgomery, K. L. (2012). Teacher involvement in school mental health interventions: A systemic review. *Children and Youth Services Review, 34*(5), 973–982.

Gilliam, W. (2005). *Pre-kindergarteners left behind: Expulsion rates in state prekindergarten systems*. Yale University Child Study Center.

Graybill, K. (2015, August 21). *P.I.E.S.: The areas of development.* https://www.familyconsumersciences.com/2015/08/p-i-e-s-the-areas-of-development/

Herbert, L., Peterson, K., & Dunsmore, K. (2019). *Literacy organizational capacity initiative. A leader's guide to trauma-sensitive schools and whole-child literacy.* https://partnership4resilience.org/wp-content/uploads/2019/05/Publisher_SEL-White-Paper_v2.pdf

Hines, C. (2018, July 10). I'm a trauma survivor; I know what it takes to teach students like me. *Teach Plus*. https://medium.com/whats-the-plus/im-a-trauma-survivor-i-know-what-it-takes-to-teach-students-like-me-3c883047bd70

Hoffman-Plotkin, D., & Twentyman, C. T. (1984). A multimodal assessment of behavioral and cognitive deficits in abused and neglected preschoolers. *Child Development, 55*(3), 794–802.

Holmes, C., Levy, M., Smith, A., Pinne, S., & Neese, P. (2015, June). A model for creating a supportive trauma-informed culture for children in preschool settings. *Journal of Child and Family Studies, 24*(6), 1650–1659. https://link.springer.com/article/10.1007/s10826-014-9968-6

Holt, M. K., Finkelhor, D., & Kantor, G. K. (2007). Multiple victimization experiences of urban elementary school students: Associations with psychosocial functioning and academic performance. *Child Abuse and Neglect, 31*(5), 503–515. doi:10.1016/j.chiabu.2006.12.006

Horn, J. L., & Trickett, P. K. (1998). Community violence and child development: A review of the research. In P. K. Trickett & C. J. Schellenbach (Eds.), *Violence against children in the family and the community* (pp. 103–138). American Psychological Association.

Hughes, H. M., Honore, M., Parkinson, D., & Vargo, M. (1989). Witnessing spouse abuse and experiencing physical abuse: A "double whammy"? *Journal of Family Violence, 4*(2), 197–209.

Hydon, S., Wong, M., Langley, A., Stein, B., & Kataoka, S. (2015). Preventing secondary traumatic stress in educators. *Child and Adolescent Psychiatric Clinics of North America, 24*, 319–333. doi:10.1016/j.chc.2014.11.003

Identifying, preventing, and treating childhood trauma: A pervasive public health issue that needs greater federal attention. (2019). Hearing before the Committee on Oversight and Reform, House of Representatives, 116th Cong., 116–45. https://docs.google.com/document/d/1BkX6C3c16M3NtQuyakZXV7BdybQd7N9 UiQaQJ3kAv1w/edit

Jaycox, L. H., Morse, L. K., Tanielian, T., & Stein, B. D. (2006). *How schools can help students recover from traumatic experiences: A toolkit for supporting long-term recovery.* Rand Gulf States Policy Institute. https://www.rand.org/content/dam/rand/pubs/technical_reports/2006/RAND_TR413.pdf

Jennings, P. A. (2019). Teaching in a trauma-sensitive classroom. *American Educator, 43*(2), 12–17.

Jimenez, M. E., Wade, R., Yong, L., Morrow, L. M., & Reichman, N. E. (2016). Adverse experiences in early childhood and kindergarten outcomes. *Pediatrics, 137*(2). https://doi.org/10.1542/peds.2015-1839

Johnson, K. (2019). Effect of inhaled lemon essential oil on cognitive test anxiety among nursing students. *Holistic Nursing Practice, 33*(2), 95–100. doi:10:1097/HNP00315

Larwood, L., & Paje, V. (2004). Teacher stress and burnout in deaf education. *Academic Exchange Quarterly, 8*(3), 261–264.

Lieberman, A., Chu, A., Van Horn, P., & Harris, W. (2011). Trauma in early childhood: Empirical evidence and clinical implications. *Development and Psychopathology, 23*, 397–410.

Lieberman, A. F., & Van Horn, P. (2009). Giving voice to the unsayable: Repairing the effects of trauma in infancy and early childhood. *Child and Adolescent Psychiatric Clinics of North America, 18*, 707–720. doi:10.1016/j.chc.2009.02.007

Manitoba Trauma Information & Education Centre. (2013). *Trauma recovery: Dissociation.* https://trauma-recovery.ca/impact-effects-of-trauma/dissociation/

Massachusetts Advocates for Children and Harvard Law School. (n.d.). *Helping traumatized children learn.* https://traumasensitiveschools.org/trauma-and-learning/the-problem-impact/

McCarthy, C. J. (2019). Teacher stress: Balancing demands and resources. *Phi Delta Kappan, 101*(3).

McEwen, B. S. (2000). The neurobiology of stress: From serendipity to clinical relevance. *Brain Research, 886*(1–2), 172–189.

McInerney, M., & McKlindon, A. (n.d.). *Unlocking the door to learning: Trauma-informed classrooms & transformational schools.* https://www.elc-pa.org/wp-content/uploads/2015/06/Trauma-Informed-in-Schools-Classrooms-FINAL-December2014-2.pdf

McKibben, S. (2018). Why schools are going to the dogs. *Educational Update, 60*(2), 1–2.

McLeod, J., Fisher, J., & Hoover, G. (2003). *Key elements of classroom management.* ASCD.

Milot, T., Ethier, L. S., St-Laurent, D., & Provost, M. A. (2010). The role of trauma symptoms in the development of behavioral problems in maltreated preschoolers. *Child Abuse & Neglect, 34*(4), 225–234.

Montgomery, S. E., Van Driel, M., & Vandendriessche, K. (2019). Mindfulness: Promoting peace in a kindergarten classroom. *Social Studies and the Young Learner, 32*(1), 26–31.

Murphey, D., & Sacks, V. (2019). Supporting students with adverse childhood experiences. *American Educator, 43*(2), 8–11.

Murphy, J. (2016). The undervaluing of school counselors. *The Atlantic.* https://www.theatlantic.com/education/archive/2016/09/the-neglected-link-in-the-high-school-to-college-pipeline/500213/

National Association for the Education of Young Children. (2009). *Developmentally appropriate practice in early childhood programs serving children from birth through age 8.* https://www.naeyc.org/sites/default/files/globally-shared/downloads/PDFs/resources/position-statements/PSDAP.pdf

National Child Traumatic Stress Network Schools Committee. (2008). *Childhood trauma toolkit for educators.* https://www.nctsn.org/sites/default/files/resources//child_trauma_toolkit_educators.pdf

National Education Association. (n.d.). *Why cultural competence?* http://www.nea.org/home/39783.htm

Neese, B. (2017, February 2). A guide to culturally competent nursing care [Blog post]. http://blog.diversitynursing.com/blog/a-guide-to-culturally-competent-nursing-care

Poag, G. (2018, November 2). *What is the difference between acute trauma and chronic trauma?* https://www.brentwoodwellnesscounseling.com/single-post/2017/07/26/What-Is-The-Difference-Between-Acute-Trauma-And-Chronic-Trauma

Perry, B., Pollard, R. A., Blakly, T. L., Baker, W. L., & Vigilante, D. (1995). Childhood trauma, the neurobiology of adaptation, and "use-dependent" development of the brain: How "states" become "traits." *Infant Mental Health Journal, 16*(4), 271–291.

Pickens, I. B., & Tschopp N. (2017). *Trauma-informed classrooms.* National Council of Juvenile and Family Court Judges.

Pryce, J., Shackelford, K., & Pryce, D. (2007). *Secondary traumatic stress and the child welfare professional.* Lyceum Books, Inc.

Putnam, F. W. (2006, Winter). The impact of trauma on child development. *Juvenile and Family Court Journal.* https://www.psychceu.com/nctsn/Putnam.impact.pdf

Saakvitne, K., Gamble, S., Pearlman, L., & Tabor Lev, B. (2000). *Risking connection: A training curriculum for working with survivors of childhood abuse.* Sidran Press.

Schore, A. N. (2001). The effects of early relational trauma on right brain development, affect regulation, & infant mental health. *Infant Mental Health Journal, 22,* 201–269.

Schwartz, D., & Proctor, L. J. (2000). Community violence exposure and children's social adjustment in the school group: The mediating roles of emotional regulation and social cognition. *Journal of Consulting & Clinical Psychology, 68*, 670–683.

Shonk, S. M., & Cicchetti, D. (2001). Maltreatment, competency deficits, and risk for academic and behavioral maladjustment. *Developmental Psychology, 37*(1), 3–17.

Sheffield Morris, A. (2008, May). Making it through a traumatic life experience: Applications for teaching, research, and personal adjustment. *Training and Education in Professional Psychology, 2*(2), 89–95.

Souers, K., & Hall, P. (2016). *Fostering resilient learners: Strategies for creating a trauma-sensitive classroom*. ASCD.

Statman-Weil, K., & Sorrels, B. (2018, April 12). *Webinar: Creating trauma sensitive classroom*. Hosted by the National Association for the Education of Young Children. https://www.youtube.com/watch?v=mjG3xNxtU1E

Sternberg, K. J., Baradaran, L. P., & Abbott, C. B. (2006). Type of violence, age, and gender differences in the effects of family violence on children's behavior problems: A mega-analysis. *Developmental Review, 26*, 89–112.

Stevens, J. E. (2012, October). *The adverse childhood experiences study – the largest, most important public health study you never heard of – began in an obesity clinic*. https://acestoohigh.com/2012/10/03/the-adverse-childhood-experiences-study-the-largest-most-important-public-health-study-you-never-heard-of-began-in-an-obesity-clinic/

Stover, C. S., & Berkowitz, S. (2005). Assessing violence exposure and trauma symptoms in young children: A critical review of measures. *Journal of Traumatic Stress, 18*(6), 707–717.

Turgoose, D., & Maddox, L. (2017). Predictors of compassion fatigue in mental health professionals: A narrative review. *Traumatology, 23*(2), 172–185.

Tustin, R. (2019). *Cultural competence in education*. https://study.com/academy/lesson/cultural-competence-in-education.html

van der Kolk, B. A. (2005). Developmental trauma disorder. *Psychiatric Annals, 35*(5), 401–408.

van der Kolk, B. A. (2014). *The body keeps the score: Brain, mind, and body in the healing of trauma*. Penguin Books.

Wright, T. (2014). Too scared to learn: Teaching young children who have experienced trauma: Research in review. *Young Children, 69*(5), 88–93.

Yellon, T., & Gurion, B. (2016, August 15–17). Touching patients: Orthodox Jewish nursing students experience. 6th World Nursing and Healthcare Conference. *Journal of Nursing & Care*. doi:10.4172/2167-1168.C1.019

Zgoda, K., Shelly, P., & Hitzel, S. (2019). Preventing retraumatization: A macro social work approach to trauma-informed practices and policies. *The New Social Worker*. https://www.socialworker.com/feature-articles/practice/preventing-retraumatization-a-macro-social-work-approach-to-trauma-informed-practices-policies/

CHAPTER 2

The Tiniest Tears
Grief and Loss in Childhood

Carolyn Oglio-Taverner

Abstract

Any child old enough to love is old enough to grieve. Every loss they experience, from a missing toy to a new school to the death of a loved one, is mourned. What they lack is the vocabulary to explain what they are feeling, in a manner adults can understand. Similar to adult grief, children's grief is intertwined with individual, temperamental, developmental, situational, interpersonal and contextual processes. They grieve in a manner and time that is most developmentally appropriate to them.

Their concerns, however, differ from those of adults and their grief tends to be more intermittent and long-term due to their more limited capacity for tolerating strong affect. Children's ability to grieve, which determines the severity and consequences of the event, is linked to the availability of caretakers who can provide a safe environment and help them tolerate painful feelings. At times, this role falls to educators who represent constants in, now, chaotic lives and introduces a need to balance academic and emotional expectations; often, without formal training in issues of grief and loss. By exploring developmental understandings of death, normative grief reactions in children and suggested methods through which children express what their vocabulary fails to provide, educators can become empowered to help their grieving students voice an experience without words.

Keywords

grief – loss – childhood – development – death – mourning – teachers – interventions – trauma

1 Introduction

It is often noted by grief counselors that "Any child old enough to love is old enough to grieve." Every loss they experience, from a missing toy, to a new school, to the death of a loved one, is mourned. Once of the first things you recognize when you work with grieving children, as I have for the past thirteen years, is that there are no "kid-sized" emotions or trivial losses. Children feel loss as deeply and profoundly as adults. What they lack is the vocabulary to explain what they are feeling in a way adults can understand. So, it is, often, difficult to understand what children are feeling. Children have a limited capacity to tolerate intense emotion so many will not cry or visibly show their feelings. They may appear cold or aloof. This is a normal reaction for children. They grieve in a manner and time that is most appropriate for them – typically out of sync with where adults are in their grief, which can be frustrating. It is important to note that children will grieve intermittently for many years. This means that they may not manifest grief symptoms for years after a loss, depending on the age of the child. When grief symptoms do occur, many are behavioral. Without a vocabulary to describe or label how they are feeling, children act out. They may become aggressive or withdrawn. They can become overly dependent and clingy or mischievous and irritable. Grades may plummet or favorite activities may no longer hold their interest. This can happen immediately after or several months or years after a loss. As such, bereavement in childhood cannot be viewed as a homogenous phenomenon nor are grief experiences in children discrete events. Rather, children's grief is a process which varies as a function of the changes that occur over time following the loss and each child's resources for adapting to those changes.

As mortality rates for middle-aged adults have risen dramatically in the last two decades, it has become increasingly likely that young children will experience the death of a parent, loved one or acquaintance. The Social Security Administration (2000) reports that 5–15% of children in the United States will lose one or both parents by the age of 15. Yet, these statistics do not account for the number of children who lose a "parental figure", such as a grandparent or other relative, that provides care (Owens, 2008). Moreover, presently, approximately 3.5% of American children under the age of 18 have already experienced the death of a parent or primary caregiver. Of equal importance, approximately 73,000 children die every year. Of these children, 83% have surviving siblings (Torbic, 2011). This makes childhood bereavement a topical and necessary conversation across multiple venues.

This is especially true with respect to education, as schools often become a safe haven for children, and teachers a force of stability amid a changing familial landscape. Statistics indicate that approximately 7 in 10 teachers (69%) have at least one student in their class who has lost a parent, guardian, sibling, or close friend in the past year (Blad, 2015). Many are caught unaware and are not trained to deal with the influx of emotions or behavioral issues that accompany mourning, especially when it is delayed. Grieving children are very concerned with being labeled "different" by their peers. Conforming to expectations and being able to fit in are especially important for children. Following a loss, where so much around them is different, this is of primary importance. Thus, returning to school is difficult following a loss. Many children are uncomfortable receiving condolences from teachers and peers, as these become badges of their difference and reminders that they are not the same as their peers. Similarly, while being excused from work or treated especially kindly can be comforting at first, over time, it also acts as a reminder of their difference. Teachers can provide a stable base for these children by maintaining a degree of normalcy and routine within the classroom. If their expectations remain the same, not everything in their lives has changed. Amid the emotional chaos of their home life, school represents an opportunity to be the normal pre-loss version of themselves and they want to be treated accordingly. Equally, grieving children are worried about the hurtful comments others may inadvertently say. This can add additional stress and pain. Peers are unprepared for the experience of loss, as many have never lost a loved one, and can be blunt in their reactions or unnecessarily cruel. Therefore, it is recommended that parents make sure the school is aware of the loss so that teachers can talk to the class before the child returns. In this way, the transition is easier for the grieving child as everyone is on the same page in terms of understanding. However, this requires teacher preparation and education in identifying and coping with grief symptoms in children.

Historically, researchers have expressed doubts about children's ability to mourn (Freud, 1915; Nagera, 1970; Wolfenstein, 1966) and concerns about the risk of pathological reactions in children while mourning (Bowlby, 1972). Such misconceptions perpetuated many of the myths associated with childhood grief. It was not until Silverman and Worden (1992) conducted their, now famous, Harvard Bereavement Study, that the concept of childhood bereavement was given both scientific and social credence. Though their study focused, solely, on parental loss, as much of the research with children does, it sparked a new conceptualization of the topic and an influx of additional research. Increased work in the area has led to the acceptance of childhood bereavement as a process of grieving which children must work through (Baker et al., 1992; Herbert, 1996; Worden, 1996; Barnard et al., 1999). Similar to adult grief, children's grief is intertwined with individual, temperamental, developmental, situational, interpersonal and contextual processes (Altschul, 1988; Furman, 1974; Silverman, 2000). Their concerns, however, differ from those of adults. Some of this is due to developmental differences in cognition and psychological processes (Thompson & Payne, 2000). Children's grieving tends to be more intermittent and long-term than adults', due to their more limited capacity for tolerating strong affect. Children are more concerned with knowing their behavior did not cause the death to happen (Nolen-Hoeksema & Larson, 1999). They worry it will happen to someone else they know or love and that there will be no one left to take care of them. Grieving children, typically, need to ask, "Did I cause it?", "Can I catch it?" and "Who will look after me?" (Stokes, 1994). Thus, the death of a loved one is a significant loss that can result in changes in multiple life domains, including the nature of children's relationships with surviving family members, daily routines and social networks (Worden, 1996). This places enormous emotional burdens on children and unique challenges for those who must care for them.

2 Developmental Understanding of Loss

Silverman and Worden (1992) refer to childhood bereavement as a dynamic interactive process to which time must be an added factor. The chronological age and developmental stage of a child affect their understanding of the loss, capacity to mourn, coping process, and the role the loss plays in ongoing development and identity formation (Baker et al., 1992; Speece & Brent, 1996). Children's experiences of grief are developmentally similar to their understanding of death in general (Black, 1998; Cohen et al., 2002; Emswiler & Emswiler, 2000; Grollman, 1995; Webb, 2000). Mostly, children want life to get back to normal and their reactions reflect this desire. However, depending upon the age of the child, the behaviors and motivations may be different.

2.1 *Universal Components in Children's Understanding of Death (Nolen-Hoeksema & Larson, 1999)*

2.1.1 Universality

Universality is the belief that all things that are now alive will one day die. Death is realized to be all-inclusive, inevitable and unpredictable. Because of children's more concrete and literal thought processes, this concept is more difficult for younger children to grasp. Often, though they claim understanding and agree with the basic tenets, there are many caveats. Everything dies – except not anyone I know and not for a very long time. In general, children are better able to grasp the idea that they will, someday, die, than the concept that anyone they love will die (Speece & Brent, 1996).

2.1.2 Non-Functionality

Non-functionality centers around the dead's inability to engage in daily activities. For children, this centers on the observable, concrete activities that they can understand. For example, the dead can no longer walk or talk or eat. Therefore, it is helpful when talking to children about death or answering the question, "What's dead?" to keep descriptions to observable events that are within the child's frame of reference. Discussions of respiration, heart rate or brain functioning, while valid, are not things children can see and are more difficult for them to comprehend. In order to reality test the situation they find themselves in, children may incessantly question whether their deceased loved one can perform basic activities. Though this may seem repetitive to adults, for many grieving children, it is a way to look for the one thing that person is able to do that makes them "not dead." It is their attempt to deny the current situation and make it not true.

2.1.3 Irreversibility

Irreversibility refers to the directionality of death. That is, a living thing can only progress from living to dead, not the reverse. Therefore, once something dies, it can never be alive again. This is an easier concept for older children, as young children tend to see death as a temporary state that one can return from. Further, the popularity of movies and television shows featuring vampires and zombies complicate the concept for many younger children who perceive a certain sense of reality in media images. According to Speece and Brent (1996), irreversibility is comprised of both Process Irreversibility and State Irreversibility. Process Irreversibility is the simple recognition that the path through life extends from life to death. State Irreversibility refers to the understanding that once the individual is in the death state, the situation is permanent. There is no reversal for death.

2.1.4 Causality

Like adults, children are plagued with the question "Why?" when a loved one dies. Yet, because of their more limited cognitive capacities, their answers tend to stem from internal rather than external causes. This is especially true for younger children, who seek concrete reasons for the loss and, by extension, look for controlling mechanisms to prevent another loss from happening. In many cases, children will blame themselves and something they said or did or some daily task they failed to do. It is a more plausible and controllable explanation than the inner mechanisms of disease and death – something they cannot see and have no access to. In this way, simply by remembering to do something or avoiding a decided upon toxic activity, children believe they can prevent another loss. Yet, children rarely voice these presumptions; worried to let the secret out or to further upset the adults in their lives. Therefore, the root cause of their behavior changes or emotional responses may remain unknown by those around them; making any treatment they receive inadequate. Often, the best gift an adult can give a grieving child is to remind them that it is not their fault. That there was nothing they could have said or done or failed to say or do that caused this to happen. Even casually mentioned, this can have enormous impact.

2.1.5 Noncorporeal Continuation

Probably the most fascinating and least studied, due to its high subjectivity, is noncorporeal continuation. All children, regardless of upbringing or education or lifestyle, have an innate belief in life after death. They will speak freely of angels or of their loved one looking down on them or visiting them. It allows them to maintain a connection to the deceased which may preclude the intense emotional reactions being experienced by the adults in their life. They "feel" the person around them so still consider them a part of their daily life. They are not gone; they are just different.

2.2 *Understanding Death across Developmental Stages*

As Silverman and Worden (1992) state, although younger children are better able than older children to express feelings, many do not have words for what they are experiencing. Due to this developmental discrepancy, school-aged children are more able to use intellectualization and isolation of affect (Baker et al., 1992) as defenses. Yet, regardless of developmental stage, reactions to loss are revived, reviewed and worked through repeatedly at successive levels of development (Krupnik, 1984).

2.2.1 Infancy

Discussions of death understanding are rarely postulated for infants. Such young children will appear distressed when a caregiver leaves the room or when a source of nurturance is removed. However, they are comforted easily and quickly when the person or object is returned or when something equally effective is provided. Games such as "peek-a-boo" provide these children with an introduction to the concepts of death (here vs. not here), but they possess no true understanding of what death is with regard to any of the components.

2.2.2 Pre-School

The first awareness and understanding of death usually occurs in preschool. Preschool children actively attempt to understand death when they encounter it, but see it as reversible and temporary. For them, things go to be dead for a while and then can come back. Most will explain dying as going to another place where it is possible for them to visit, vacation with or at least telephone their loved one. As such, preschool children wait for bugs that have been stepped on to come back to life or may, repeatedly ask when their loved one's will be coming back ("Grandma will be back for my birthday, right? She always comes to my birthday!") This can happen even amid direction from parents or caregivers locating the deceased in a place like Heaven and reinforcing that children cannot visit them there, nor can the deceased come back. For preschool children death is a place people go to. Since it has a location, like all places, in their minds, people can travel back and forth at will. Forever is too large a concept for children at this age. In a comprehensive qualitative study by Christ (2000), processes of mourning in children aged three to seventeen were viewed developmentally. Mourning experiences within age groups were distinct. Three to five-year-old children understand the permanence of death several months after the event in theory. While children at this age can assert that their loved one is dead forever, they are not ready to admit that they will never come back. For pre-school children these concepts are not intrinsically linked. In their thinking, a person can be dead forever in the same way a person moves to a new house or goes to a new school. Neither of those things preclude being able to still see each other. Death is somewhere their loved ones went to and they are adamant that there must be a way to visit. They have no frame of reference for the idea that a person can go to a place from which they can never return. Therefore, despite being in agreement that their loved onesare dead, children at this age will repeatedly search for ways to connect. They wonder, "If we can't visit, can we at least call Grandpa and tell him about my soccer trophy?"; "Let's go to Heaven for summer vacation this year! I bet it would be better than an amusement park or the beach!"; "Does Heaven have a gift shop? Maybe Grandma can send me something I can bring to school for show and tell!" Though, often, frustratingly repetitive for adults, preschool children need to explore concepts of death in their own cognitive format.

It is important to note that, at this age, children are very literal thinkers. They are bound by the things they can observe or have a frame of reference for. They may be concerned with how the deceased will perform life functions in the small space of a coffin or a how person can be buried in ground and still be in "Heaven." Preschool children will put snacks in the coffin "in case they get hungry" or may provide the deceased with their favorite stuffed animal to keep them company. "They can return it when they stop being dead." For them, nothing has changed in what the deceased needs and they are waiting for everything to return to normal. Children's need for concrete, literal explanations where loss is concerned, is, often, a counterintuitive aspect for adults. Instinctually, most adults seek to "soften" things for children and explain death and loss in ways that are more metaphoric than literal. They say things like, "They (deceased) are just sleeping" or "They are gone/passed away." These can be confusing and may reinforce misconceptions. Namely, that there is a type of sleep you do not wake up from (which guarantees no one will ever sleep soundly in the house again) or that the loss is temporary until the deceased comes back from being "gone." Difficult though it may be, the best way to explain loss to preschool age children is to be honest: "They died." Giving them the vocabulary will also allow their questions to arise from their understanding of death (or lack thereof) rather than their attempts to untangle and understand the metaphor.

As they are increasingly faced with the absence of their loved ones and attempts to find a venue for connection are thwarted, preschool children experience the full impact of the loss. Their mourning is, often, manifested in increased regressive behavior (such as a return to thumb sucking or wanting to sleep in their parents' beds). Subconsciously, they seek to return to a time when their deceased loved one was present and life was "normal." They may also display irritability, which is more an expression of frustration at the changes in their life and the lack of information they are receiving from adults, and develop physical symptoms similar to those of their deceased loved one (they will be sick, too, in the hopes that this is the way to get to Heaven and see the deceased again). They can also experience intense separation anxiety. They worry, when people are missing or out of sight for a period of time, that they have gone to be dead too. As difficult as permanency is for children of this age to understand, the, seeming, unpredictable randomness of who goes to be dead is even worse. Moreover, because of what dead seems to do to all the adults around them who are not dead. Preschool children are very overwhelmed by the grief reactions of the other adults in their lives. They seek to comfort them, repeatedly questioning about the deceased loved ones return. Even at this young age, children seek to protect adults as much as adults are seeking to protect them.

2.2.3   Elementary Age

By the middle childhood years, children have acquired an understanding to the irreversibility of death as well as its universality. At this point, understanding internal causes may also be added to external ones. That is, children can conceptualize that their loved one dies of cancer or a heart attack, even though they cannot physically see these things. However, it is also at this point that death ceases to be a place people go to and becomes personified as a being (presumably with the black hood, sickle and bony hand) that comes to get people. This helps elementary age children explain those internal causes of death. Yet, they still use personal frames of reference to understand the concept. For example: "Once, I had a race with my Grandma and she was so slow! I was all the way down the block before she even got a little way. That's why she died

– because when people get old, they can't run very fast and so Death can catch them!" The same can be said of those who are very sick with reference to a time these children remember being on the couch, home from school and not being able to do anything. This not only, helps them explain the causality of death but also helps them exert perceived control over the universality of death. Young people and people who are not really sick will not die because they can outrun Death when he comes. There is comfort in that for children even if, for adults, there is no practicality to it. As their understanding grows, however, their questions about death may become more graphic ("Why is a dead body cold?"; "What happens to a body after it dies?"; "Does the skin really fall off?"). These questions are often used to discern what is permissible to discuss. Any topic from which adults change the subject or recoil in horror is considered taboo and won't be brought up again. Yet, in this technological age, not answering these questions openly or working toward finding an answer together, will open the door for them exploring the answers online which can be more detrimental and will leave them feeling as though they have no one to talk to or turn to. Especially for elementary age children, questions require true answers, even if they are difficult to hear. Yet, this is also an opportunity to utilize the concrete descriptions of Nonfunctionality children are able to understand. Instead of recoiling or deflecting it is possible to say something like: "I'm not sure of the exact answer to that but remember how we said that a dead person can't feel anything anymore. Whatever happens is not painful for them. Maybe later we can find out the answer together so we both understand?" Children at this age respect that because it makes the adults in their lives approachable. If adults can handle those questions with honesty, children are more willing to come to them with the other, difficult aspects of grief.

Typically, it is not until at least six or seven years of age that children can understand the finality and irreversibility of death (Baker et al., 1992; Speece & Brent, 1996). However, fantasies about the return of the lost loved one may persist well into middle childhood (Baker et al., 1992). Like adults, it is hard for children to come to terms with the fact that they lost someone they love and that they are never coming back. To combat such heavy and intense emotions, six to eight-year-old children will immerse themselves in those important positive memories of the deceased loved one to ensure that expressions of sadness, anger and dejection are brief. While there remain elements of the physical symptoms experienced in preschool children, elementary age children have a greater ability to tolerate the negative emotions associated with loss. They can verbalize feelings of fear, sleep disturbances and separation anxiety. Further, at this age, there is greater expression of a desire to die in order to be with or visit their loved one. Yet, they are also eager to talk about their deceased loved one to anyone who will listen and, typically, constructed a benevolent image of the person comprised of all their best memories. The memories, and the sense that their loved ones' lives had value are deeply protective factors as children of this age grieve. It is incomprehensible to them that pictures should be put away or clothes donated in the wake of a death. It feels as though the person is, somehow, being erased and did not matter and they worry that the same will happen to them if they are not around. So, they cling to and cherish the stories and the memories and all the small mementos that make up a lived life. In this way, they were able to maintain a connection to the deceased (Christ, 2000). As they are gaining independence and control over their lives, it is hard for them to believe death can happen to them or anyone else they know. Many children at this age will externalize and personify death as a figure that comes to take people away. This is why death happens to the elderly, sick or handicapped – they could not outrun it and escape death.

2.2.4   Pre-Adolescence

Nine to eleven-year-old children were the first, according to Christ (2000), to be intolerant of the strong emotional experience, in both themselves and others, that accompanies loss. Further, this is the period of time during which understanding of death becomes akin to that of adults. Preadolescent children no longer personify death or consider it an external location people go to. Rather, they understand it more abstractly and comparable to an adult. Death is a state of being. Thus, despite requiring more detailed factual information about the events leading up to the death in an attempt to gain control, they are more likely to attempt to find external activities which would allow them to escape their grief. Despite their more mature cognitive understanding, emotionally, they are unable to tolerate elongated, intense grief emotions. They appear to rely on denial and projection, which can distort their perceptions of reality. So, they may want to play with friends instead of going to the wake or funeral. They may immerse themselves in a video game or activity when memories are being shared. Many prefer to grieve in private equally, because they cannot process such intense emotions adequately and for fear that their emotional expressions will upset the surviving adults in their lives – another attempt to shield and protect their surviving loved ones from the full emotional impact of the loss. Yet, given the opportunity and a space within which they are emotionally ready, elementary age children will talk openly, yet briefly, about their deceased loved one and their emotional responses. For the most part, however, children at this stage of development will show their grief rather than talk about it. They can engage in indirect mourning such as being messy, stubborn, argumentative or withdrawn. Grades may drop abruptly or there may be distinct personality alterations that are decidedly different from the norm. However, because these displays are, often, out of sync with where the adults in their lives are in terms of their own grief, the connection is often not made. Surviving adults will rationalize that it is just a "phase" or the result of a more difficult workload at school. The connection to the loss is easy to miss and, because these children are lax to discuss their emotions, there is little guidance or direction provided.

Yet, even if their emotions do not directly display their grief, children at this age are more likely to treasure material possessions from their deceased loved one as a way of maintaining connections. Unlike their preschool counterparts, elementary age children will leave notes or gifts in the coffin that reflect activities they shared with that person. It is their private way of saying "Goodbye" and honoring the relationship they shared. Nothing more needs to be said for them. This may be misleading, however.

2.2.5 Adolescence

Adolescent children closely match grief experiences reported by adults with intense emotional reactions and mature defenses such as denial and adamant optimism. The major underlying issue for adolescent grievers is the susceptibility of incorporating their loss into their burgeoning identity formation. They come to define themselves as someone who loses and this can have detrimental effects on how they engage with the world and find their place within it. Similarly, adolescents have a difficult time finding the help and support they need, especially externally. Too old for most children's bereavement groups and too young for adult bereavement groups, they can have a difficult time finding a place to belong even in their grief. As a result, adolescents who are grieving are, often, at greater risk of escaping into drugs or alcohol to mask the pain they feel they have no place to process (Black, 2005). Many thrive in groups specific to their developmental stage where concerns can be discussed among those who understand all the challenges of this stage.

3 Grief in Childhood

Bereavement in children is manifested in varying ways depending on the family's modeling and support of emotional expression, religious and cultural beliefs, and mourning rituals, as well as the child's own developmental level, cognitive and expressive style. What is essential is that children be allowed to grieve according to their unique parameters. Children experience death as intensely as adults do and, forced (through a desire to protect the child) or voluntary (through the child's desire to protect the surviving adults), suppression of emotions or opportunities to maintain connections leave children vulnerable to mental health issues. By allowing bereaved children to express their grief and participate in rituals such as funerals and memorial services, they are encouraged to celebrate the life of their deceased loved one. In the context of a supportive environment, this can make all the difference.

3.1   *Behavioral and Emotional Manifestations*

Despite agreement concerning the presence of grief reactions in childhood, little consensus is found regarding the precipitators, gender differences and outcomes of mourning in childhood.

Early bereavement has been linked to increases in a child's susceptibility to depression or depressive symptoms (Worden & Silverman, 1996), problems at school and delinquency or conduct problems (Weller et al., 1991; Silverman & Worden, 1992), social withdrawal (Dowdney, 2000; Lutzke et al., 1997; Worden & Silverman, 1996) and anxiety (Worden & Silverman, 1996). Being teased at school and feeling different seems to be of a particularly common for children who develop mental health problems as a result of bereavement (Worden & Silverman, 1996). Overall, there is more consistent evidence regarding the risk for depression and anxiety in bereaved children that the risk for conduct problems (Lutzke et al., 1997). Yet, Harrington and Harrison (1999) argue that bereavement does not emerge as a strong predictor of depression and, in many cases, bereaved children do not require professional intervention. Research has not demonstrated definitely that bereavement is correlated with mental or behavioral disorders in young people (Kessler et al., 1997; Chase-Lansdale et al., 1991; Velez et al., 1989). Further, there is evidence to suggest that most bereaved children do not display serious symptoms or dysfunctional behavior (Silverman and Worden, 1992) and that children of divorced parents have a higher risk of mental illness in later life than parentally bereaved children (Rodgers & Pryor, 1998).

According to Worden et al. (1999), boys are generally more affected by loss and are at a higher clinical risk than girls. Preteen parentally bereaved boys reported more thought problems and exhibited more withdrawn behavior, often, having trouble articulating their views or feelings. This correlates with mounting evidence that children's inhibition of their experience of negative emotions relates positively to mental health problems (Pennebaker et al., 2001). As a result, boys are more likely to be placed in at-risk groups. This is especially prevalent during the first year of bereavement for boys who had lost their father. However, despite these findings, several studies have shown that boys speak more often than girls (Dyregov, 1991; Silverman & Worden, 1992) suggesting that variables other than gender play a more significant role in bereavement outcomes.

Luther and Cushing (1999) argue that such inconsistencies may be due to children functioning well in one domain, as seen by one rater, but showing serious problems in other domains. For example, parents and teachers may rate a bereaved child as not having behavioral problems, yet the same child may self-report clinically significant levels of depression or anxiety. This dichotomy may also relate to evidence suggesting that a bereaved child may recognize that adults in their life become easily upset or anxious when talking about the deceased. Typically, these children will engage in restorative behaviors such as not talking about the person who died or behaving in a way that distracts the grieving adults (Stroebe & Schut, 1995, 1999).

Distinct child variables may also explain the inconsistent findings. Negative life events follow the death of a loved one and may reduce a child's internal locus of control by inducing feelings of helplessness or impairing the surviving adults' ability to provide a responsive environment. These negative life events may also lead to reduced self-esteem by directly devaluing the child, through criticism or rejection by surviving adults, exposing the child to some self-devaluing stigma, or decreasing opportunities to engage in esteem-enhancing activities (Seifer et al., 1992). Maintaining high self-esteem buffers the effects of negative life events by allowing bereaved children to appraise stressful events in ways that are less threatening to their self-worth (Kliewer & Sandler, 1992). Children with high self-esteem are more able to integrate stressful experiences with less negative arousal by using adaptive coping mechanisms (Harter, 1986). In a study by Haine et al. (2003) self-esteem significantly mediated child and parent reports of internalizing problems. Thus, lower mental health problems may be positively related to bereaved children's ability to maintain a positive sense of self, either through self-esteem or locus of control, in the face of adversity (Haine et al., 2003; Worden & Silverman, 1996) and belief in their efficacy to cope with future stressors (Lawrence, 1995).

Among family variables, surviving adults' mental health (especially that of the primary caregiver) consistently predicts children's mental health following a loss. While Cerel et al. (1999) reported that suicidally bereaved children were more likely to experience anger, anxiety, shame and have pre-existing behavioral problems, Dowdney et al. (1999) did not find a statistical relationship between the manner of death and children's level of psychological disturbance but, rather, reported children's distress as being associated with probable psychological distress in surviving adults. Conjugal bereavement studies indicate that young widows and widowers are particularly prone to psychological distress, including higher levels of acute grief, restlessness and irritability, physical distress and drug use (Stroebe & Stroebe, 1993). Surviving spouses living alone with dependent children report greater distress than those living without children or those living with children and someone else, such as a relative (Stroebe & Stroebe, 1993; Vachon, 1976). Thus, there is considerable evidence that the mental health problems of bereaved adults are associated with the mental health problems of their children (Kalter et al., 2002; Kranzler et al., 1990). There is also considerable evidence that bereaved children's mental health problems are related to lower levels of acceptance, warmth and support provided by surviving family members (Elizur & Kaffman, 1983; Raveis et al., 1999; West et al., 1992). For example, in an epidemiological study, Bifulco, Brown and Harris (1987) found that bereaved girls who experienced disinterest, neglect and a failure to discipline from surviving adults were twice as likely to suffer depression during adulthood. These findings are consistent with other studies that show that the parent-child bond and family routines promote children's healthy adjustment following a loss (Elizur & Kaffman, 1983; Raveis et al., 1999; Saler & Skolnick, 1992; Sandler et al., 1992; West et al., 1992) and that inadequate care, including neglect and a failure to discipline (Harris et al., 1990) increases bereaved children's risk for psychological problems. Children are as worried about you as you are about them. They bear witness to all the intense emotions grief brings to the adults in their lives and do not want to add to the sadness. So, they might make sure not to talk about the deceased in front of you, may be the one holding your hand or being strong. This does not mean they are not grieving. Many will cry in private or turn to other means of expression to work through their emotions, such as writing, art or play.

3.2   *Secondary Losses*
Familial death precipitates a series of negative life events, known as secondary losses. These include, but are not limited to, separation or addition of family members, parental distress, financial difficulties and relocation, which, in turn, can lead to increased mental health problems (West et al., 1991) through burdens on the child's self-system processes (such as locus of control) and environmental resources. If the family has to relocate, children may also have to leave their school, peers, place of worship and other social supports (Thompson et al., 1998). The accumulation of these stressful events, not simply the state of being bereaved, is related to higher levels of mental health problems in children (Elizur & Kaffman, 1983; Silverman & Worden, 1992; Thompson et al., 1998; West et al., 1991) and may also lead to reduced self-esteem by directly devaluing the child, through criticism or rejection by parents or caregivers, exposing the child to some self-devaluing stigma, or decreasing opportunities to engage in self-esteem enhancing activities (Seifer et al., 1992). Secondary

losses can be just as traumatic for the child and require the same capacity to adapt. Equally, they place enormous emotional burdens on the child and unique challenges for those who must care for them. Children are as worried about the adults in their lives as those adults are worried about them. They bear witness to all the intense emotions grief brings and do not want to add to the sadness. So, they might make sure not to talk about the deceased in front of adults or may be the one holding an adult's hand or being strong. This does not mean they are not grieving. Many will cry in private or turn to other means of expression to work through their emotions such as writing, art or play. These are the methods through which children express what their vocabulary fails to provide – a way to voice an experience without words.

3.3   Childhood Traumatic Grief

Consideration must also be paid to the nature of the loved one's death which can impact the mourning processes of the child. Childhood Traumatic Grief (CTG) refers to a condition in which a child or adolescent has lost a loved one in circumstances that are objectively or subjectively traumatic and in which trauma symptoms impinge on the child's ability to negotiate the normal grieving process (Elder & Knowles, 2002; Nader, 1997; Rando, 1993). In essence, children with CTG cannot get their minds off the traumatic and threatening circumstances of the death and thus the loss itself cannot be fully experienced and the pain of the grief cannot recede. They demonstrate diminished interest in normal activities, feeling emotionally distant or detached from others, a restricted affect range, and a sense of foreshortened future similar to all parentally bereaved children. Atypically, such children also experience symptoms of Post-Traumatic Stress Disorder (re-experiencing the traumatic event that led to the loved one's death; avoidance of reminders of the traumatic event, the death and the loved one; and physiological hyperarousal). They either avoid acknowledging any similarities between themselves and the deceased, for fear they will also share the fate of the deceased by dying in a horrifying and premature manner (Nader, 1997), or over-identify with the deceased, to the point of taking the deceased's name or only wearing articles of clothing that used to belong to the deceased, as an attempt to avoid accepting the reality of the death and thereby avoid the accompanying pain (Nader, 1997).

Many children with CTG blame themselves for the death, experience survival grief, or have rescue and revenge fantasies. As a result, the danger and trauma associated with the circumstances of death are taking priority over the loss itself in the child's mind. Positive reminiscing (thinking about happy times with the deceased) segues into thoughts, memories and emotions related to the traumatic nature of the person's death (Cohen et al., 2004). The experience is further complicated in cases of stigmatized deaths, such as a death from AIDS or because of drunk driving. These children receive less public sympathy or financial support, which leads to secondary losses and further complicates their grief.

4   Helping the Grieving Child

Given the wide range of reactions and individualized experiences of grief and loss, helping bereaved children can be a challenge. Though there is some evidence to suggest that early bereavement is linked to increases in child susceptibility to depression or depressive symptoms (Worden & Silverman, 1996), problems and school delinquency or conduct problems (Weller et al., 1991; Silverman & Worden, 1992), social withdrawal (Dowdney, 2000; Lutzke et al., 1997) and anxiety (Worden & Silverman, 1996), most bereaved children do not seek out traditional, individualized therapy. As there are no diagnostic criteria pertaining specifically to grief (which can have implications for insurance coverage and necessitate the child being labelled with an approved diagnostic category), families are left with few psychological resources at their disposal. Further, as was stated earlier, many children do not openly display their grief emotions and are, therefore, considered "fine" by their families and to be coping well. Having worked with many such "fine" children, it is important to note that when a child is not openly discussing a situation, there is definitely a problem and they are, assuredly, not "fine."

Most children who are grieving a loss do not display serious symptoms or dysfunctional behavior (Silverman & Worden, 1992). In fact, there is evidence to suggest that children of divorced parents have a higher risk for mental illness later in life than parentally bereaved children (Rodgers & Pryor, 1998). Mostly, children want life back to normal and their reactions reflect this desire. Depending upon the age of the child, the behaviors and motivations may be different, but the desire is the same. They do not want to be different from their peers or treated cautiously by those around them. It is for this reason that many children benefit from a child-focused bereavement group. As many parents are reluctant for their child to acquire a psychiatric record, these services play a role in normalizing the experience of bereavement by avoiding stigmatization and the view of grief as an illness. Further, psychiatric interventions often require lengthy and costly professional input that may be targeted at one child in particular. Often, this child becomes the focus of negative family attention and a useful distraction from the needs and hurts of others (Stokes et al., 1997). Community interventions also allow for flexibility such that services respond positively to the context-specific challenges of the local area, acknowledging particular social and cultural issues (Young & Papadatou, 1997). Similarly, the outcome measures they afford are particularly relevant to the needs of the children. These include: providing information, enhancing coping strategies, improving family communication, and providing an opportunity to meet others with similar experiences (Stokes et al., 1997). Such interventions have been shown to assist in facilitating the accomplishment of normal developmental tasks while satisfying important motivational needs (a sense of secure social ties, environmental control, or self-worth) that are, often, disrupted by bereavement (Sandler, 2001). These considerations may explain the low attrition rates observed in established community-based services.

Many interventions focusing on the prevention of mental health problems in bereaved children target self-esteem (Silverman & Worden, 1992), either through positive interactions with caregivers or involvement in activities for which children receive positive recognition. Child-focused programs provide bereaved children with competency-enhancing experiences and teach adaptive coping strategies to increase self-esteem. They are based on evidence which suggests that children's perception of their efficacy to cope with life stressors was negatively related to clinically significant mental health problems (Lin et al., 2004). Much of this efficacy to cope revolves around maintaining connections to the deceased through reviewing memories, keeping photographs and objects belonging to the deceased, and identification (Furman, 1974; Altschul, 1988). Silverman et al. (1992) in a study of six to seventeen-year-old children, discovered five strategies in trying to maintain connections to the deceased. These included: making an effort to locate the deceased (74% of those studied believed in Heaven), actually experiencing the deceased in some way (watching or communicating with them, dreams), reaching out to initiate a connection (visiting cemeteries), remembering (four months after the death 90% of the children reported thinking of their loved one several times a week) and keeping something that bonds with the deceased, even passed the time of eventual recovery. However, to date, there are no studies exploring circumstances and expressions in which ongoing connections are either adaptive and helpful or problematic.

Child-focused group programs provide bereaved children with competency-enhancing experiences and teach adaptive coping strategies to increase self-esteem. Typically staffed with highly-trained volunteers who understand children's unique perspectives on grief and loss, there is always someone to talk to or spend time with, eliminating much of the loneliness experienced by children who come home to an empty house where the silence is deafening. Children will also have the opportunity to participate in a wide range of expressive activities encompassing aspects of art, music, drama and sports. In this way, every child's strength can be harnessed and explored. Much of the work that is done is art-based. Studies of childhood bereavement support the use of art and art therapy techniques as a way to help grieving children identify feelings and understand loss through sensory means (Rozum, 2012; Griffith, 2003; Webb, 2003; McIntyre, 1990). Many children are hesitant to speak when they first enter group and would prefer to listen to others' stories, fearful of judgement or of toppling those carefully built defenses of "fine-ness" they have built up for the adults in their lives. However, as they become more engaged in whatever creative endeavor they undertake, their defenses slowly subside and they are more open to sharing, honestly, what the experience has been like for them. There is mounting evidence to suggest that children's inhibition of their expression of negative emotion relates positively to mental health problems (Pennebaker et al., 2001) so this expression can be invaluable. Not only will it build self-esteem in children who often feel defined by their loss and fundamentally different from their peers, it will also allow them to use their existing skills as coping tools. Whether they are making masks to represent inner emotions or creating mock stained-glass candle holders so they feel less lonely when they miss their loved one, taking advantage of the natural way children communicate (art and creativity) can help unleash what, for most, are traumatic memories of loss and change. Lusebrink (2004) suggests that art integrates both sensory and emotional stimuli and, therefore, is a beneficial vehicle to access and integrate traumatic memories. For this reason, it is essential to use a variety of mediums beyond drawing materials. Clay and play-dough are excellent ways to release anger, one of the lesser acknowledged grief emotions in children. It can be pounded or torn apart or serve as a physical personification of the pain inside through sculpture. Children utilize stickers and shapes and scrapbooking materials to personalize their creations and individually express their unique reactions. The only criteria should be that it makes sense to them and, through a process of voluntary sharing, that creation comes to make sense to the others in the group. Often, the narrative unlocks the words and the emotions buried deep inside. Within the safe environment of a group setting where children have the opportunity to share their unique grief experiences with others who are in similar situations and providing them with a sense of community they might not otherwise have, they can safely express their traumatic experiences through their artwork and, ultimately, process their negative memories. Further, much of their efficacy to cope revolves around maintaining connections to the deceased through reviewing memories, keeping photographs and objects of the deceased and identification (Furman, 1974; Altschul, 1988). This commemoration is essential for children and this is, often, ignored by the adults in their lives who cannot bear tangible reminders of the deceased. For this reason, Memory Boxes can be an invaluable resource for grieving children. These plain, simple cardboard boxes are decorated by the child in honor of their loved one and filled with their treasured memories, which they bring to share with the group. Though most share cherished photographs, of equal importance is the last Matchbox car their loved one gave them or those plastic eggs that come out of the machines in the supermarket because even though their parents called them "junk," Grandma always had an extra quarter or two. These are their reminders that their loved one existed; that the life had value and that they deserve to be remembered.

Silverman and Worden (1992) suggest that one of the tasks of early bereavement is to develop a language that gives children the tools to talk about death. This is, often, best accomplished in group interventions which allow grieving children access to others who are experiencing similar situations. Studies (Silverman & Worden, 1992) have demonstrated the effectiveness of such peer support in helping children cope with loss by normalizing the experience and allowing them to be around others who "get it." There is something deeply authentic about not needing to justify or explain their experiences. Moreover, the bonds they form with other grieving children are profound, lasting and decidedly different from any other peer relationships they have. Without fear of ridicule or stigmatization, children blossom and the bond is instant. To witness it as it unfolds is pure magic. There is truly no feeling in the world like watching the light find its way back into a child's eyes as they finally give into the laughter they don't feel they have a right to as a mourner. It is hard to smile when everyone you love and have left is sad. All you want to do is protect your family and it makes you grow up very fast. These group interactions are there to remind them that they are still children and allowed to have fun, even when they are hurting. Supported by their peers and a group of caring adults, they will slowly begin to believe that and heal. There is no loftier goal than to hold a child's story and give voice to one who may not feel able to speak for themselves.

Beyond singularly child-focused programs are programs involving multiple family members. These are designed to encourage parents or primary caregivers to increase parenting behaviors, such as consistency and warmth, that provide a supportive environment and promote self-esteem in bereaved children (Skinner, 1985). Such programs also promote decreasing the occurrence of negative events in the family, such as serious conflicts between caregivers and children and increasing adaptive beliefs about why negative events occur. This extends from evidence suggesting that these variables are related to the mental health of bereaved children (Lutzke et al., 1997; Worden & Silverman,

1996). Caregivers are encouraged not to involve children in stressors that are primarily the caregiver's responsibility, such as financial troubles (Lutzke et al., 1997) and focus on consistency in discipline (Silverman, 2000). Sandler et al. (1992) randomly assigned seventy-two families to such a family-based program. The program was delivered using family groups, in-home sessions with the whole family, and individual meetings with parents. At post-test, the program improved parents' reports of warmth in their relationships with their children and their feelings of social support, and increased family discussion of grief-related issues. Overall, the program reduced conduct and depression problems for older children (ages eight to eleven). Similar positive outcomes have been demonstrated in parentally-bereaved families with open communication (Silverman & Worden, 1992), including an increase in children's beliefs that their feelings were understood by their caregivers and a reduction in their need to inhibit the negative expression of grief-related feelings (Gottman et al., 1997; Gross & Levenson, 1997). Studies further demonstrate that family-based interventions can reduce morbidity in children one year after bereavement from 40% to 20% (Weller et al., 1991).

Regardless of type, bereavement interventions have been shown to assist in facilitating the accomplishment of normative developmental tasks while satisfying important motivational needs (a sense of secure social ties, environmental control, or self-worth) that are, often, disrupted by bereavement (Sandler, 2001). Still, Worden (1996) argues that professional intervention is not appropriate for all bereaved children and that only certain behaviors or circumstances, such as low self-esteem or the manner/suddenness of the death, indicate a need for professional referral. Moreover, vulnerable clients may be harmed by services delivered with the best of intentions (Schilling et al., 1992). This may explain why, in a meta-analysis of programs, Curtis and Newman (2001) found only a small amount of quantitative evidence that community interventions benefit parents and children within a bereaved family. Presently, evidence is too weak to make judgements about the relative effectiveness of different models of community-based interventions. What appears to be salient, however, is the need for a measure of selectivity, based on known risk factors, especially the etiology of the condition and the capacity of the immediate family to provide support.

5   The Grieving Student

Teachers are in a very unique position with respect to grieving students in their classroom. They are, simultaneously, one of the few harbingers of "normalcy" in lives of these children while also having very little formal training in what to do when outward expressions of grief enter the classroom. Equally, with the current, strong focus on academic progress within the classroom, teachers may have difficulty finding time within the school day to address the concerns of grieving children (Lytje, 2018). While formal, in school bereavement groups would be an ideal in all schools, this is not a global reality. Therefore, it is left to the classroom teacher to deal with the emotional and behavioral responses of grieving children. In many cases, because they represent an agent of normalcy, teachers may be the first ones to observe the emotional and behavioral changes associated with grief. Families who are steeped in their own grief coupled with children who seek to protect the adults in their lives, may make it difficult for children's grief to be recognized as overtly at home. Teachers are objective and have the capacity to recognize the subtleties and intervene on behalf of the child. They key is knowing what to look for within the classroom and feeling comfortable intervening.

5.1 Before the Loss

Proactively, it would be beneficial to address issues of grief in the curriculum conference at the beginning of the year. Teachers can stress their need to be informed of any significant life changes in the lives of their students – divorce, separation, death, family move, etc. Presented as a desire to create a unified plan of care for children, it opens the door for conversations that may otherwise be overlooked. No matter how trivial the loss seems to adults, it may have a significant impact in the lives of children. Information is a teachers most powerful tool. Even a generalized statement without specific details can alter teachers to potential behavior changes or explain those already witnessed. Phrases such as:

> I am so honored to be teaching your children this year and to be a part of this important time in their lives. Because so many things can happen both in school and at home, please let me know if anything changes in your family while your child is in my class. I may see the effects in school or it may help to explain something I have already noticed in your child's behavior. Even something that happened some time ago can have an impact. Please feel free to send me a note, or make a call to the school or even schedule an appointment with me. We are all on the same team for your child to ensure their success both inside the classroom and outside it. Communication is the key to that.

Similarly, teachers can familiarize themselves with developmentally appropriate literature and community resources for families that may be affected by loss throughout the schoolyear. Having books on hand that children can take home and share with their families is a wonderful way to connect with a grieving child without being too formal. It also opens the possibility for a family discussion about loss that might not otherwise have happened. In the same way, knowing where children and families can turn for external support in the form of therapeutic intervention or support groups is invaluable. Grieving parents, often, do not even know where to begin in order to help their children. Eliminating their need to navigate those resources themselves and, possibly, become overwhelmed in the process can be an essential form of support teachers can provide. Sometimes, simply knowing where to go for help makes all the difference in the world.

5.2   *After the Loss*

When a child suffers a loss during the schoolyear, the entire class is affected. It alters the dynamic and presents a new set of challenges to teachers which can feel impossible to navigate. In the absence of Professional Development to equip teachers to cope with grieving children in their classrooms, most are left on their own to find a way to help. This can lead to burnout in teachers who feel as though they cannot handle the emotional and academic needs at the same time. Yet, what is necessary to help grieving children is, often, simpler than one imagines.

5.2.1   Grieving Children Need Consistency

To the best of the teacher's ability, it is important not to single out grieving children for special treatment or to excuse them from their academic responsibilities. Initially, such measured show comfort and understanding and are appreciated. In the long-term, however, they signify another change in their lives that these children neither asked for not want. If school is the one normal place that remains, then it should be normal. At the core, they want to be like all of their peers, not constantly be reminded that they are different. Moreover, they become ostracized from the support system their peers can provide if they are viewed as receiving special treatment. Compassion can be shown without negating all expectations. Grieving children should be responsible for completing all work assignments on time or along with the rest of the class. In this way teachers can note behavior changes or emotional responses to material in the controlled environment of their standardized classroom. If grieving children are treated differently, it is difficult to truly know if they are responding to the loss or the change in treatment.

5.2.2   Grieving Children Need Opportunities to Grieve

It is impossible to guarantee that children are doing the appropriate amount of griefwork at home, as has already been noted. In what is often referred to as a conspiracy of silence, children seek to protect their grieving parents as much as their parents seek to protect them. As such, no one may be discussing the loss directly so there is no real opportunity to grieve. Likewise, parents may

also believe that because their children are not talking about the loss, they are not aware or affected by it. In reality, if children are not talking about something significant in their lives to anyone who will listen, it is the first sign that there is a problem. Teachers can bridge that silence both directly and indirectly during the course of a school day in the following ways:
- Look for Teachable Moments – The loss of a class pet or a tragic current event are opportunities for teachers to discuss aspects of grief and loss objectively with their students. This can, often, open the door to personal reflections from students, regardless of whether parents have provided direct information. This can be an important avenue for identification and intervention for teachers.
- Prepare the Classroom before Grieving Children Return to School – Ideally, teachers would have the opportunity to speak with parents prior to children returning to school to discuss what children know about the loss and any details that might be important for teachers to be aware of (Black, 2005). For example, children are, often, shielded from the manner of death, especially in cases of suicide or murder, and establishing such boundaries prior to the return to school can make things more seamless. Further, without going into too many details, it is essential to prepare the other students in the classroom for the return of a child who has just suffered a loss. Sadly, children can be callous and cruel to each other and arming other students with some appropriate responses ("I am so sorry for what happened."; "I hope you are feeling a little better"; "We missed you and we are happy to have you back") can not only be empowering for the other students but can remove a cumbersome obstacle as grieving children try to acclimate back to "normal."
- Construct Read-Alouds around a Theme – If teachers know there is a child experiencing a loss within their classroom and are not comfortable confronting the child directly, introducing a story to the class that has aspects of loss inherent in it and asking them to respond can be a powerful tool. Equally, as everyone in the class will be responding to the same information, the child will not feel singled out in their loss but, rather, a normal member of the class. Not only is writing an essential therapeutic intervention for children, but the information provided will provide the teacher with a better sense of the child's emotional state than they could ever put into words.
- Label Emotions as Necessary – If children feel comfortable enough to discuss the loss with a teacher, they may not have the vocabulary to describe what they are feeling. It can be helpful to give them the labels they lack. For example, saying things like: "It sounds to me like you are frustrated" or "You seem disappointed" provide them with a broader vocabulary that they will take with them throughout their grief journey. For younger children,

especially those in their preschool years, asking "What color do you feel like today?" and then gently probing for why they chose that specific color, can yield much deeper and more authentic information than a more direct, "How are you feeling?"
- Allow for Constructive Expressions of Grief – Children are not born knowing how to cope with loss, they learn from the adults in their lives. So, it can be important to help them express their, at time, nameless emotions in a way that best serves them. That may be by providing additional opportunities to write about their experience or borrowing from therapeutic techniques to deal with outbursts of anger or sudden waves of sadness. Having items like clay or bubbles in the classroom can provide these children with a better way or expressing their emotional state without calling too much attention to their situation in a classroom setting.
- Art – It can be extremely helpful to allow the grieving children in a classroom a space to draw or engage in an artistic representation of their grief. Art, especially, is a powerful tool for grieving children as they cope with new and resurging emotions throughout their journey. Visual representations of what they are feeling and experiencing require no words or explanations. They simply stand as they are and can tell far more than any dialogue whether they choose to share or not.
- Parent Teacher Conferences – Even when a presentation was made during the curriculum conference asking for information about significant life changes, not all parents will follow through or imagine it applies to their family, especially if the loss happened in what they consider the distant past. When discussing noted academic or behavior changes, it may prove beneficial to visit the idea of loss before approaching developmental delays or learning disabilities. Briefly talking through a child's history may reveal an underlying cause neither teacher nor parent has considered. Similarly, when a loss has been identified and relayed, a conference with the parent is a way to check-in and make sure everyone is working toward a consistent agenda.
- Listen! – Dealing with issues of grief and loss can be intimidating for teachers who do not feel as though they have adequate training to meet the needs of this population. Yet, one of the most essential things teachers can to help grieving children is to listen. Ultimately, there are no words teachers can say to magically make the experience better. They cannot bring children's loved ones back or normalize their families. Teachers also do not have answers to the more difficult questions children will ask like, "Why did this happen to me?" In reality, children are not looking for answers and respect a return of "I don't know" over a platitude that offers little comfort. They simply want to be heard – when it doesn't make sense and the words won't come or when

there is so much to say it runs into a stream of consciousness. They want to know that there is a safe space to go to where they can say out loud what they may not admit to those closest to them. Yet, it is equally important for teachers not to force a student to talk if they are not ready to. Despite what teachers may believe is best for the child, this is that child's grief and it has to evolve in their way. The role of the teacher is to act as a collaborative partner (Lytje, 2018). So, simply opening the door – "I know this is a really hard time for you and your family and I want you to know if you ever want to talk about it, I will listen." Then, do so. Make the time in a swamped school day and minimize the distractions during the conversation. Grieving children, especially those who are entrusting teachers with their stories and memories, deserve full attention. The second a teacher is distracted; the conversation ends and may never be revisited again.

6   Challenges for Teachers

6.1   *Cross Cultural Differences*

Before teachers can determine whether children's grief is abnormal or problematic, it is essential to become familiar with the cultural background of the family in question. Teachers must suspend any preconceived ideas regarding how children should grieve or any assumptions based on information read in a textbook (Rosenblatt, 2013). Understanding what grieving children are socialized to believe about death and loss is essential for teachers. Such information can be hard to come by, however. Academic journals provide generalizations that may not reflect children's lived experience and families may not be open to discussing their practices, especially if they are culturally taught to keep such emotions and information inside. Without an intimate knowledge of the grief practices children are taught, it is impossible to know the correct way to intervene. This may require teachers to open general classroom discussions regarding how children deal with difficult situations at home.

6.2   *Personal Grief Experiences*

One of the largest obstacles for a teacher who has a grieving child in their classroom is their personal response to grief. Often, our own frame of reference clouds what we are actually witnessing and averts our presumptions about the child in question. Therefore, teachers need to be introspective before they attempt to help a child who is grieving. An examination of how their family death with grief and what their personal beliefs are, will prevent them from projecting those beliefs onto the children they are trying to help or creating a measurable comparison between their reactions and those of the children (Black, 2005). Further, dealing with grief experiences in the lives of students may make teachers vulnerable to personal, unresolved grief experiences in their own lives. It is important for teachers to self-reflect when working with grieving students to determine when and whether their own grief is encroaching. Such self-awareness is essential as both a protective factor for teachers and an assurance that the help they are providing is solely about the students' grief and not an extension of their own. If they suspect that they are experiencing grief reactions that stem from their own lives, teachers should reach out. The community resources teachers recommend to grieving students and families are also available for teachers to help them navigate the residual feelings they may be experiencing.

6.3   *Institutional Barriers*
School exist as academic institutions and, as a result, activities that privilege that agenda are stressed. Emotional well-being is, often, relegated to the family and not considered the role of the school or teacher. Therefore, when grief and loss enter a school, there is little support in place. Even when a child within the school dies, grief counselors are called in only for a day or two and students must find the time to see them. This negates the cognitive lag that can accompany loss for children and leaves teachers at the forefront when cognition and emotion catch up to reality. Few schools have in place, consistent bereavement groups for children or a ready list of resources for families who may need additional help outside of the school. This leaves teachers struggling on their own to cope with a situation they were not trained for while still maintaining the academic standards they must adhere to. It requires conversations between teachers and administration to create a proactive approach to an unavoidable situation.

6.4   *Long-Term Support Is a Struggle*
Children are in a teacher's class for a short period of time. Even if that time encompasses a significant one in their lives, they move on to another teacher and grade the following year and there is no way for the previous teacher to know if the supports they put in place to help that child remain. With a new group of students and new challenges to face, teachers, often, lose track of former students as more than just a passing thought every once in a while. Further, outside of everyday, classroom interaction, former teachers, typically, do not reach out to families unless such parameters have been established and maintained. This means that, though a grieving child may have thrived under the support of a teacher last year, if their new teacher does not share in those

supports, they may backslide in their grief. This further speaks to the need for institutional agreement and collaboration in the ways to help children who have experiences a loss in their lives.

7 Final Thoughts

While there is evidence to suggest that children who experience the loss of a loved one, most notably a parent, are at increased risk for developing psychiatric problems (Weller et al., 1991; Black & Young, 1995), this is not an absolute. Children's ability to grieve, which determines the severity of the consequences of the event, is linked to the availability of caretakers who can provide a safe environment which allows them to tolerate painful feelings (Furman, 1974; Altschul, 1988). Families where communication is open, feelings are shared, problems are solved creatively, roles are flexible, resources are sought and used, reorganization to change is adaptive, individual differences are tolerated and beliefs are confronted, are better able to focus on their child's needs during bereavement (Davies et al., 1986). However, such situations are not always possible. Bereaved adults are often too concerned that they will say or do the wrong thing and want to believe their children are coping well (Stokes et al., 1997). Moreover, they seek to protect children from painful experiences. In doing so, however, children are, often, left confused and alone with their fears and fantasies (Monroe, 1995; Thompson, 1995). This is further complicated by surviving adults who may be struggling with their own grief, as well as trying to understand the child's. In such cases, children try to protect those around them to personal detriment. Often, children in unsupportive family environments grieve privately and escape detrimental effects by maintaining a connection to the deceased. As a whole, children appear to do this readily (Silverman, 2000; Silverman et al., 1992; Silverman & Worden, 1992; Worden, 1996) and it has been found to be adaptive (Baker et al., 1992).

It is essential for adults to remember that children are not immune from exposure to concepts of death and dying, no matter how strongly they seek to protect them. As Sedney (1999) has pointed out, deaths portrayed in children's films provide lessons, not only about death, but, potentially, about the grief process. In films such as *The Lion King* and *The Land Before Time*, grief is portrayed as a complex process that occurs across time and involves sadness, anger, blame, tears, seeking the deceased, imagined sightings of the deceased, remembering, developing new connections to the deceased as well as other symptoms such as somatic complaints. These grief narratives represent portrayals of how characters respond, over time, to the death of a loved one. They can form part of the context for children dealing with a death and provide entrance into family discussions.

What is essential is that children be allowed to grieve according to their unique parameters. Children experience death as intensely as adults do and forced (through desire to protect the child) or voluntary (through the child's desire to protect the adults) suppression of emotions or opportunities to maintain connections leave children vulnerable to mental health issues. By allowing bereaved children to express their grief and participate in rituals such as funerals and memorial services, they are encouraged to celebrate the life of their deceased loved one. In the context of a supportive environment, this can make all the difference. Despite their different levels of understanding and unique reactions and coping skills, the best way to help a grieving child is to be there. To know how it feels to lose someone or something you love and to recognize that in them. There is no greater honor than being entrusted with a child's story, for they do not give it lightly. When you can spare a few extra moments, or stop and answer the myriad of questions or stand steadfast through the flood of emotions, you provide a voice to a population that we, often, fail to listen to as closely as we should. For with every little hand held or tear dried, a difference is made. The smallest gestures mean the world to a grieving child. To be seen and recognized as a mourner is a powerful, life changing event and, it ensures that, no matter how lonely a grieving child may feel, no child will ever have to grieve alone.

References

Altschul, S. (1988). Trauma, mourning and adaptation: A dynamic point of view. In S. Altschul (Ed.), *Childhood bereavement and its aftermath* (pp. 3–15). International University Press.

Baker, J., Sedney, M., & Gross, E. (1992). Psychological tasks for bereaved children. *American Journal of Orthopsychiatry*, 62(1), 105–116.

Barnard, P., Morland, I., & Nagy, J. (1999). *Children, bereavement and nurturing resilience*. Jessica Kinglsey.

Bifulco, A., Brown, G., & Harris, T. (1987). Childhood loss of parent, lack of adequate parental care and adult depression. *Journal of Affective Disorders*, 12(2), 115–128.

Black, D. (1998). Coping with loss, bereavement in childhood. *British Medical Journal*, 316(7135), 931–933.

Black, D., & Young, B. (1995). Bereaved children: Risk and preventive intervention. In B. Raphael & G. Burrows (Eds.), *Handbook of studies of preventive psychiatry*. Elsevier.

Black, S. (2005). When children grieve. *American School Board Journal*, 192(8), 28–30.

Blad, E. (2015). Educators often overlook student grief, experts say. *Education Week, 34*, 12–13.

Bowlby, J. (1972). Pathological mourning and childhood mourning. *Journal of American Psychoanalytic Association, 11*(3), 500–541.

Cerel, J., Fristad, M., Weller, E., & Weller, R. (1999). Suicide-bereaved children and adolescents: A controlled longitudinal examination. *Journal of the American Academy of Child and Adolescent Psychiatry, 38*(6), 672–679.

Chase-Lansdale, P. L., Mott, F. L., Brooks-Gunn, J., & Phillips, D. (1991). Children of the national longitudinal survey of youth: A unique research opportunity. *Developmental Psychology, 27*(6), 919–931.

Christ, G. H. (2000). Impact of development on children's mourning. *Cancer Practice, 8*(2), 72–81.

Cohen, J. A., & Mannarino, A. P. (2004). Treatment of childhood traumatic grief. *Journal of Clinical Child and Adolescent Psychology, 33*(4), 819–831.

Cohen, J. A., Mannarino, A. P., Greenberg, T., Padlo, S., & Shipley, C. (2002). Childhood traumatic grief: Concepts and controversies. *Trauma, Violence and Abuse, 3*(4), 307–327.

Corr, C. A., & Corr, D. M. (1996). *Handbook of childhood death and bereavement*. Springer.

Curtis, K., & Newman, T. (2001). Do community-based support services benefit bereaved children? A review of empirical evidence. *Child: Care, Health and Development, 27*, 487–495.

Davies, B., Spinetta, J., Martinson, I., McClowry, S., & Kulenkamp, E. (1986). Manifestations of levels of functioning in grieving families. *Journal of Family Issues, 7*(6), 297–313.

Dowdney, L. (2000). Childhood bereavement following parental death. *Journal of Child Psychology and Psychiatry and Allied Disciplines, 41*(7), 819–830.

Dowdney, L., Wilson, R., Maugham, B., Allerton, M., Schofield, P., & Skuse, D. (1999). Psychological disturbance and service provision in parentally bereaved children: Prospective case-control study. *British Medical Journal, 319*(7206), 354–357.

Dyregov, A. (1991). *Grief in children*. Jessica Kingsley.

Elder, S. L., & Knowles, D. (2002). Suicide in the family. In N.B. Webb (Ed.), *Helping bereaved children* (pp. 128–148). Guilford.

Elizur, E., & Kaffman, M. (1983). Factors influencing the severity of childhood bereavement reactions. *American Journal of Orthopsychiatry, 53*(4), 668–676.

Emswiler, M. A., & Emswiler, J. P. (2000). *Guide your child through grief*. Bantam.

Freud, S. (1915). *Mourning and melancholia*. Hogarth Press.

Furman, E. (1974). *A child's parent dies: Studies in childhood bereavement*. Yale University Press.

Gottman, J. M., Katz, L. F., & Hooven, C. (1997). *Meta-emotion: How families communicate emotionally*. Erlbaum.

Griffith, T. (2003). Assisting with the "big hurts, little tears" of the youngest grievers: Working with three-, four-, and five-year olds who have experienced loss and grief because of death. *Illness, Crisis and Loss, 11*, 217–225.

Grollman, E. A. (1995). *Bereaved children and teens: A support guide for parents and professionals*. Beacon.

Gross, J. J., & Levenson, R. W. (1997). Hiding feelings: The acute effects of inhibiting negative and positive emotions. *Journal of Abnormal Psychology, 106*(1), 95–103.

Haine, R. A., Ayers, T. S., Sandler, I. N., Wolchik, S. A., & Weyer, J. L. (2003). Locus of control and self-esteem as stress-moderators or stress-mediators in parentally bereaved children. *Death Studies, 27*(7), 619–640.

Harrington, R., & Harrison, L. (1999). Unproven assumptions about the impact of bereavement on children. *Journal of the Royal Society of Medicine, 92*(5), 230–232.

Harris, T., Brown, G. W., & Bifulco, A. (1990). Loss of parent in childhood and adult psychiatric disorder: A tentative overall model. *Development and Psychopathology, 2*(3), 311–328.

Harter, S. (1986). Processes underlying the construction, maintenance, and enhancement of self-concept in children. In J. Suls & A. G. Greenwald (Eds.), *Psychological perspectives on the self* (Vol. 3, pp. 137–181). Lawrence Erlbaum Associates.

Herbert, M. (1996). *Supporting bereaved and dying children and their parents*. British Psychological Society.

Judd, J. (1989). *Give sorrow words*. Free Association Books.

Kalter, N., Lohnes, K. L., Chasin, J., Cain, A. C., Dunning, S., & Rowan, J. (2002). The adjustment of parentally bereaved children: Factors associated with short-term adjustment. *Omega, 46*(1), 15–34.

Kessler, R. C., Davis, C. G., & Kendler, K. S. (1997). Childhood adversity and adult psychiatric disorder in the U.S. National Comorbidity Survey. *Psychological Medicine, 27*, 1101–1119.

Kliewer, W., & Sandler, I. N. (1992). Locus of control and self-esteem as moderators of stressor-symptom relations in children and adolescents. *Journal of Abnormal Child Psychology, 20*(4), 393–413.

Kranzler, E., Shaffer, D., Wasserman, G., & Davies, M. (1990). Early childhood bereavement. *Journal of the Academy of Child and Adolescent Psychiatry, 29*(4), 513–520.

Krupnik, J. L. (1984). Bereaved during childhood and adolescence. In M. Osterweiss, F. Solomon, & M. Green (Eds.), *Bereavement: Reactions, consequences, and care* (pp. 99–141). National Academy Press.

Lawrence, G. B. (1995). *The impact of coping and perceived control on adjustment in children who have lost a parent* (Unpublished doctoral dissertation). Columbia University.

Lin, K. K., Sandler, I. N., Ayers, T. S., Wolchik, S. A., & Luecken, L. J. (2004). Resilience in parentally bereaved children and adolescents seeking preventive services. *Journal of Clinical Child and Adolescent Psychiatry, 33*(4), 673–683.

Lusebrink, V. (2004). Art therapy and the brain: An attempt to understand the underlying processes of art expression in therapy. *Art Therapy: Journal of the American Art Therapy Association, 21*(3), 125–135.

Luthar, S. S., & Cushing, G. (1999). Measurement issues in the empirical study of resilience: An overview. In M. Glanz & J. L. Johnson (Eds.), *Handbook of children's coping: Linking theory and intervention* (pp. 215–243). Plenum Press.

Lutzke, J. R., Ayers, T. S., Sandler, I. N., & Barr, A. (1997). Risks and intervention for the parentally bereaved child. In S. A. Wolckik & I. N. Sandler (Eds.), *Handbook of children's coping: Linking theory and intervention* (pp. 215–243). Plenum Press.

Lytje, M. (2018). The Danish bereavement response in 2015 – Historic development and evaluation of success. *Scandinavian Journal of Education Research, 62*(1), 140–149.

McIntyre, B. B. (1990). Art therapy with bereaved youth. *Journal of Palliative Care, 6*(1), 16–25.

Monroe, B. (1995). It is not impossible to communicate – helping the grieving family. In S. Smith & M. Pennells (Eds.), *Interventions with bereaved children* (pp. 87–106). Jessica Kingsley.

Nader, K. O. (1997). Childhood traumatic loss: The intersection of trauma and grief. In C. R. Figley, B. E. Bride, & N. Mazza (Eds.), *Death and trauma: The traumatology of grieving* (pp. 17–41). Taylor & Francis.

Nagera, U. (1970). Children's reactions to death of important objects: A developmental approach. *Psychoanalytic Study of Childhood, 25*(1), 360–400.

Nolen-Hoeksema, S., & Larson, J. (1999). *Coping with loss*. Lawrence Erlbaum Associates.

Owens, D. (2008). Recognizing the needs of bereaved children in palliative care. *Journal of Hospice and Palliative Nursing, 10*(1), 14–16.

Pennebaker, J. W., Zech, E., & Rime, B. (2001). Disclosing and sharing emotion: Psychological, social and health consequences. In M. S. Stroebe, R. O. Hansson, W. Stroebe, & H. Schut (Eds.), *Handbook of bereavement research: Consequences, coping and caring* (pp. 517–543). American Psychological Association.

Rando, T. (1993). *Treatment of complicated mourning*. Research Press.

Raveis, V. H., Siegel, K., & Karus, D. (1999). Children's psychological distress following the death of a parent. *Journal of Youth and Adolescence, 28*(2), 165–180.

Rodgers, B., & Pryor, J. (1998). *Divorce and separation: The outcomes for children*. Joseph Rowntree Foundation.

Rosenblatt, P. C. (2013). Culture and socialization in grief, death and mourning. In D. K. Meagher & D. E. Balk (Eds.), *Handbook of thanatology* (pp. 121–126). Routledge.

Rozum, A. L. (2012). Art therapy with children in grief and loss groups. In C. A. Malchiodi (Ed.), *Handbook of art therapy* (pp. 422–432). Guilford Press.

Saler, L., & Skolnick, N. (1992). Childhood parental death and depression in adulthood: Roles of surviving parent and family environment. *American Journal of Orthopsychiatry, 62*(4), 504–516.

Sandler, I. N. (2001). Quality and ecology of adversity as common mechanisms of risk and resilience. *American Journal of Community Psychology, 29*(1), 19–61.

Sandler, I. N., West, S., Baca, L., Pillow, D., Gersten, J., & Rogosch, E. (1992). Linking empirically based theory and evaluation: The family bereavement program. *American Journal of Community Psychology, 20*(4), 491–521.

Schilling, R., Abramovitz, R., & Gilbert, L. (1992). Bereavement groups for inner-city children. *Research on Social Work Practice, 2*(3), 405–519.

Sedney, M. A. (1999). Children's grief narratives in popular films. *Omega, 39*(4), 315–324.

Seifer, R., Sameroff, A. J., Baldwin, C. P., & Baldwin, A. (1992). Child and family factors that ameliorate risk between 4 and 13 years of age. *Journal of the American Academy of Child and Adolescent Psychiatry, 31*(5), 893–903.

Silverman, P. R. (2000). *Never too young to know: Death in children's lives*. Oxford University Press.

Silverman, P. R., Nickman, S., & Worden, J. W. (1992). Detachment revisited: The child's reconstruction of a dead parent. *American Journal of Orthopsychiatry, 62*(4), 494–503.

Silverman, P. R., & Worden, J. W. (1992). Children's reactions in the early months after the death of a parent. *American Journal of Orthopsychiatry, 62*(1), 93–104.

Skinner, E. A. (1985). Action, control judgments, and the structure of control experience. *Psychological Review, 92*(1), 39–58.

Social Security Administration. (2000). *Immediate assumptions of the 2000 trustees report*. Office of the Chief Actuary of the Social Security Administration.

Speece, M. W., & Brent, S. B. (1996). The development of children's understanding of death. In C. A. Corr & D. M. Corr (Eds.), *Handbook of childhood death and bereavement* (pp. 29–50). Springer.

Stokes, J. (1994). Anticipatory grief in families affected by HIV/AIDS. *Progress in Palliative Care, 2*(2), 43–48.

Stokes, J., Wyer, S., & Crossley, D. (1997). The challenge of evaluating a child bereavement programme. *Palliative Medicine, 11*(3), 179–190.

Stroebe, M. S., & Schut, H. (1995, June 26). *The dual process model of coping with loss* [Conference presentation]. International Work Group on Death, Dying, and Bereavement, Oxford, UK.

Stroebe, M. S., & Schut, H. (1999). The dual process model of coping with bereavement: Rationale and description. *Death Studies, 23*(3), 197–224.

Stroebe, W., & Stroebe, M. (1993). Determinants of adjustment to bereavement in younger widows and widowers. In M. Stroebe, W. Stroebe, & R. Hanson (Eds.), *Handbook of bereavement: Theory, research and intervention* (pp. 208–226). Cambridge University Press.

Thompson, F. (1995). *Where is dead? A study of bereaved children's questions to doctors* [Unpublished doctoral dissertation]. Southampton University.

Thompson, F., & Payne, S. (2000). Bereaved children's questions to a doctor. *Mortality*, *1*(5), 74–96.

Thompson, M. P., Kaslow, N. J., Price, A. W., Williams, K., & Kingree, J. B. (1998). Role of secondary stressors in the parental death-child distress relation. *Journal of Abnormal Child Psychology*, *26*(5), 357–366.

Torbic, H. (2011). Children and grief: But what about the children? *Home HealthCare Nurse*, *29*(2), 67–79.

Vachon, M. L. (1976). Stress reactions to bereavement. *Essence*, *1*(1), 23–33.

Velez, C., Johnson, J., & Cohen, P. (1989). A longitudinal analysis of selective risk factors for childhood psychopathology. *Journal of the American Academy of Child Adolescent Psychiatrists*, *28*(6), 861–864.

Webb, N. B. (2000). The child and death. In N. B. Webb (Ed.), *Helping bereaved children* (pp. 3–18). Guilford.

Webb, N. B. (2003). Play and expressive therapies to help bereaved children: Individual, family and group treatment. *Smith College Studies in Social Work*, *73*(3), 405–422.

Weller, R., Weller, E., Fristad, M., & Bowes, J. (1991). Depression in recently bereaved pre-pubescent children. *American Journal of Psychiatry*, *148*(11), 1536–1540.

West, S. G., Sandler, I., Pillow, D. R., Baca, L., & Gersten, J. C. (1991). The use of structural equation modelling in generative research: Towards the design of a preventive intervention for bereaved families. *American Journal of Community Psychology*, *19*(4), 459–480.

Wolfenstein, M. (1966). How is mourning possible? *Psychoanalytic Study of the Child*, *21*(1), 93–123.

Worden, J. W. (1996). *Children and grief: When a parent dies*. Guilford Press.

Worden, J. W., Davies, B., & McCown, D. (1999). Comparing parent loss with sibling loss. *Death Studies*, *23*(1), 1–15.

Worden, J. W., & Silverman, P. R. (1996). Parental death and the adjustment of school-age children. *Omega*, *33*(2), 91–102.

Young, B., & Papadatou, D. (1997). Childhood death and bereavement. In C. Parkes, P. Laungani, & M. Young (Eds.), *Death and bereavement across cultures* (pp. 191–205). Routledge.

CHAPTER 3

Techniques for Creating Trauma-Sensitive Learning Environments for Children

Jennifer Lauria

Abstract

Mindfulness methods and a growth mindset approach can serve as effective social and emotional learning (SEL) supports, both in school and at home, to foster healing and self-empowerment in students who have experienced trauma in their lives. Introductory techniques for creating trauma-sensitive learning environments for children, including mindfulness methods as SEL tools for students, use of children's literature, and a growth mindset approach, along with implications for teacher education programs. will be discussed. A focus on wellness for educators as an essential element for creating a trauma-sensitive learning environment is highlighted in the context of techniques for creating trauma-sensitive learning environments for children. In addition to providing practical SEL strategies educators can implement in the classroom, techniques that can be used by caregivers in the home environment are shared in this chapter. Recommendations for expansions of teacher education curricula to adequately prepare future educators to implement effective use of SEL supports, mental health and wellness initiatives, and create safe and respectful learning environments are presented.

Keywords

grit – growth mindset – mindfulness – resilience – social and emotional learning (SEL) – trauma-sensitive

1   Introduction

Master educators tend to exhibit key dispositions that serve as determinants of high quality learning experiences for students of all ages, and significantly contribute to overall teaching excellence and resultant student successes. Educators of distinction genuinely care about meeting students' unique needs and positively impacting students to help them thrive by instilling passion for learning. Their caring ethic is evident in everything they do-- from creative planning to implementation of innovative instruction to motivating students to excel, and providing meaningful feedback during the assessment process.

A genuine ethic of caring is a vital disposition for teacher candidates to embody in order to be able to become successful, transformative, and professionally fulfilled educators. This disposition is equally important to the requisite content knowledge and pedagogical skills sets required to earn professional teaching certification, if not more, because it guides the multitude of daily decisions educators make, thus shaping the culture and climate of the learning environment for students. Caring is central to shaping meaningful relationships and happens when children sense the adults in their lives respect and accept them. Caring is a product of learning communities that deem all members important, believe everyone has something to contribute, and that everyone counts (Elias et al., 1997).

Central to the educational philosophies of caring teachers is the belief that all students deserve a dedicated, safe, nurturing, and inspiring place to learn, but for students who have survived trauma, and especially those currently enduring traumatic ordeals, caring teachers, and safe, nurturing, and inspiring learning environments are essential elements for high quality learning. It's important that all stakeholders in a child's life and educational journey become informed about identifying and utilizing appropriate strategies to help create trauma-sensitive classrooms rather than shy away thinking they should leave that type of support up to trained mental health professionals. Unfortunately, not all schools provide students access to support from mental health professionals for a variety of reasons. In such instances, all stakeholders, collectively, can make a difference toward helping students begin to overcome obstacles stemming from trauma with mental health supports (while awaiting professional mental health services). Attention to the effects of trauma can occur at the classroom level, and, when possible, through partnership and communication with students' families and caregivers. Therefore, educators need to be trauma-informed and trauma-sensitive when planning appropriate learning experiences for children impacted by trauma as that added degree of support can make a world of difference.

Ironically, during the writing of this chapter about supportive techniques educators and families can use with children who have experienced trauma, I was faced with a personal trauma of my own, concurrently, as our world suddenly was confronted with a global pandemic of monumental proportions. The trauma-sensitive techniques I'd shared in the chapter up until that point were focused on supporting children's needs in a range of unfortunate and traumatic circumstances, prior to the pandemic and the drastic changes it caused to all facets of life as it once was known. Then, rather suddenly, we all were challenged with navigating the terrifying scenario of a global pandemic most never imagined possible, causing many to experience life-altering events as traumatic on many levels. Compounded with the new and previously unfathomable life stressors every one has encountered, thoughtfully selected, trauma-sensitive techniques, not solely for learners affected by trauma, have become necessary. They are even more imperative at this pivotal time, during such a sudden shift to remote learning, to support learners' emotional needs and to guide continuation of academic, social, and emotional growth.

Similarly, although part of the focus of the chapter was on the need for educators to attend to their own wellness in order to be prepared to help students who have experienced trauma, once the pandemic developed rather rapidly, the need to include wellness strategies for educators became even more evident. Educators and caregivers need to support their own wellness in order to be able to help young learners thrive during times of such unprecedented uncertainty, anxiety, and fear brought on by a global pandemic. My current work as an independent educational consultant has provided several opportunities to respond to the educators' increased needs for health and wellness supports while navigating the stress of needing to learn new teaching techniques so quickly with minimal support during such troubling times of uncertainty.

Additionally, surviving my own trauma provided uniquely relevant insight, through a different lens and perspective, into what it takes to be trauma-sensitive and meet the needs of someone coping with trauma from walking in their shoes and feeling what it might be like for a student with unexpected new challenges – such as difficulty sleeping, focusing or calming anxiety, obstacles that simply weren't there prior to the traumatic event and can't be ignored. Personally, day to day living became a completely different experience and some seemingly simple tasks became challenging due to the after effects of the trauma, for which I needed to find coping techniques. These unanticipated obstacles caused me to consider recommendations for trauma sensitive learning environments in new ways as I could relate very differently to how students who've experienced trauma would have to adjust to new modes of daily classroom life. It's helpful to keep in mind that if educators are unaware of a student's trauma, it can be challenging to realize a student needs additional support. Therefore, employing trauma-sensitive techniques for all students embedded in a strategically crafted respectful classroom climate can be a good supportive measure, particularly at this time when so many stakeholders in the education process are struggling with unforeseen obstacles – students, teachers, and caregivers, alike.

2   Social and Emotional Learning

In recent years, the topic of social and emotional learning has been widely discussed in terms of its benefits and potential integration in the academic curricula of PreK-12 schools. As an advocate of high quality and personalized education for all learners, I'm an avid proponent of providing students with a plethora of tools to help them navigate any challenges they may face, both in school and in life outside the classroom. I've experienced countless instances throughout my career as an educator thus far, in which students benefited tremendously from being taught how to maximize their strengths, develop areas needing improvement, and develop SEL skills, such as self-regulation, to help them overcome obstacles to learning. Having taught diverse and challenging student populations in the New York City school system for nearly a decade spanning PreK-5, immediately followed by almost 2 additional decades working as a full time professor of education, I firmly attest to the need to avoid a one size fits all approach to teaching and supporting students well. Therefore, the need for infusion of social and emotional learning skills into academic curricula of PreK-12 schools and higher education teacher preparation programs resonates profoundly with me. Now, more than ever, as schools unexpectedly scramble to provide the best remote learning scenarios possible due to the global Covid-19 pandemic, SEL supports can be beneficial to all stakeholders.

Social and emotional learning has been defined by Reilly (2017–2018) as an instructional approach that takes into account emotional components that either facilitate or impede learning built on safe, positive relationships cultivated between educators and students. She described the cumulative goal of education as "offering students interrelated academic, personal, and social competencies that have long term impact on their lives and stressed two key tenets of a social-emotional approach to learning as a caring, responsive school climate for both students and adults, along with children's emotions, behaviors, learning, and regulation being inextricably intertwined" (Reilly, 2017–2018, p. 57). Key to SEL, students' emotional wellness comprises a substantial component of their overall well-being and mental health. Curiosity and joy for learning can become substantially diminished when social and emotional struggles become part of the equation. While modern educational systems continually have been developing programs to help educators and families support students' social and emotional health, more work needs to be done to help provide students with the tools they need to thrive, despite incremental stressors ever present in our modern global society that can function as potential obstacles to their academic success.

Within the realm of SEL, the use of mindfulness techniques is on the rise in a variety of educational settings. Mindfulness can be defined, generally, as consciously focusing on the present moment. Mindfulness expert, Jon Kabat-Zinn (2017), defined mindfulness as paying attention, intentionally, in the present moment, and non-judgmentally. Some researchers, who have discussed mindfulness practices in terms of breathing and focusing exercises that enhance attention and awareness, have reported the benefits of incorporating mindfulness to support social and emotional learning, and identified the ability to manage stress and pay attention as important determinants of well-being and successful learning (Titone, Feldman, & DeRosato, 2017–2018). A literature review revealed school-based mindfulness research that included a specific focus on social and emotional learning. Broderick and Metz (2009) successfully piloted a mindfulness curriculum for adolescent learners in 2009. Later, social and emotional learning was examined by Schonert-Reichl, Oberle, Lawlor, Abbot, Thompson, Oberlander, and Diamond (2015). Significant gains in cognitive control, stress physiology, empathy, perspective-taking, emotional control, optimism, school self-concept, and mindfulness were reported for the children who received an SEL program with mindfulness components. Some of the many benefits of mindfulness for all young learners (and adults), particularly those who have been affected by trauma, are increased capacity for self-compassion, reduced anxiety and stress levels, improved self-esteem and alertness. All of these benefits provide supports to help children focus and work through the adverse effects of trauma.

Schwartz (2019) outlined clinical psychologist, Dr. Sam Himelstein's, description of how to be trauma-informed while still using mindfulness in classrooms, in which he suggested guidelines for teachers to be sure mindfulness practice with youth is helping, not hurting, as mindfulness practice can bring up uncomfortable feelings that when combined with existing trauma can be frightening or psychologically dysregulating. He stressed that students shouldn't be forced to close their eyes or sit a certain way because kids can feel vulnerable when attempting to be present in the moment. Therefore, a focus on physical safety is necessary.

Toward that end, while developing classroom culture – ,building at the beginning of each school year to create a safe and welcoming learning environment for all, it would be helpful if teachers would pay extra attention to incorporating elements that help students feel safe, respected, and accepted as valued members of the of the classroom, to set the stage for use of mindfulness methods to come. Another strategy for avoiding any potential challenges with the use of mindfulness for students who have experienced trauma could be to ensure all students know right from the start that there will always be choices to implement the mindfulness activities in ways that best suit them individually, one of which always will be to opt out of participating if they don't feel comfortable in any way. Teachers also might want to let students know there will be other options that would allow them to participate in their own preferred way, which can include keeping eyes open rather than needing to close them or not being required to sit in the manner dictated by the activity instructions. If students know beforehand that flexibility for preferences always will be permitted, they may feel safer to opt in.

3 Practical Applications

As a complementary extension of social and emotional learning, a focus on mindfulness can be particularly beneficial in childhood education settings as a foundation for future self-care, caring for the welfare of others, and development of stress management tools and self-regulation. Various modes of utilization of mindfulness approaches to help foster students' social and emotional development have been highlighted in mindfulness literature. Such evidence warranted personal reflection about how teacher education programs prepare future educators to enter their chosen profession and prompted careful consideration of more prominent infusion of SEL elements in curricular redesign of teacher preparation programs that aim to nurture caring, competent, and confident educators.

My comprehensive work as a PreK-5 classroom teacher in a diverse and challenging urban New York City public school, followed by nearly two decades as a professor of education preparing future teachers, revealed common threads regarding the need for SEL supports for teacher candidates, and the young students they are preparing to teach. In conjunction with substantial faculty teaching and scholarship, serving as Director of both undergraduate and graduate Childhood Education programs for a combined 18 years, granted the flexibility to redesign course curricula, including health education methods courses to expand the mental health components toward a more in-depth focus on SEL.

From the onset of a strategic focus on SEL supports, teacher candidates consistently requested even more work with the SEL components to inform their classroom practice. Serving as an unanticipated outcome each semester, without fail, several students would comment on how they began to apply many of the SEL supports explored in courses to their own personal and professional lives. They lamented that they believed mastering such support techniques as much younger learners would have helped them tremendously throughout their earlier years of schooling. That dynamic prompted my sharing of how I'd used many of the SEL supports myself as a classroom teacher, then as a professor brand new to higher education and navigating demanding tenure and promotion processes up through earning the rank of full professor. I continue to implement them to this day, particularly the deep breathing techniques and meditation, which can be used almost anywhere and at any time without anyone being aware that you are doing so! Such candid discussions regarding realities of teaching stressors and coping strategies for use in tackling them contributed to the community building components of our classroom learning environment. Through leading by example, strategies for implementation of SEL supports which teacher candidates would be expected to utilize in their professional field placements with diverse students in grades 1–6 were modeled. Soon afterward, cooperating mentor teachers in field placements were partnered with the teacher candidates, and the young students' families, were offered opportunities to learn about the SEL supports to be implemented in the classroom by our teacher candidates, such as mindfulness methods, including meditation, yoga for children and families, breath work, gratitude journaling, etc. The cooperating mentor teachers were receptive to learning new techniques for their own professional development and helped facilitate the scheduling of modes of SEL outreach to families.

More specifically, the mindfulness strategies shared included: (a) implementation of a growth mindset approach to providing effective, actionable feedback that helps foster communication between teachers and students to develop professional relationships and establish a rapport conducive to learning, (b) cultivating kindness and nurturing a culture of mutual respect in which students feel valued and safe to take academic risks; and (c) mindfulness methods that help manage stress and foster resilience.

In several teacher education methods courses, mindfulness techniques and a growth mindset approach were modeled consistently spanning 37 semesters in total. Undergraduate and graduate level students learned about the benefits of self-care as crucial for success, rather than merely a welcomed enhancement, and focused on guided meditation, a growth mindset approach, yoga for children, movement breaks, deep breathing, body scanning, kindness strategies, nutritional tutorials, high quality sleep strategies, journaling, and relaxation. The mindfulness techniques were taught and modeled in an effort to support SEL and provide stress management training to help foster higher levels of resilience, overall wellness, and self-confidence. Some techniques were modeled through "thinking out loud" to demonstrate how and when mindfulness strategies such as kindness training and use of growth mindset language could be beneficial in each scenario and how they might be utilized in diverse childhood education classroom field placements. Others were modeled through active demonstration requiring substantial student participation, including guided meditation, deep breathing, yoga for children, and body scanning. For instance, we began course sessions with mini meditations, paused for brief movement breaks, and ended class with deep breathing during the debriefing and reflection portions of our lessons, which provided teacher candidates with opportunities to observe the implementation of the supports, become active participants, and reflect on the experiences from a child's perspective prior to implementing each technique in their classroom field placements. Teacher candidates were encouraged to implement the mindfulness methods learned in their teacher preparation courses in corresponding professional classroom field experiences in preparation for the upcoming immersive student teaching semester.

Table 3.1 presents easily accessible, cost-free resources and techniques that were utilized with implementation of mindfulness methods in my teacher education courses,as well as in diverse childhood education settings, to help support students' social and emotional learning. Several of the children served

TABLE 3.1　Mindfulness resources and beginning techniques for educators

Easily accessible mindfulness resources	Getting started with mindfulness techniques
1. Mindfulschools.org	Strategic self-care
2. Mindsetworks.com	Guided meditations
3. GoZen.com	Deep breathing
4. MindBodyGreen.com	Dissolve-A-Thought
5. MeditationDojo.com	Quality sleep
6. KidsYogaStories.com	Body scanning
7. MindfulInquiry.org	Purposeful nutrition
8. Littlefloweryoga.com	Mindfulness breaks
9. Mindful.org	Fun physical exercise
10. YourTherapySource.com	Movement in learning activities
11. Shambalakids.com	Feelings Yoga/Yoga for Children
12. Mamarooyoga.com	Journaling
13. TheMindfulClassroom.wordpress.com	Growth mindset language/behaviors
14. Calm.com/schools	Kindness Measures
15. Sleepbeditations.com	PLAY!

in the professional classroom field placements were coping with serious life circumstances, including homelessness and extreme poverty and were in dire need of stress relief and tools to help them process feelings of hopelessness, fear, and despair.

4   Children's Literature for SEL

Another technique for use in a trauma-sensitive learning environment is the use of children's literature. Works of children's literature can serve as wonderful resources for use in helping educators and children communicate and begin to explore the effects of trauma in a non-threatening manner. Books addressing real-life situations are effective with a wide range of age levels because their story lines ring true and they evoke real feelings (Roberts & Crawford, 2008). Although educators need to be careful in determining a child's readiness to communicate and selecting appropriate texts, a child may be able to relate to the plight of a character as presented in the text and begin to realize they are not alone in dealing with the problems they are shouldering. Perhaps experiencing the character's journey through the reading experience and discovering how the character dealt with adversity might inspire the courage to work through their own hurt and begin the healing process. A reading response discussion or journal-writing expression of feelings can open the lines of communication on challenging topics.

Roberts and Crawford (2008) described how quality works of children's literature offer much for the social-emotional needs of young readers because authentic literature can inform, comfort, and provide models of coping strategies. Additionally, they emphasized the importance of being sensitive to children's circumstances and personalities when selecting children's books, and honoring children's unique responses to stories, as individuals will have differing responses to the same book. Therefore, providing opportunities for different responses to literature such as oral responses, artistic expression, or dramatic play, can allow children to find their genuine, honest, and caring voices and engage in discussions about the tough topics the literature presents. Roberts and Crawford (2008) warned that children should be introduced to the book's content beforehand so as not to be shocked by sensitive issues presented and noted that children coping with loss often will repeatedly request a particular book. Although older children may read books independently, educators and caregivers can conduct read-alouds and follow-up discussions or writing exercises/ reading response journals, to help them navigate difficult or traumatic topics. With guidance from educators and caregivers, children can comprehend and make sense of both the subtle and complex messages presented in the stories.

There are countless, free resources readily available for assistance with selecting appropriate works of children's literature to help children cope with trauma and stressors, such as book lists of suggested titles categorized by specific traumatic circumstances (family illness, death or incarceration of a loved one, divorce, military deployment, etc.) that can be found through a basic search process online, along with corresponding reading response activities. Reading a book with a child is a good start, but the follow-up discussions and responses to the text are where the real healing and support for children affected by trauma will begin. Educators can facilitate these reading response experiences in school, through remote learning, or recommend similar activities for families to use at home. Families can use reading together as a special bonding experience in the home. Treasured books can be read over and over and tend to help children feel safe and loved as they reflect on memories of reading each text with family members or other caregivers. These experiences help develop trust.

An early experience from my first year as a professor of education that occurred during clinical supervision of student teachers at a New York City elementary school has stayed with me to this day. As I was observing a fifth grade literacy lesson, the classroom teacher was continually interrupting my student teacher's lesson to scold a little girl who was tuned out from the lesson because she was looking down to try to read a book of her own inside her desk. The child was startled each time the classroom teacher yelled at her for doing so and clearly was embarrassed that the other students were looking at her as she was getting reprimanded. I asked about the incident when I met with my student teacher afterward. He shared that the little girl did that often because he learned that her father had given her that book as a gift and read a portion of it each night to her at bedtime. Sadly, they were halfway through the book when her father, a NYC firefighter, was killed during the September 11th terrorist attacks at the World Trade Center five months earlier. The child was using the book as a security blanket of sorts that helped her feel close to him as she was grieving. Although the book was a bit too difficult for her to finish on her own, she tried very hard to keep reading without assistance whenever she could. It turned out that the day of my student teacher's observation lesson was her father's birthday and she wanted to be able to read more of their special book as a gift to him in Heaven. Clearly, that was all she could focus on that day and, unfortunately her teacher hadn't established a sufficient rapport with her to know how much she still was suffering from the trauma of losing her father.

Two lessons emerged from that saddening experience. The first was witnessing the power of children's literature as a healing tool and, the second, the need for teachers to cultivate genuine relationships with students in order to become trauma-sensitive. Had the teacher developed a better rapport with the student, she may have realized what was happening and reacted differently, sparing the child that unnecessary unpleasantness while she was still grieving the loss of her father.

Use of works of children's literature can be an effective mode of exploring elements of social and emotional learning as children often can relate to the dilemmas characters may be faced with in each story better than they might be able to when taught these concepts by an adult. Special focus should be devoted to selecting a multiculturally inclusive collection of texts to represent the cultural diversity of many modern classrooms. Similarly, a variety of texts representing other types of diversity, such as children with exceptionalities, health challenges, differing socio-economic levels, LGBTQ, nontraditional family models, etc. should be included as well. Students' recognition of characters they can identify with can enhance the reading experience in powerful ways.

The *Huffington Post* published a list of children's books that offer poignant lessons about friendship, acceptance, kindness and compassion (Bologna, 2019), some of which are included in Table 3.2, along with helpful resources for training educators on how to begin implementing mindfulness methods, meditation, and movement as social and emotional learning supports for children.

5 Resilience

Souers and Hall (2016) identified resilience as a crucial element that needs to be taught in schools to adequately prepare students for life beyond graduation, along with responsibility, respect, and relationship building. They stressed that students carrying the burdens of trauma, neglect, and abuse into the classroom have altered the educational landscape in schools and that learning only happens when the learner is in a learning condition. Trauma can be toxic to the brain and can affect development and learning in a multitude of ways (Souers & Hall, 2016).

When considering how trauma affects the learning process, fostering children's capacity for resilience should be a primary goal in order to help children develop the skills they'll need to overcome the impact of the trauma. In her book, *Outward*, Aguilar (2018) partially defines resilience as a way of being that allows us to bounce back quickly from adversity, and stronger than before, so that we can fulfill our purpose in life.

TABLE 3.2 Children's literature on mindfulness, meditation, and social and emotional learning elements

Text	Theme and publisher
I Am Enough	*Acceptance* – Scenarios about self-acceptance and accepting others. Balzer + Bray
Lovely	*Acceptance* – Explores the many ways we can be different and how everyone is lovely in their own unique way. Creston Books
Chocolate Milk, Por Favor!	*Empathy* – A story of a boy's friendship with a new classmate who doesn't speak English. Cardinal Rule Press
Empathy Is My Superpower!	*Empathy* – Recognizing emotions in others and discovering the power of compassion. Boys Town Press
Hey, Little Ant	*Empathy* – Considering the feelings of others. Penguin Random House
I Am Human	*Empathy* – Understanding and accepting our imperfections and loving our flawed selves and peers. Abrams Books
Just Feel	*Empathy* – Helping children learn to understand and navigate their own emotions and develop empathy for others. Running Press Kids

(cont.)

TABLE 3.2 Children's literature on mindfulness, meditation, and social and emotional learning elements (*cont.*)

Text	Theme and publisher
Wonder	*Empathy* – How one person's struggles can inspire change and impact the lives of many. Knopf Books for Young Readers
We're All Wonders	*Empathy* – A version of *Wonder* for younger readers about popular character Auggie's desire for acceptance. Penguin Random House
You, Me, and Empathy	*Empathy* – Development of empathy and understanding modeled by compassionate main character. Educate2Empower Publishing
Save Me a Seat	*Friendship* – Tale of discovery of commonalities between two children from different backgrounds, develop a friendship based on understanding and acceptance. Scholastic
Be Kind	*Kindness* – Examples of compassion through kindness. Roaring Brook Press
Each Kindness	*Kindness* – Anti-bullying messages, impact of small actions. Penguin Random House

(*cont.*)

TABLE 3.2 Children's literature on mindfulness, meditation, and social and emotional learning elements (cont.)

Text	Theme and publisher
Enemy Pie	*Kindness* – Ways to treat our "enemies" with kindness. Chronicle Books
Last Stop on the Market Street	*Kindness* – Observations of kindness and joy on a bus ride. Penguin Books *Newbery Medal Winner
I Walk With Vanessa	*Kindness* – Small acts of kindness can inspire communities and make a huge difference. Penguin Random House
If You Plant a Seed	*Kindness* – The power of being thoughtful. Balzer + Bray
Kindness Is Cooler, Mrs. Ruler	*Kindness* – The value of being nice and doing good deeds. Simon & Schuster
Little Blue Truck	*Kindness* – A tale of an unlikely friendships and the beauty of helping others. Houghton Mifflin Harcourt
Otis and the Scarecrow	*Kindness* – Messages about standing up for people and showing compassion. Penguin Random House

(cont.)

TABLE 3.2 Children's literature on mindfulness, meditation, and social and emotional learning elements (*cont.*)

Text	Theme and publisher
The Invisible Boy	*Kindness* – Depicts the power of friendship and inclusion when one feels left out. Penguin Random House
Lost and Found Cat	*Kindness* – The beauty of strangers helping strangers. *Based on a true story Penguin Random House
Pass It On	*Kindness* – Spreading positivity in everyday life. Philomel Books
Superheroes Club	*Kindness* – Ways to help others and use kindness as a superpower. My Bench Productions
Those Shoes	*Kindness* – A story of generosity and selflessness amidst peer pressure. Candlewick Press
A Handful of Quiet	*Meditation*

(*cont.*)

TABLE 3.2 Children's literature on mindfulness, meditation, and social and emotional learning elements (cont.)

Text	Theme and publisher
Meditation is an Open Sky	*Meditation* Quaker Books
Meditate with Me	*Meditation* Penguin Random House
Calm Kids	*Mindfulness* – Relaxation Techniques for Children Floris Books
I am Peace	*Mindfulness* Abrams
Mad to Glad	*Mindfulness* – Lessons to help children cope with changing emotions Mindful Aromatherapy, LLC
Master of Mindfulness	*Mindfulness* – How to be your own superhero during stressful times Instant Help

(cont.)

TABLE 3.2   Children's literature on mindfulness, meditation, and social and emotional learning elements (*cont.*)

Text	Theme and publisher
Mindful Kids	*Mindfulness* – Activities for kindness, focus, and calm
	Stewart, Whitney; Box Crds edition (October 1, 2017)
My Magic Breath	*Mindfulness*
	Harper Collins
What does it Mean to Be Present?	*Mindfulness*
	Little Pickle Books
The Art of Mindfulness for Children	*Mindfulness*
	Create Space
Unstoppable Me!	*Mindfulness*
	Hay House
Good Morning Yoga	*Movement*
	Sounds True

(*cont.*)

TABLE 3.2   Children's literature on mindfulness, meditation, and social and emotional learning elements (*cont.*)

Text	Theme and publisher
Listening with My Heart	*Self-compassion* and love help foster empathy and kindness. Skinned Knee Publishing
Most People	Emphasizes the vast amount of good amidst other things in the world that seem frightening. Tilbury House Publishers

Note: A complete list of references is provided at the end of the chapter.

Resiliency is a vital factor inherent to the healing process and can be developed through supportive and trusting professional and personal relationships to prevent children from having to cope on their own, both at school and at home. Imagine the heartbreaking plights of the children who were suddenly forced to learn at home during this pandemic without any support measures in place and how much better off they'd have been with some tools to help them cope, particularly if the home environment was the source of the trauma and going to school every day was a welcomed escape. Knowing a trusted adult is consistently at school to help, or just yearning to be in their presence, can become a motivating factor to keep trying to survive the effects of childhood trauma rather than succumb to it or feeling helpless to overcome it. How can educators and families help cultivate resilience in young learners?

Helping children and educators develop resilience can aid in filtering stress and staying calm in stressful situations, thus reducing the ill-effects of stress on the body and mind. Nurturing our relationships with students can help students feel supported and connected, which provides extra support and can reduce feelings of isolation. Human connection is at the core of good relationships and needed to build strong, positive relationships between educators and students. Feeling the genuine support of a trusted teacher can help a child maintain a positive outlook when dealing with the stress brought on by trauma. Research clearly depicts strong, responsive and supportive adult relationships are the strongest predictors for mitigating the impact of chronic and toxic stress on children. Being aware of the messages we are sending through our tone of voice and body language will assist children in building a sense of personal safety through consistent and predictable interactions (Stuart, 2016).

Professional relationships have been the common theme pervasive throughout my 28 years as a professional educator. Devoting substantial amounts of time for establishing, building, and nurturing those professional relationships was necessary for creating welcoming, safe, supportive and respectful learning environments for children – and such relationships certainly are essential for creating trauma-sensitive classrooms.

Educators can begin with some basic relationship-building techniques and expand as they begin to build a good rapport with students, their families, and other colleagues. First day of school community building and getting to know one another activities work well toward this end. One year, when teaching third grade, I used a classroom quilt to celebrate the diversity within the class, foster belonging, and to honor each child's unique contributions to the classroom learning community via their individual square on the quilt that represented special things they wanted to share about themself. Each child's square was sewn into the quilt, together with those of their peers, to form a cohesive and inclusive class quilt as a community building exercise and served as a visual reminder that although our diversity made us stronger as a united community of learners We used the quilt all year long for community building activities and reflections on how we valued the unique qualities each child brought to the classroom community. Another community building activity I implemented that year was a classroom Bill of Rights. All members of the class contributed to deciding on characteristics important for good citizens to exhibit, acceptable and unacceptable behaviors, etc. All stakeholders signed the enlarged poster of the Bill of Rights for members of our classroom community for accountability and buy-in purposes. We displayed it proudly on our classroom wall as a daily reminder of how we should treat one another respectfully at all times.

6 Growth Mindset

Beyond using mindfulness methods and meditation as social and emotional learning supports to help children cope with the effects of trauma, adoption of a growth mindset approach can support children during the healing process as well. Overcoming feelings of poor self-worth and established habits of negative self-talk, sometimes prevalent with children who are suffering, also, can be improved through use of a growth mindset approach. Educators can model self-empowering language and behavior, as well as communicate their belief in children's abilities to excel through consistent use of growth mindset-oriented language during regular interactions with students, including instruction and assessment feedback. Families can be encouraged to continue the growth mindset approach in the home environment as well, to help shape new habits and create optimism for children's potential to overcome adversity. The power of our words and actions can shape children's thoughts for the better.

Dweck (2006), who conducted extensive research on growth versus fixed mindsets and their implications for learning success, defined mindsets as beliefs about yourself and your most basic qualities in terms of fixed mindsets that are givens and therefore, fixed, and growth mindsets that can be cultivated throughout one's life through passionate practice, dedication and effort. She shared her belief that cherished qualities can be developed, thus creating a passion for learning; each successive learning opportunity will provide more experience with careful consideration of someone else's position on a selected topic or understanding another's problem-solving strategies, develops their capacities for critical thinking, deeper levels of reflection and effective communication skills through collaborative learning. She stressed that educators can help foster the development of growth mindsets as students strive to improve and grow, rather than rely solely on the strengths they already possess and areas in which they presently excel. Another motivation technique proposed by Dweck (2006) was to make students believe they can achieve by removing negative, defeating talk, along with the word "can't," from their vocabularies and to make a habit of consistently using the term "yet," as in "I can't do this YET!" and surrounding oneself with people who will challenge you to grow.

Busch (2018) discussed growth mindset as the idea that intelligence can be developed in his synopsis of growth mindset research written for educators in which he synthesized results of multiple studies and reported other advantages of a growth mindset approach beyond academic attainment, such as students coping better with transition, higher self-regulation, and pro-social behavior. Furthermore, he identified mental health benefits of adoption of a growth mindset, including less aggression, higher self-esteem, and fewer symptoms that can be associated with anxiety and depression. He also shared recommendations centered on teachers carefully considering word choice in praise and feedback to describe strategies for improvement rather than more commonly used generalized modes of praise, which tend to omit more specific feedback to help students grow.

Consistent use of growth mindset language can help educators clearly communicate their belief in students' abilities to improve, along with their commitment to help them strategize how to do so. It sets a tone on partnership in the teaching-learning process between teacher and students, which can motivate learners to persevere, rather than one of criticism that often closes down lines of communication. Through use of growth mindset-based communication, children aren't left feeling defeated in accepting a grade with no additional feedback. Rather, their effort might be acknowledged more positively, coupled with specific comments on components needing more work. For instance, an educator might communicate the following comment to a student that demonstrated much effort but still hasn't achieved mastery. The comment might be framed as "I'm proud of the extra time you've put in to work on your problem-solving skills, but let's conference soon to figure out where you are still experiencing difficulty and construct a plan for improvement together." This sends a message to the student that the teacher recognized the effort expended and is offering further support, indicating a more collaborative teacher-student partnership, rather than simply indicating the work was not completed successfully with a low grade and no feedback (Lauria, 2016).

The following growth mindset language prompts retrieved from www.mindsetworks.com can be utilized as well. When providing more feedback to learners who struggle despite strong effort, language such as "I realize you didn't do as well as you wanted to. Let's look at this as an opportunity to learn. You are not there/here yet. When you think you can't do it, remind yourself that you can't do it yet!!" or "You might be struggling, but you are making progress. I can see your growth in ____. Look at how much progress you made on this. Do you remember how much more challenging this was (yesterday/last week/last year)?" can be effective. Another example used for this same purpose provided by mindsetworks.com was "I admire your persistence and I appreciate your hard work. It will pay off!" For communicating a learning goal at the onset of a lesson, a teacher might choose to say "Today's learning objective will give everyone an opportunity to stretch beyond your comfort zone. I do not expect you to know this concept already and am here to help you learn challenging material. We're in the learning zone today. Mistakes are our friends!" Or, in order to communicate high expectations, "Let's make mistakes together! I have seen you stretch and succeed in the past. Let's do it again!" is a recommended prompt.

During adoption of a growth mindset approach, it was one thing to motivate teacher candidates to want to try the techniques when providing feedback to children in classroom field experiences and teach them how to do so, but quite another for them to be properly equipped to implement the techniques on their own. Beginning with intensive modeling and practice in the teacher education courses prior to implementation, the clear and focused growth mindset language prompts provided by www.mindsetworks.com proved to be very effective tools. The positive responses teacher candidates received from young learners when using the growth mindset approach to communicate feedback resulted in higher levels of motivation and confidence for both the children and teacher candidates alike.

Use of such specific, supportive, and encouraging language may help a learner recognize the teacher's belief in their ability to improve, which can help to encourage the student to continue working toward mastery. A growth mindset approach to classroom communication and modes of feedback can help children develop self confidence in their own abilities, begin to appreciate the power of perseverance, and believe in their own potential for success. Dweck (2006) explains, in her revolutionary work on mindsets, that a growth mindset thrives on challenge and sees failure not as evidence of lack of intelligence but as a promising springboard for growth and for stretching our existing abilities. Additionally, along with motivating and supporting struggling students, growth mindset-oriented feedback can inspire successful students to even higher levels of achievement.

Closely related to a growth mindset approach is the concept of grit. Duckworth (2016) defines grit as a unique blend of passion and long-term perseverance. The willingness to put in the hard work to obtain the desired outcome, as needed for those who believe mistakes are good opportunities for growth and that determination will lead to improvement, grit is a necessary ingredient for victory. Hoerr (2013) felt educators tend to underestimate their value as role models and that it's important that our students need to know that we used grit to find our success. He felt sharing our own vulnerabilities and examples of grit can be powerful lessons to our students.

Stemming from the aforementioned teacher education curricular expansions, the same SEL supports were also infused throughout a reading intervention program. This was designed to help first grade, at-risk children in a New York City public school learn calming techniques for relaxation, anxiety relief, and focusing attention for use in coping with the disappointment that can arise when experiencing reading difficulties, along with other academic and life stressors. This proved to be particularly helpful for many student participants who were experiencing rather extreme hardships beyond their academic struggles and clearly needed support in managing their emotions and frustrations in order to be able to focus and concentrate on literacy development. One of the program's primary goals, beyond use of the SEL tools when experiencing high levels of emotional frustration and lack of focus while learning, was that

TABLE 3.3   Recommended works of children's literature for exploring growth mindsets

Text	Theme
Beautiful Oops!	Mistakes are learning opportunities
Your Fantastic Elastic Brain	Learning by stretching one's brain
Mrs K Begins Again: A Story of Resilience	Perseverance and resilience
Thanks for the Feedback	Feedback for growth
The Girl Who Never Made Mistakes	Mistakes are welcomed growth opportunities
The Most Magnificent Thing	The benefits of perseverance

Note: A complete list of references is provided at the end of the chapter.

children would continue to utilize some of the mindfulness techniques and growth mindset language used in the reading intervention program in their daily lives, both in and out of school, going forward after program completion.

The mindfulness components proved to be essential program elements, teaching children simple techniques for calming their minds and bodies to prepare to focus on learning, as well as cope with frustrations they may face both in and out of the classroom. Some of the mindfulness techniques were deep breathing, guided meditation, yoga for children, journaling, and energizing through movement. Many of the deep breathing exercises corresponded directly with the characters in the daily reading texts, such as "Moose Breathing" for the Morris the Moose text and the "Elephant Sigh" stress release exercise for Horton Hears a Who, a Dr. Seuss text in which the main character, Horton, was an elephant.

Children reflected in personal "My Mindfulness" journals each day after participating in the mindfulness exercises. Each entry highlighted the name of the day's technique and included either a drawing of the exercise or a few words about how students felt about it. At the end of the program students took the journals home as a resource to support continued mindfulness practice and journaling. Student testimonials, journal reflections, and qualitative attitude surveys evidenced predominantly positive responses to the mindfulness techniques and growth mindset language implemented throughout the duration of the program. Many students began to self-correct with use of growth mindset language toward the end of the program through replacement of their former negative responses, frustrations, and/or tantrums characterized by consistent "I can't" language with "I can't do this yet, but these are the things I will do to improve so that I can." A related program objective was to help struggling readers improve their attitudes toward reading, and to believe in their abilities to grow as young readers, despite multiple reading difficulties. Consistent use of growth mindset-oriented language and behaviors were modeled to encourage students to embrace the idea of learning as a growth process full of mistakes needed for improvement and development of perseverance. It helped the children begin to view literacy mistakes as learning opportunities rather than defeats, and validated students' expressions of frustration they experienced with literacy struggles, while providing encouragement and support strategies to help them overcome hurdles. It eventually became evident that the slight shift toward feeling more supported while experiencing reading difficulties helped the children to become more optimistic toward improving their literacy skills. Simultaneously, many participants demonstrated higher levels of self-confidence regarding literacy skills and willingness to persevere, along with more positive dispositions toward reading. Observation of students utilizing some of the mindfulness techniques and growth mindset language on their own, when needed, truly was a program highlight.

The ethic of caring as a disposition has a prominent role in social and emotional learning, as it provides a basis for students to develop empathy, compassion, a sense of justice, positive values, and the capacity to take action. For learners of all ages, caring thinking includes caring for oneself and caring about others. Students involved in caring thinking recognize what they value and acknowledge their feelings about pertinent issues, as well as the feelings of others. Prior to teacher candidates' implementation of a growth mindset approach through instructional methods and both verbal and written feedback for young learners in classroom field placements, it was imperative to ensure they were placed in classrooms that exhibited a safe, respectful, and caring learning environment in which students would be willing to take risks and challenge themselves. The goal was that meaningful and regular use of the suggested growth mindset language prompts might help children begin to appreciate that although taking risks might lead to some mistakes, they could learn from and didn't need to fear making mistakes during the learning process. Fostering growth mindsets can support students' social and emotional learning and help students enjoy learning in ways that aren't possible when evaluation of progress is perceived through a more critical lens. Students can experience lifelong benefits, including improved self-confidence, positivity, and perseverance, from working with caring educators that encourage growth mindsets, which can be especially beneficial for students impacted by trauma and wanting to feel safe, accepted, and generally good about themselves again. Dweck (2006) expressed that the passion for stretching yourself and sticking to it, even, or especially, when it's not going well, is the hallmark of the growth mindset and allows people to thrive during some of the most difficult times.

Several cooperating mentor teachers that partnered with the teacher candidates in classroom field experiences expressed interest in continuing the practice of utilizing SEL supports when the placements ended, due to the improvements they had observed in children's achievement, work ethic, attitudes, and levels of motivation. Some commented that they were pleasantly surprised how incorporation of mindfulness methods and focus on a growth mindset approach could shift the dynamic of classroom culture so positively, particularly since they had not learned to use SEL supports in their own teacher training or professional development endeavors. Learning more about the role of SEL in students' overall academic success can help educators to better prepare children to face the inherent challenges of striving to become productive, caring citizens of our multidimensional global society and cope with the increasingly complex challenges they will inevitably face. A logical next step could be incorporating training on use of SEL supports and consideration of a growth mindset approach into professional development endeavors for employed teachers and infusing training into course curricula and corresponding professional field experiences in more teacher education programs. Additionally, focus on other wellness strategies for students, teachers, and families, such as guidance on healthy living (nutritional coaching, importance of daily movement, quality sleep, and overall stress relief elements) would add value as effective supports for key stakeholders working in partnership to best serve students' needs, while also teaching elements of healthful living to children.

My college's teacher preparation programs have grown in breadth and depth through expansion of course curricula to include more strategic focus on techniques for infusing SEL supports in pedagogy, implemented in diverse classroom field placements, in order to help teacher candidates guide young learners in managing how to cope with stressors. The curricular adjustments were well received by the teacher candidates, many of whom expressed gratitude for the experiences of guided support while learning how to implement mindfulness methods and a growth mindset approach. They were confident in their abilities to be able to effectively incorporate these methods into their pedagogy once certified to teach, and several planned to use the SEL supports in their future classrooms. Again, an unexpected outcome of integrating mindfulness methods and a growth mindset approach into curricula of multiple teacher education courses arose as the majority of teacher candidates continually expressed how much the mindfulness techniques they were learning to implement with diverse student populations were beneficial to them as adult learners in helping them balance the challenges of pursuing dual childhood (1–6) teaching certification in both general and special education. Consistent themes prevalent in course evaluations included sentiments such as, "I can only imagine how much more enjoyable school might've been for me if I'd had access to support strategies like simple meditation or deep breathing work I could've use on my own without needing help from an adult because I wouldn't have felt so overwhelmed." Or, "I hadn't realized the power of my word choice and just how negative my mindset had been, when being kinder to myself with more positive self-talk would've made my life less stressful." Acknowledging one's own effort, focusing on the progress being made, and persevering, despite challenging circumstances, are important life skills students can develop though use of mindfulness methods and a caring, growth mindset approach as SEL supports that can extend far beyond using them to overcome academic, social, and emotional adversities throughout their schooling.

Similarly, the young first grade children who participated in the literacy intervention program began to express positive comments about using the new SEL supports they'd learned. Although some couldn't articulate exactly what was working as they participated in the guided meditations, yoga for children, pictorial journaling, or deep breathing exercises, their smiles, lower levels of aggressions, and improved social skills were indicative of beneficial outcomes. By the last week of the program, parents and visitors noted a difference in the children's behavior and improved ability to focus on reading. Program evaluations and feedback inspired consideration of a second phase through which quantitative data would be collected for analysis.

Infusion of mindfulness methods in teacher preparation programs can begin slowly, with perhaps just a few techniques, and can create a shift toward positive changes with potential for substantial impact on students' social and emotional development, which can empower educators with practical tools to support struggling students, as well as those who are ready to aim even higher. The SEL supports infused into teacher education course curricula and, later, implemented in classroom field placement work with students in grades 1–6, were simple to incorporate. They included mini-meditations at the beginning of class to help focus our attention and calm our minds, brief movement breaks when needed to energize our bodies and minds, yoga, and as an element of closure, guided deep breathing and journaling during debriefing and reflection portions at the end of class. None of the techniques took much time, yet were very impactful components of the learning experience. Teacher candidates were asked to envision themselves as the young learners they'd be implementing each strategy with, to get a sense of how children may perceive these unfamiliar additions to the daily classroom experience.

A myriad of free and easily accessible online resources utilized as supplemental course resources were presented in Table 3.1 to help educators experiment with SEL supports. Additionally, these resources can be shared with families through home-school partnerships to continue mindfulness practice at home. Jain (2017) believed mindful children react differently to challenges. She touted mindfulness as a skill that can improve children's impulse control, calmness, kindness, patience, compassion, empathy, executive function, and attention spans, as well as contribute toward development of self-respect and self-compassion. In light of the multifaceted challenges modern learners face in today's global society, consideration of infusing a focus on mindfulness in teacher education programs and, in turn, diverse classroom settings, can benefit all stakeholders with minimal effort and cost, and a substantial return on investment. Although SEL supports shared were geared toward teaching young learners new ways to cope with the frustration of ongoing learning challenges and obstacles, such as multiple academic struggles and life stressors, techniques presented can be adapted for use with other audiences and age groups as supports for coping with inevitable life stressors in the personal and professional realms.

7 Practical Applications

Mulvahill (2019) described how some schools have experimented with bringing therapy dogs into the classroom to support children's emotional needs. A dog's calming presence helped some children with effects of trauma and others with reading interventions. The presence of a therapy dog contributed to more positive school climate and the positive impact on students' social-emotional development was very beneficial. Desautels (2019) recommended starting the day with a simple calming routine to help young students recovering from trauma transition into the school day in a relaxed manner, which helps them become ready to learn.

Schwartz (2018) provided a snapshot into the transition to trauma-informed practices in her account of how a school in Nashville, Tennessee is implementing changes focused on trust and relationship building and setting the tone that students will be heard. Their trauma-informed practices were designed to help students fell safe and well supported. She highlighted their use of a peace corner in each classroom, hiring of a trained trauma-informed practitioner to help implement trauma informed approaches, and a daily individual goal setting Check-In and Check-Out system for students with a staff member. The Peace Corner is a place where students have the time and space to calm down and practice the type of reflection required to build self-regulation skills and the Check-In/Check-Out system helped build positive relationships between students and staff by providing accountability for daily goal setting and advice for students on how to accomplish meeting their goals, which served as a good support strategy (Schwartz, 2019).

My former grade school students had very stressful lives and were carrying the burden of some types of life stressors and trauma that adults wouldn't be able to handle well. At times, I felt they needed to express what they were dealing with before they were even ready to think about academics. Providing that outlet for just a few moments each morning through a journal writing activity, artistic expression, or a small group morning meeting discussion often was just enough for them to be able to release what was upsetting them and refocus to begin our day in the classroom. Schools using techniques that help students affected by trauma are brainstorming ways in which to make students feel safe and supported and to let students know that someone there really cares. These small, yet powerful, shifts can positively impact children in countless ways and, therefore, are well worth the extra effort needed for implementation.

8 Wellness Strategies for Educators

Psychologists and mental health practitioners report that the impact of trauma goes far beyond the kids experiencing the effects of trauma and reaches into the lives of educators who work closely with them every day (Minero, 2018). Therefore, it's important for educators to find time for their own wellness while working in such a physically and emotionally demanding profession in order to continue thriving and functioning at peak performance. I recommend that educators schedule self-care time right into their daily calendars as they would an urgent appointment. When the time comes, they will go directly to that appointment as they would another meeting on the calendar for that day. Otherwise, it's likely that self-care time will be replaced by something else that needs to be done. Some suggestions for self-care include nurturing oneself through movement, healthy eating, relaxation (meditation, yoga, prayer, napping, reading), socialization, nurturing personal relationships, spiritual reflection, or just plain fun! Without short breaks to recharge, it's difficult to maintain the stamina necessary to be a highly effective educator and self-care time is crucial for inspiring innovation and creativity.

Aguilar (2018) stressed the importance of teachers cultivating their own resilience. She explained that the moment when we cultivate resilience is the moment between something that happens and how we respond, because that space in time is when we have the power to choose our response. She warned that each of those actions will have intended and unintended consequences, ripples of impact on ourselves, our class, and our relationships with individual students. She stressed the importance of making thoughtful choices in those moments and the need to cultivate resilience so that all children feel that they belong to a resilient community.

9 Implications for Enhancement of Teacher Education Curricula

In order for educators to be adequately prepared to support students' SEL needs, modeling of effective techniques should be provided through course work and professional field placements with teachers skilled in the areas of social and emotion learning and use of a growth mindset approach. Additionally, mentors could be provided early on for teacher candidates. A focus on SEL, along with health and wellness strategies, can be incorporated into teacher education programs to model stress management and coping strategies for teacher candidates, in order for them to emulate effective techniques for use with the modern learners they'll be teaching in diverse classroom environments. Adoption of a growth mindset approach by teacher candidates and their young students can foster empowerment to strive for excellence. The need for expansion of teacher education curricula to include more instruction on techniques for supporting students who have experienced trauma and methods for creating safe, nurturing, and trauma-sensitive learning spaces is pressing. Infusion of SEL elements throughout curricula in schools would support all children, but is particularly important for those trying to balance the additional burdens of dealing with the effects of trauma. Teachers need to be adequately prepared to do so.

It can take a long time for students experiencing academic difficulties or emotional hardships, including dealing with traumatic life events, to receive school-based support until completing all the proper evaluation protocols. Therefore, it's imperative that teachers be armed with as many tools as possible to provide support for such students at the classroom level until targeted, specific trauma-related support can be provided by mental health professionals. Creating trauma-sensitive learning experiences and environments can serve as a beginning step for children who are suffering.

10   Conclusion

It's important that teachers aiming to integrate mindfulness practice are aware that, as with any educational endeavor, not all techniques work the same way for all children, as they are unique and special beings. In a trauma-sensitive classroom, teachers will need to be flexible and open to feedback. However, a solid first step would be to figure out ways to communicate to students that they are supported and have an advocate in their corner ready to do whatever it takes to help them succeed if they are willing to put in the dedication and effort. It will be safe to assume that not all children sense that type of unwavering support from their families and caregivers at home, which means the majority of that role will be placed on teachers' shoulders in those cases. Educators up for the challenge and the extra effort it may require will get that back tenfold; once students feel their teachers truly believe in them, the possibilities are endless for how much they'll be able to achieve with the support of a special teacher.

Children tend to possess a natural sense of resilience and can thrive in a positive and supportive environment. However, being left to fend for themselves when trying to overcome trauma can be a recipe for disaster for many young learners. It's important that their teachers become trauma-informed in order to ensure they can establish the safe, nurturing, and inspirational learning environments these students—rather—all students deserve. Educators of distinction continually yearn to improve to best meet the needs of their students.

Henderson (2013) stressed that schools can be havens in which resilience can flourish when educators and all caring adults in the school claim their role as agents of internal protective factors, that included relationships, service, humor, perceptiveness, flexibility, love of learning, self-motivation, perseverance, creativity, and self-worth. The world's recent, sudden and unexpected transition to remote learning, with minimal preparation and planning time, made that even more important. While educators are finding their way through the new educational landscape that extends far beyond teaching academic knowledge and skills, and now requires effective remote learning with little preparation time, they should try to process the emotions involved in such a stressful scenario so they can successfully model how students can process their own emotions. Brackett and Simmons (2015) stress the importance of understanding and connecting with our emotions as it's our best hope for safe, caring, and effective schools and reinforce that boredom, anxiety and fear disrupt concentration and interfere with the learning process.

Ward-Roncalli (2018) supported the effectiveness of SEL to mitigate the effects of trauma. Use of mindfulness methods and a growth mindset approach, as SEL supports, can shape a learning environment that's safe, secure, and supportive. Educators can model use of both in the classroom, and in turn, teach children how to do so on their own when encountering obstacles to their academic, social, and emotional development. A multitude of SEL supports can be utilized by educators to cope with daily stressors in their own lives to better equip them to support their students' SEL toward that same end, which is imperative for students coping with trauma. We know student struggling to survive trauma in their lives have extra burdens to bear, which require trauma-sensitive techniques and carefully chosen words and behaviors from their teachers. It's important to keep in mind that students can hear every message we send, whether overt or implied, about their capacity to learn and succeed (Tomlinson, 2015). We need to handle each situation with care. She stressed the combination of a good mind and heart as being key for developing emotionally healthy kids. While it may seem like a tall order to be so many things to all students, the reward of positively impacting so many young lives makes it all worthwhile.

Glossary

Dispositions   attitudes of ways of thinking about a particular topic or comcept.

Grit   a unique blend of passion and long-term perseverance and willingness to put in the hard work to obtain the desired outcome, needed for those who believe mistakes are good opportunities for growth and that determination will lead to improvement, a necessary ingredient for victory (Duckworth, 2016).

Growth mindset   a growth mindset thrives on challenge and sees failure not as evidence of lack of intelligence but as a promising springboard for growth and for stretching our existing abilities. (Dweck, 2006).

Mindfulness   paying attention, intentionally, in the present moment, and non-judgmentally (Zinn, 2017).

Resilience   a way of being that allows us to bounce back quickly from adversity, and stronger than before, so that we can fulfill our purpose in life (Aguliar, 2018).

Social and emotional learning (SEL)   an instructional approach that takes into account emotional components that either facilitate or impede learning built on safe, positive relationships cultivated between educators and students (Reilly, 2017–2018).

Trauma-sensitive   an approach that aims for every student being healthy, safe, engaged supported, and challenged (Souers & Hall, 2016).

References

Aguilar, E. (2018). *Onward: Cultivating emotional resilience in educators.* Wiley/Jossey-Bass.

Bologna, C. (2019, August 31). *35 books that teach empathy and kindness.* Huffingtonpost.com. https://www.huffpost.com/entry/childrens-books-empathy-kindness_l_5d52e7b1e4b0c63bcbee2699

Brackett, M., & Simmons, D. (2015). Emotions matter. *Educational Leadership, 73*(2), 22–27.

Broderick, P. C., & Metz, S. (2009). Learning to BREATHE: A pilot trial of mindfulness and curriculum for adolescents. *Advances in School Mental Health Promotion, 2*(10), 35–46.

Busch, B. (2018, January 4). Research every teacher should know: Growth mindset. *The Guardian.* https://www.theguardian.com/teacher-network/2018/jan/04/research-every-teacher-should-know-growth-mindset#:~:text=There%20is%20a%

20wealth%20of,the%20realities%20of%20classroom%20practice.&text=This%20time%2C%20we%20consider%20growth%20mindset

Desautels, L. (2019, July 26). *Starting the day with a calming routine: Exercises that help young students who've experienced trauma transition into the school day in a relaxed and ready state.* Edutopia.org. https://www.edutopia.org/article/starting-day-calming-routine

Duckworth, A. (2016). *Grit: The power of passion and perseverance.* Scribner-Simon and Schuster.

Dweck, C. (2006). *Mindset.* Random House.

Elias, M., Zins, J., Weissberg, R., Frey, K., Greenberg, M., Haynes, N., Kessler, R., Schwab-Stone, M., & Shriver, T. (1997). *Promoting social and emotional learning: Guidelines for educators.* ASCD.

Henderson, N. (2013). Havens of resilience. *Educational Leadership, 71*(1), 22–27.

Hoerr, T. (2013). *Fostering grit.* ASCD.

Jain, R. (2017, April 21). *How mindful children react differently to challenges.* Huffpost.com. https://www.huffpost.com/entry/how-mindful-children-react-differently-to-challenges_b_6347654

Kabat-Zinn, J. (2017). *What is mindfulness? Explained.* https://positivepsychologyprogram.com/what-is-mindfulness-definition/

Lauria, J. (2016). Fostering development of 21st century competencies and global citizenship through constructivist-based and learning-style responsive pedagogy. In K. Gonzalez & R. Frumkin (Eds.), *Handbook of research on effective communication in culturally diverse classrooms.* IGI Publishing.

Minero, E. (2018, May 3). Student trauma impacts teachers, too. In *Taking care of yourself isn't a luxury-it's a necessity.* Edutopia.org. https://www.edutopia.org/article/student-trauma-its-ok-set-boundaries#:~:text=Student%20trauma%20impacts%20teachers%2C%20too,a%20luxury%E2%80%94it's%20a%20necessity.&text=But%20psychologists%20and%20mental%20health,with%20them%20day%20to%20day

Mulvahill, E. (2019, October 25). *Dogs in the classroom improve SEL, cognitive, and even reading skills.* WeAreTeachers.com. https://www.weareteachers.com/dogs-in-the-classroom/

Reily, N. (2017–2018). The bonds of social-emotional learning. *Educational Leadership, 75*(4), 56–60.

Roberts, S., & Crawford, P. (2008). Literature to help children cope with family stressors. *Beyond the Journal: Young Children on the Web,* NAEYC, 1–8.

Schonert-Reichl, K., Oberle, E., Lawlor, M., Abbot, D., Thompson, K., Oberlander, T., & Diamond, A. (2015). Enhancing cognitive and social-emotional development through a simple-to-administer mindfulness-based school program for elementary school children: A randomized controlled trial. *Developmental Psychology, 51*(1), 52–66.

Schwartz, K. (2018, October 3). *A glimpse inside the transition to trauma-informed classrooms.* Mindshift.org. https://www.kqed.org/mindshift/52267/a-glimpse-inside-the-transition-to-trauma-informed-practices

Schwartz, K. (2019, April 8). *Nine ways to ensure your mindfulness teaching practice is trauma informed.* Mindshift.com. https://www.google.com/search?q=Nine+ways+to+ensure+your+mindfulness+teaching+practice+is+trauma+informed.&oq=Nine+ways+to+ensure+your+mindfulness+teaching+practice+is+trauma+informed.&aqs=chrome..69i57.15463j0j7&sourceid=chrome&ie=UTF-8

Souers, K., & Hall, P. (2016). *Fostering resilient learners: Strategies for creating a trauma-sensitive classroom.* ASCD.

Stuart, J. (2016, October 13). *Are you trauma-informed?* ExchangeEveryDay.com

Titone, C., Feldman, E., & DeRosato, M. (2017). Getting the buffalo off their chests. *Educational Leadership, 75*(4), 74–77.

Tomlinson, C. (2015). Being human in the classroom. *Educational Leadership, 72*(3), 74–77.

Ward-Roncalli, S. (2018, January 18). *How social and emotional learning can mitigate the effects of trauma.* Transformingeducation.org. https://transformingeducation.org/how-social-emotional-learning-can-mitigate-the-effects-of-trauma/#:~:text=In%20other%20words%2C%20the%20more,the%20child's%20brain%20is%20impacted.&text=These%20studies%20show%20that%20SEL,manage%20anger%2C%20and%20avoid%20distractions

Children's Literature Resources

Boelts, M. (2009). *Those shoes.* Candlewick Press.
Byers, G. (2018). *I am enough.* Balzer and Bray/Harper Collins Publishers.
Chopra, M. (2019). *Just feel.* Running Press Kids/Hachette Book Group.
Cook, J. (2013). *Thanks for the feedback.* Boys Town Press.
Cuyler, M. (2007). *Kindness is cooler, Mrs. Ruler.* Simon and Schuster.
Deak, J. (2010). *Fantastic elastic brain.* Scholastic.
DeLaPena, M. (2015). *Last stop on market street.* Penguin Books.
DiOrio, R. (2010). *What does it mean to be present?* Little Pickle Books.
Dismondy, M. (2015). *Chocolate milk, por favor!* Cardinal Rule Press
Dyer, W., & Tracy, K. (2006). *Unstoppable me.* Hay House.
Garcia, G. (2017). *Listening with my heart.* Skinned Knee Publishing.
Gates, M. (2019). *Breathe with me.* Sounds True.
Gates, M. (2017). *Meditate with me.* Penguin Random House.
Gates, M. (2016). *Good morning yoga: A pose by pose wake up story.* Sounds True.

Gates, M. (2015). *Good night yoga: A pose by pose bedtime story.*
Grossman, L. (2016). *Master of mindfulness.* Instant Help.
Hanh, T. N. (2008). *A handful of quiet.* Penguin Random House.
Harris, A. (2015). *Mad to glad.* Mindful Aromatherapy.
Henn, S. (2017). *Pass it on.* Philomel Books.
Hong, J. (2017). *Lovely.* Creston Books.
Hoose, P., Hoose, H., & Tilley, D. (1998). *Hey, little ant.* Penguin Random House.
Kaminsky, A. (2017). *Mrs. K begins again.* Create Space Independent Publishing.
Kerascoet. (2018). *I walk with Vanessa.* Penguin Random House.
Kuntz, D., & Shrodes, A. (2019). *Lost and found cat.* Penguin Random House.
Leannah, M. (2017). *Most people.* Tilbury House Publishers.
Long, L. (2014). *Otis and the scarecrow.* Penguin Random House.
Ludwig, T. (2013). *The invisible boy.* Penguin Random House.
Miller, P. Z. (2018). *Be kind.* Roaring Brook Press/Macmillan.
Munson, D. (2000). *Enemy pie.* Chronicle Books.
Murray, L. (2012). *Calm kids.* Floris Books.
Nelson, K. (2015). *If you plant a seed.* Balzar and Bray/Harper Collins.
Ortner, N., & Taylor. A. (2018). *My magic breath.* Harper Collins.
Palacio, R. J. (2017). *We're all wonders.* Penguin Random House.
Palacio, R. J. (2012). *Wonder.* Knopf Books for Young Readers.
Pett, M., & Rubenstein, G. (2011). *The girl who never made mistakes.* Sourcebooks Jabberwocky.
Reddy, A. (2014). *The art of mindfulness for children.* Create Space.
Rippin, S. (2015). *Meditation is an open sky.* Quaker Books.
Saltzburg, B. (2010). *Beautiful oops.* Workman Publishing.
Sanders, J. (2017). *You, me, and empathy.* Educate2 Empower Publishing.
Schertle, A. (2008). *Little blue truck.* Houghton Mifflin Harcourt.
Smith, B. (2018). *Empathy is my superpower.* Boys Town Press.
Spires, A. (2019). *The most magnificent thing.* Kids Can Press.
Stewart, W., & Braun, M. (2017). *Mindful kids.* Stewart, Whitney; Box Crds Edition.
Verde, S. (2020, September). *I am human.* Abrams Appleseed Books.
Verde, S., & Reynolds, P. (2017). *I am peace: A book of meditation.* Abrams.
Weeks, S., & Varadarajan, G. (2016). *Save me a seat.* Scholastic Press.
Woodson, J. (2012). *Each kindness.* Penguin Random House.

CHAPTER 4

Mindfulness in the Trauma Informed Classroom
Using Yoga and Meditation to Infuse Classrooms with Coping Skills, Resilience, Self-Expression, and Safety

Deryn A. Susman

Abstract

American student stress levels are at an all time high, as shown by the correlation between the increase of high stakes testing and the increase of childhood mental illness (Streeter et al., 2007). Many members of the American education community are becoming increasingly frustrated with the situation at hand, and their perceived lack of ability to influence impactful change (Nankin & Fenchel, 2019). However, some educators have begun to utilize the philosophies and practices of Yoga within their classroom and school communities, and have seen incredible results (Nankin & Fenchel, 2019). In order for Yoga practice to be fully integrated into a classroom setting, especially a public classroom setting, it must be clearly stated that *Yoga is **not** a religion*. It is an ancient spiritual and philosophical practice (Nankin & Fenchel, 2019). This chapter will describe and defend the different possible uses of Yoga within a classroom structure, while listing possible benefits that have been observed as a result of a classroom Yoga practice.

Keywords

yoga – meditation – mindfulness – Social Emotional Learning (SEL) – stress responses – parasympathetic nervous system – sympathetic nervous system

1   Stress and Our Students

Recently, the World Health Organization reported "that mental illness makes up 15% of the global burden of disease" (Streeter et al., 2007, p. 425). A large portion of this startling statistic can be attributed to the distortion of the human fight, flight, or freeze response displayed in most First World Societies (Nankin & Fenchel, 2019, p. 171). The human brain evolved to assess a given stimulus in order to detect danger. When triggered to feel unsafe, the brain releases epinephrine, more commonly known as adrenaline, throughout the body, indicating to every biological system that danger is present. During this time, the heart races, breathing increases, and metabolism slows (Nankin & Fenchel, 2019, p. 171). Additionally, the majority of brain activity is reverted to the midbrain, "which is responsible for controlling sensory processes" (Napoli, Krech, & Holley, 2008, p. 104). The rest of the brain, which is responsible for the more, "higher-ordered cognitive processes [is]generally inactive" (Napoli, Krech, & Holley, 2008, p. 104). In other words, during a situation which the brain has deemed unsafe, the brain is not thinking, it is simply reacting.

This response is not a bad thing. In fact, it is what has enabled all of us, and our ancestors, to live our fullest lives. Sensing danger helps keep us safe. However, when the input of recognizing danger becomes corrupt, this life-saving system can become very damaging. Reva et al. (2014) suggests:

> When a given stimulus is initially appraised as challenging, harmful, or threatening, an activation of physiological systems involved in the stress response co-occurs with a subjective experience of distress. A persistent trend of overestimating the significance of the negative events leads to excessive emotional reactivity and wear-and-tear to visceral systems. (p. 195)

These high stress levels are often caused by unnecessary stressors, which have almost become a bragging point in our culture. How many extra classes are you taking? How late are you staying at work? How many sports and extra-curriculars is your child enrolled in? How many of those are you volunteering with? How late did you stay up last night? How little sleep did you get?

Yet, everytime the human mind perceives something as stressful, even if it is something as 'small' as getting stuck in traffic, the sympathetic nervous system is activated and adrenaline is released throughout the body. Our systems can also be triggered by intense stressors, such as hospitalizations. Chronic exposure to stress hormones, which can be caused by small or intense stressors, is detrimental to the physical and mental body (Butzer et al., 2015, p. 41). It can lead to high blood pressure, digestion problems, sleep problems, depression, and anxiety – and this is not limited to adults in our society. Toscano and Clemente (2013) state "modern life has not only created stress and pressure for adults, but also children" (p. 16). When children come to school experiencing stress responses due to home environmental factors outside of their control, carrying the weight of their Adverse Childhood Experiences (ACEs), or if the school culture itself is activating the students' stress responses due to high pressure, competition, test anxiety, discipline challenges, time management, and more, then the brain is not activating in a way that can cognitively process information (Arbeua, 2015, p. 35; Harper, 2010, pp. 99–100; Napoli, Krech, & Holley, 2008, pp. 100–104). This means that "during these stressful occurrences, meaningful learning is infrequent" (Napoli, Krech, & Holley, 2008, p. 104). When a student is experiencing these stress responses several times throughout the school day, then the likelihood of them actually learning anything is extremely low.

Students are often having their symptoms of stress and trauma labeled as either an 'attention problem' or a 'lack of motivation' (Ruiz, 2014). Few adults are recognizing that "with all of these challenges facing them, focusing on schoolwork can take a heroic effort on the part of many children" (Harper, 2010, p. 100). Children experiencing high levels of stress often struggle to stay on task, are unorganized, need constant redirection, and have a below-expected academic performance (Peck et al., 2005, pp. 415–416). Additionally, students' overactive stress response may be impacting their socialization skills, which, in turn, affect their self-esteem and ability to participate in group work. This then affects their academic performance, which could continue to contribute to their poor socialization, starting a vicious cycle (Harper, 2010, p. 104).

Thankfully there is a simple solution to all of this: what if we provided children with the tools to quiet their overactive stress response systems? We have the opportunity to provide them with resources to help self-regulate their emotions, learning, and behavior. That's where Yoga comes in.

2   What Is Yoga?

"Yoga" is an ancient Sanskrit word that roughly translates as "unite" (Nankin & Fenchel, 2019, p. 17). When most Americans hear the word "yoga," they tend to picture the physical movements and stretches, traditionally referred to as "asanas," which directly translates from Sanskrit to English as "posture." However, these postures were actually created as a way to prepare the body for meditation, or intense, deep focus (Arbeau, 2016, p. 35). Practicing Asana is favored by teachers and young children, especially in physical education, because it develops "a balance of strength and flexibility" (Nankin & Fenchel, 2019, p. 222). It is a low-pressure activity, that is "non-judgemental and non-competitive," while placing an emphasis on "working at one's own pace" (Tummers, 2013, pp. 15–36). Practicing Asana also encourages bringing mindful awareness to the body, and a sense of accepting oneself fully and in the moment, while being "rooted in the idea that practicing and improving yourself are what indicate success" (Harper, 2010, p. 101).

However, Yoga is so much more than only Asana. In fact, Yoga first emerged in India thousands of years ago as a philosophy, "[T]o connect, to merge. To unite mind and body, breath and movement, spirit and humanity. Thus, Yoga is a path toward uniting seeming opposites and cultivating harmony in our lives" (Nankin & Fenchel, 2019, p. 222). It is, "a holistic approach that includes ethical and moral principles, physical postures, breathwork, and various types of meditation for the purpose of uniting mind, body, and spirit" (Nankin & Fenchel, 2019, p. 17). Yoga also incorporates mindfulness – the metacognition of presence and awareness – and meditation – the practice of mental silence and observation.

In order for Yoga practice to be fully integrated into a classroom setting, especially a public classroom setting, it must be clearly stated that *Yoga is **not** a religion*. It is an ancient spiritual and philosophical practice that is sometimes associated with religions. While Yoga persists in many religious contexts, Yoga is not a religion, but a philosophy and practice (Nankin & Fenchel, 2019). People may be apprehensive about beginning a Yoga practice because there is a common misconception that such a practice will break their existing ties with their religious background. Others may worry about 'indoctrinating' children into a religion during the school day. It is much easier to discuss Yoga as a way of thinking, which Asanas and other elements can support. Some teachers choose to only refer to Yoga practices as mindfulness throughout the school day, but I prefer using "Yoga." To me, it is far more encompassing than the word "mindfulness," and it honors the history of the tradition rather than appropriating it. Therefore this chapter will refer to the philosophy and practices as Yoga.

Additionally, there are several variations of the Yogic philosophies. This chapter will mostly focus on the Raja Yoga Path, which revolves around an Eight-Limbed Path to achieving union, and the Yoga Sutras of Patanjali (Nankin & Fenchel, 2019). However, other related philosophies, such as chakra energy systems and Buddhist's meditation practices may be referenced.

3   Physiology of Calm

Did you know that breath is the only vital function that can be both controlled and automated in the human body? By voluntarily connecting to the breath, we "can help cue which [nervous] system will operate" (Nankin & Fenchel, 2019, p. 172). In many cultures, including the Yoga Tradition, breath equates to life force: as long as we are breathing, we are alive. When attention is given to the breath, switching the function from an automated function to a consciously controlled action, it is considered Pranayama, or life force restriction. The Yoga Tradition is filled with dozens of methods of Pranayama, each serving its own purpose within the tradition and within the body. Almost every aspect of Raja Yoga is accompanied by breath control.

Regardless of the Pranayama methods being used, breath control is constantly associated with the calm and relaxed feeling people will often report after an empowering Yoga practice. Part of the reason for this is due to the vagus nerve, which lies along our back body. When enacting breath control, the diaphragm, or the muscle that primarily controls the acts of inhalation and exhalation, slides along the vagus nerve, stimulating it to activate the parasympathetic nervous system (Nankin & Fenchel, 2019, p. 172). Actually, "ninety percent of the nerves that relay sensory information of the brain run through the respiratory diaphragm. Breathing deeply slides the diaphragm along the vagus nerve, sending calming signals" (Nankin & Fenchel, 2019, p. 172).

Our nervous system is broken down into several sub-categories, including the sympathetic and parasympathetic nervous systems. These two systems make up "the autonomic nervous system, which primarily regulates involuntary activity such as heartbeat and respiration" (Peck et al., 2005, p. 417). The sympathetic nervous system is responsible for the fight, flight, or freeze reaction – the reaction that is currently causing great harm in most Westernized human beings (Nankin & Fenchel, 2019, p. 171). When the sympathetic nervous system is activated, body functions that are deemed unnecessary for immediate survival, such as digestion or higher order cognition, are completely shut down as adrenaline courses through the body (Nankin & Fenchel, 2019, p. 172). If this sympathetic nervous response is used briefly and effectively, it can lead to a high bodily performance in a short span of time, "but [it can be] very harmful when prolonged" (Nankin & Fenchel, 2019, p. 172). Shallow breathing or gasping breaths automatically activate the sympathetic nervous system, sending distress signals to the brain (Nankin & Fenchel, 2019, p. 172).

In direct contrast, the parasympathetic nervous system allows the body to "rest and digest" (Nankin & Fenchel, 2019, p. 171). The parasympathetic nervous system is activated when the vagus nerve is stimulated, allowing all bodily functions and systems to work to the best of their ability meaning the brain can think, food can digest, and the body can heal (Nankin & Fenchel, 2019, p. 172). As with most elements of Yoga, the two-part autonomic nervous system acts in a system of balance and counterbalance:

> Although these systems generally control the same muscles and glands, they work in opposition to each other. The sympathetic system utilizes

stored energy and prepares the body for 'fight or flight' by increasing heart rate and blood sugar level. In contrast, the parasympathetic division conserves energy and is active in relaxed situations. Activities of this division include a decrease in heart rate and activation of the digestive system. (Peck et al., 2005, p. 417)

Because of Yoga's emphasis on breathwork and Asana's tendency to stimulate the vagus nerve, "the process of yoga deactivates the sympathetic division and stimulates the parasympathetic system resulting in a sense of calm, emotional balance, tranquility, and increased concentration" (Peck et al., 2005, p. 417). By creating more of a habitual existence with the parasympathetic nervous system, students may find "alleviation [of] the psychological stressors encountered by youth" (Butzer et al., 2015, p. 42). This practice may also help prevent further stressors from accruing.

4 Yoga and the Emotional Body

In Raja Yoga, Pratyahara is the practice of noticing the senses, acknowledging the information they provide, and then distancing the self from the experiences, especially when it comes to emotions. This may seem harsh at first: Is Yoga about being an unfeeling robot? Absolutely not! In fact, when experienced meditators were exposed to a physically uncomfortable sensation, their brains showed a bigger reaction than the control group (McFarlin et al., 2012). However, the meditators were also able to recover from the experience far quicker than the control (McFarlin et al., 2012). Reva et al. (2014) states that "Yoga meditators can hardly be seen as [a] general flattening of the emotional responses to external events, but rather as the ability to prevent intense experiences and full-scale, potentially harmful, physiological reactions in response to strong stimuli" (p. 199).

Meditators actually experience feelings more deeply than non-meditators; however, they are able to recover much quicker from the experiences. Yoga teaches us to remember that emotions are fleeting: if our minds were a pond, emotions could be the ripples. They may distort the pond momentarily, but, after a moment, the ripple will calm, and the pond will once again be still. By distancing ourselves from our sensory inputs and our reactions to those inputs, we can see the whole pond instead of being constantly caught up in the ripples. That practice is Pratyahara. It is easier said than done, but, by breaking it down into manageable action items, it can be accessible for students of all ages.

To begin, practitioners must learn to assess their stimuli without judgement. No matter what causes the ripples in our ponds, the ripples must always be completely accepted. If we view all ripples with love and gratitude, they stop affecting us deeply. There are no such things as good nor bad ripples in our ponds. By practicing this nonjudgement, our attention can shift from "being fixated on evaluation language," and shifting our focus to "metacognitive awareness of thoughts and feelings, so [we are] able to let go of clinging to memories of the past and hopes and fears of the future, based on habitual patterns of thought" (Reva et al., 2014, p. 195). In other words, when our thoughts and feelings are distanced enough that they can be seen as passing ripples, they stop holding so much value – meaning it is easier for us to let them go.

One study found that meditating seems to create the space necessary to evaluate emotional stimuli as it occurs, before deciding if and how to respond to it (Reva et al., 2014, p. 195). Simply by acknowledging the emotions in an internal dialogue can help diffuse the intensity of the feeling, in a similar sense to how venting about a feeling to a close friend can help diffuse that tension (Reva et al., 2014, p. 199). This study found "that due to meditation practice the process of appraisal of an event's motivational significance undergoes a change which allows an individual to control emerging emotions; moreover, this change gradually becomes automatic" (Reva et al., 2014, p. 195). Once a regular meditation or Yoga practice has been established, the process of having an internal dialogue of labeling stimuli happens without thinking.

Teaching students to reflect on their emotions can help them not only become increasingly aware of what they are thinking and feeling, but also what others are thinking and feeling (Shapiro et al., 2015, p. 23). It could also help them with understanding character traits and motivations in different literature work. Awareness of emotions can then lead to "the practice of Manifesting With Emotions [which] supports us in cultivating emotions we want to experience and letting go of those that no longer serve us" (Nankin & Fenchel, 2019, p. 90). Once a regular nonjudgement practice has been established, and internal labeling has occurred, students can then use Pratyahara to help them focus on the positives instead of the negatives by letting go of the emotions they do not want to feel and hanging on to the emotions they do want to feel. People who have a regular Yoga, meditation, and mindfulness practice were actually found to see more positives than negatives in a given situation. During an eye-tracking experiment, meditators would "shift [their] attention towards happy faces ... [revealing a] positive affect bias" (Reva et al., 2014, pp. 196–199). In other words, this experiment showed that those who hold a meditation practice naturally focus on positives rather than negatives, when provided with a complex visual stimulus. Pratyahara can help us identify our feelings, let go of the feelings that do not serve us, and focus our attention on the feelings that are serving us.

This means students can use Yoga to build emotional resilience, which, of course, every teacher knows to be a crucial characteristic of a strong learner, especially if they are overcoming their own ACEs. Increased resilience is also often associated with decreased stress and anxiety, making the practice of Pratyahara a powerful loop of anti-anxiety thought patterns and behaviors. Countless studies have shown that practicing Yoga helps reduce anxiety in students (Butzer et al., 2015, p. 42; Harper, 2010, p. 106; Napoli, Krech, & Holley, 2008, p. 103). Shapiro et al. (2015) found that:

> Research with children indicates that mindfulness training reduces anxiety in a range of populations, including adolescent outpatients with psychiatric disorders … inner city children … and typically developing first, second, and third graders … Mindfulness practice also appears to reduce depressive symptoms in children and adolescents … including rumination and intrusive thoughts. (p. 22)

As one researcher points out, through a practice of Pratyahara, some students may experience relaxation, peace, and true resilience for possibly the first time in their lives (Harper, 2010, p. 106). The overall practice can help students "develop stress management skills" that could help to combat and prevent the high number of stress-related disorders currently seen in children, or those disorders which may develop due to unaddressed ACEs (Butzer et al., 2015, p. 42). The incorporation of these practices into the school classroom can lead to higher academic performance, mood, and positive community behaviors (Napoli, Krech, & Holley, 2008, p. 105). Generally speaking, Pratyahara can help teachers raise more well-rounded humans, better equipped to take on the challenges of the world around them.

5 Social Emotional Learning

The word "yama" means "restraint." It is a foundational part of Raja Yoga philosophy that provides the practitioner with a specific lists of 'do nots' in order to achieve this idea of union: Ahimsa (non-violence), Satya (non-lying), Asteya (non-stealing), Brahmacharya (correct use of energy), and Aparigraha (non-greed) (Nankin & Fenchel, 2019, p. 120). When initially read, the Yamas obviously have to do with interpersonal interactions, but upon deeper consideration, each Yama also applies to one's own intrapersonal relationship. How can we ensure that our inner dialogue aligns with the concepts of non-violence, non-lying, non-stealing, non-greed, and the appropriate use of energy?

In the classroom, the Yamas can be incorporated in a way that mimics a social-emotional learning curriculum, as students explore what it means to self-regulate through their inner dialogue, and to use that to regulate their interpersonal relationships. These benefits in no way require the teaching of the Yamas, either. They can be observed even after Asana and mindfulness instruction, as one third grade teacher observed:

> Chelsea Jackson taught her students a few poses and simple breathing exercises and found positive results including 'fewer fights and arguments among students; better student decision making; increased self-awareness and self-esteem; improves concentration and retention; and more efficient use of class time.' (Arbeau, 2016, p. 36)

Other studies have also shown positive results. For example, "a brief (5-week) course on mindfulness improved preschool children's theory of mind understanding," which is their ability to recognize that another's thoughts and emotions are different than their own (Shapiro et al., 2015, p. 23). Another found that, "participation in yoga class decreased [undesirable] behavior among students, which was measured by school discipline referrals" (Tummers, 2013, p. 35). The physiological benefits discussed above are benefitting classroom cultures and social-emotional well being.

A large contributor to increased social awareness is the increased self-regulation, or the management "of emotions that arise automatically in the context of important events" (Shapiro et al., 2015, p. 21). This concept can go hand in hand with a regular Yoga practice, which "gives students a framework for processing and handling their emotions" (Harper, 2010, p. 101). In a study done with long term adult meditators, it was determined that their internal dialogue has been altered in a way that labels emotions in a more neutral way, "thus allowing more flexible responses to affective challenges" (Reva et al., 2014, pp. 199–200). Self-regulation skills are crucial for developing children because of the adaptability and flexibility it allows. Shapiro et al. (2015) states, "boosting children's self-regulation may initiate a cascade of benefits in which children become less likely to be disruptive, move likely to form positive relationships with teachers and peers, and more motivated and better able to learn" (p. 2).

And yet, self-regulation is only one way researchers think Yoga may benefit children's social lives. The Yamas apply as much to the self as they do to interpersonal interactions. In alignment with that, one study showed that "as a result of participation in yoga, there was a 20 percent improvement in the students' positive feelings about themselves" (Tummers, 2013, p. 35). Essentially, by building from the inner self outwards, Yoga is able to help children develop a positive sense of self which can then shine outwards into positive relationship skills (Shapiro et al., 2015; Toscano & Clemente, 2013). Tummers (2013) suggests that practice itself, which usually happens on a mat, can help instill a sense of personal space in younger students (p. 36). Overall, Yoga practice can help improve classroom environments (YJ Editors, 2016), and "these improvements in social and emotional learning competencies of self-management, social awareness, and responsible decision-making suggest that yoga may have beneficial effects" on classroom culture (Butzer et al., 2015, p. 46).

6   Your Brain on Yoga

Meditation is a paramount attribute of Yoga, especially when the goal is to achieve union of breath, mind, and body. In 'true' meditation, the mind is relaxed in such a way that all focus is lost and the practitioner is able to "attain a state of consciousness that is different from the normal waking state" (Nankin & Fenchel, 2019, p. 18). Before that state can be reached, it helps to practice with something to focus on – Dharana. Yogis may use several tools during a Dharana practice, including music, bells, chanting, silently reciting a mantra, or simply giving all of the attention to the breath to help them tune into a calm mind – a state of being free from racing thoughts and feelings. The mind will wander several times, and that should be expected. The mind is the blue sky; even though grey clouds of thought may cover the sky, we know the blue sky still exists behind it. We simply need to remember the blue sky and shift our focus back to that. Dharana can act as the guide to help us find the blue sky when the clouds cover our vision.

Mindful Yoga is the practice of regulating attention, and is often attributed to exercising the ability to focus, on and off of the mat, despite any possible surrounding distractions (Shapiro et al., 2015, p. 2; Harper, 2010, p. 101). As Shapiro et al. (2015) states:

> Research specifically related to children indicates that mindfulness meditation, a form of contemplative practice which emphasizes intentionally attending to one's moment-to-moment experiences, improves executive function in school-age populations. In child and adolescent psychiatric outpatients, for example, weekly group mindfulness-training sessions have been found to reduce attention problems … In community samples, bimonthly mindfulness-training activities (implemented over the course of the school year) have been found to improve second and third graders'

ability to sustain attention ... Such activities may be especially beneficial for children with limited executive function .... (Shapiro et al., 2015, p. 21)

And like Shapiro et al. (2015) suggests, Yoga helps regulate the focus and attention of those students who have ADHD, ADD, or other challenges related to prolonged attention. One study showed that "yoga can improve the ability of students with special needs to focus, attend, and follow directions in fine and gross motor activities" (Tummers, 2013, p. 36). One teacher even recalled "My students would always ask, 'When is yoga time?' ... And as soon as we practiced our mindful movement, my students would calm down and focus in ways that seemed impossible before" (YJ Editors, 2016). Whether through a Dharana practice or not, Yoga has been proven to increase the ability to focus, as well as increase attention spans, in all of our students.

Sometimes, after practicing Dharana and focusing on one singular aspect of reality, the mind may begin to slip into Dhyana, or what could be considered 'true' meditation. The mind is completely blank. There is nothing. As soon as the mind has realized it is in this state, it has left the state of Dhyana. It is very difficult to achieve Dhyana Meditation, especially for our students. So, it may be easier to teach a path to meditation that is much more accessible and mainstreamed.

Mindfulness meditation "is characterized by mental state of 'thoughtless awareness,' or 'mental silence'; in general, the outcome of this meditative technique, as most others, is a sense of relaxation and positive mood and a feeling of benevolence toward oneself and others" (Reva et al., 2014, p. 196). It is "the cognitive propensity to be aware of what is happening the moment without judgement or attachment to any particular outcome" (Napoli, Krech, & Holley, 2008, p. 99), or in other words, it is the total acceptance of each fleeting moment as it passes. That includes an "accepting awareness of our breath, body, emotions, and thoughts" (Nankin & Fenchel, 2019, p. 18); as well as our surroundings and the breath, body, emotions, and thoughts of others. Napoli, Krech, and Holley (2008) shares that:

> When we are mindful, we can both implicitly and explicitly (1) view a situation from several perspectives, (2) see information presented in the situation as novel, (3) attend to the context in which we are perceiving the information, and, eventually, (4) create new categories through which the information may be understood. (pp. 101–102)

One researcher went so far as to say "If one class, one student lives in mindfulness, the entire class is influenced" (Napoli, Krech, & Holley, 2008, p. 103).

Mindfulness meditation is probably the most popular form of Yoga and meditation at this point in Western Culture.

Thanks to the ever-increasing popularity, and the multitude of accessible resources available to practice with – including apps like Headspace, Calm, Insight Timer, and GoNoodle – mindfulness meditation, and its many benefits, can continue to spread in and out of our classrooms. Breathe for Change, an organization dedicated to equipping educators with Yoga techniques to help themselves and their students, noted that "as we continue to practice Mindfulness ... we may notice that the distinction between our life and meditation practice decreases" (Nankin & Fenchel, 2019, p. 102). The more we practice, the more habitualized the elements of the practice become, and the more we can internalize the habits. They become a routine thought process instead of a special practice.

A very interesting 2013 study explored how meditation could help us in our day-to-day lives by observing the correlation between mindfulness meditation and brain wave coherence. This is significant because:

> [Brain wave] coherence reflects the number and strength of connections between two brain areas. Higher coherence indicates that these two points of the brain are working more closely together. Similarly, higher coherence is associated with more integrated and effective thinking and behavior, including greater intelligence, creativity, learning ability, emotional stability, ethical and more reasoning, self-confidences, and reduced anxiety ... Everything good about the brain depends on its coherent, orderly functioning. (Ganpat, Romarao, & Selvi, 2013, pp. 349–351)

Specific brain wave coherences are also associated with improved "mental performance and overall health," as well as "wakefulness and vigilance and ... 'student efficiency'" (Ganpat, Romarao, & Selvi, 2013, p. 351). Essentially, this study shows that all of the qualities teachers hope to instill in their students, including creativity, intelligence, and the ability to learn, can be improved on a neurological level through meditation. During a meditation practice, "the ordinary thinking process settles down," which helps the left, logical side of the brain better synchronize with the right, intuitive side of the brain (Ganpat, Romarao, & Selvi, 2013, p. 351). Overall, the study showed that this practice will help children continue to become better students.

A neurological study done by Streeter et al. (2007) proved that Asana is beneficial to the practitioner, regardless of body type, ability level, or other body diversity factors. By analyzing regular Yoga practitioners' GABA levels, a type of neurotransmitter associated with mood disorders and mental illnesses, they found that after a 60 minute Asana practice, their GABA levels rose by an average of 27%. The elevation of GABA levels post Asana practice may indicate that Asana "may be efficacious treatment for low GABA states" (Streeter et al., 2007, p. 424).

7 Yoga for Academic Data

It is extremely easy to implement Yoga in a classroom setting because there are so many possible variations to how it can be done. Teaching students an Asana practice is not (and should not be) a teacher's only option: "for example, a breathing exercise could be used at the beginning of a lesson to provide a smooth and focused transition from the previous classes. Or, a relaxation pose could be done before sending students back to their classes" (Tummers, 2013, p. 36). Asanas, Pranayamas, mindfulness, and meditations also make great brain breaks throughout the academic day. One teacher used Yoga Philosophies "to implement mind-body practices in her classroom, creating a peace corner in her room, and leading group breathing exercises during transitions" (YJ Editors, 2016).

When students experience and practice mindfulness – the act of focusing on the present moment – they are more likely to think creatively and exhibit traits of a growth mindset, which means they "are able to better use information to enhance memory for instructional retention" (Napoli, Krech, & Holley, 2008, p. 102). So, students who are exposed to Yoga use more of their brains to think, and are able to retain more information that they learn. Additionally, students who practice Yoga are able to be more engaged in their learning and use their emotional regulation to increase their overall academic achievement (Shapiro et al., 2015, pp. 22–25). Teachers also have the opportunity to use different Asana poses as a part of the Total Physical Response method of language learning, or as a kinesthetic addition to help students retain information better (Arbeau, 2016, p. 36).

Students who practice Yoga are able to demonstrate their increased learning on different exams, partially because they were more focused, relaxed, and could manage any test-taking anxiety (Napoli, Krech, & Holley, 2008, p. 103). They also indicate that Yoga is benefitting students with special needs as well, particularly students who have ADHD/ADD, or exhibit similar behavior patterns. These students actually "provided the greatest variance in terms of performance improvement" after exposure to a regular Yoga practice (Napoli, Krech, & Holley, 2008, p. 113).

Over and over again, Yoga has proven to be a viable alternative to medical intervention in children's mental health and attention challenges, while also decreasing school discipline challenges (Peck et al., 2005, pp. 417–422). One study in particular demonstrated the incredible difference Yoga made as an intervention with children, specifically with their performance on several formal assessments, including the ADD-H Comprehensive Teacher Rating Scale (ACTeRs), the Test Anxiety Scale (TAS), and two variations of the Test for Everyday Attention for Children (TEA-Ch) – Selective (Visual) Attention Measures, and Sustained Attention Measures (Napoli, Krech, & Holley, 2008, pp. 108–109). The results were astounding. Students who participated in a yoga-based intervention improved every aspect they were tested on. There is no mistake: Yoga works.

8   Stay Trauma Informed

In addition to being a useful resource for all students in their learning and self-regulation, Yoga has also been proven to support those who have trauma. Every single person in the world has experienced traumatic events and has witnessed trauma, but that does not mean they have been traumatized. A traumatized person's brain struggles to process the traumatic event: meaning it can not be stored as a memory that occurred in the past. A trauma memory is reexperienced not as a story with a beginning, middle, and end, but as a series of images and vivid sensory recalls (Van Der Kolk, 2014). These intense recollections may occur in the form of flashbacks, nightmares, or intrusive thoughts when triggered by a stimulus. This reaction is different from a stress response, where the person is triggered by a connected stimulus (a student fell and scraped their knee, and is now crying). A trauma response is a reaction to a trigger that may seem unrelated to the stimulus (a teacher wears a perfume, and the child cries). Yoga, which focuses on the present moment, helps trauma survivors begin to distinguish the difference between past and present.

A physical Yoga practice, either through Pranayama (breath control) or Asana (physical postures), can also help survivors reconnect with their bodies. Some trauma survivors report feeling disconnected from their bodies. There have even been documented instances where survivors cannot register a physical sensation at all (Van Der Kolk, 2014). While helping survivors connect with their bodies in the present moment, Yoga also guides them to explore how their psychological symptoms may manifest in their physiology. For instance, a survivor may be so caught up in their psychology that they did not realize they were holding (medically unexplainable) pain in their right ankle.

It should be stated that Yoga has not been proven to 'heal' a person's trauma. It is not a therapy or doctor, and Yoga instructors, even those who have

Trauma-Informed training, are not medically trained professionals. However, Yoga has been proven to be one useful tool in a survivor's toolbox during their journey of healing their trauma (Van Der Kolk, 2014).

Even without training, any teacher can ensure that their Yoga instruction, as well as their academic instruction, remains trauma-informed. An easy starting point is to simply ask students "what can we do to make you feel more comfortable in this space?" It is wise to avoid using the words 'safe' or 'unsafe' because there are some survivors who never truly feel safe, and they should feel supported in knowing that their reactions are not bad or wrong.

To help continue this air of comfort, teachers should offer choice throughout the practice. When doing a movement practice, a Trauma-Informed teacher would provide two or three options for what the movement may look like, and also state that choosing stillness is also a possible option. When doing a meditation, a Trauma-Informed teacher would offer a variety of positions to be in, and also state that having eyes open or eyes closed are both acceptable options. Yoga practices should always be offered as an invitation the teacher is offering. Nothing the teacher says to do must be done. The students are the ones who know their bodies the best, and they should feel comfortable in giving themselves what they need, even if it is different than the invitation.

All teachers should also be aware of possible triggers that are common for survivors to have, such as lights turning on and off, physical touch, and loud sounds. It is almost impossible to intentionally accommodate for every single person's triggers, so teachers must also be reflective and open to feedback from their students.

9   Conclusion

It seems that Yoga can provide teachers with endless possibilities of resources to support their students' learning, social-emotional well being, and stress management. Yoga has also been proven to be a positive support for children and adults who are trauma survivors. The body of research, which is continually growing, makes it apparent that Yoga should be an integral part of a trauma informed classroom setting.

Teachers can benefit from in-person or online training to increase their knowledge of how to effectively implement these Yoga-based interventions, but that is not a requirement. All that is necessary is having a curious mind, and a willingness to try new activities. Below are a list of resources and activities to help all teachers create a more trauma-informed classroom through Yoga.

10   Practical Tools and Techniques for a Trauma-Informed Classroom

The rest of this chapter will explore a small selection of the hundreds of possibilities for incorporating Yoga practices into a day-to-day classroom. These resources are a mix of traditional Yoga practices (dating back thousands of years), activities I have observed teachers use in classrooms, and scripts that I have created myself. Each activity can easily be adapted to fit any age group.

10.1   *Social Emotional Learning Tie-Ins*
Yoga is about finding the union of mind, body, spirit, emotions, relationships, everything. In order to venture through the Eight Limb Path, we must be willing to explore what it means to be our highest, or best, selves. Who am I when I am being my ideal person? How do I hope other people would describe me when I am not in the room? By teaching this to our students, we are encouraging them to partake in a reflection process, wherein they can identify if they are acting in a way that reflects their Best Self.

One possible method of facilitating these conversations is to have the students decorate a stick figure version of their Best Self with a handful of traits they would associate with that state of being. Then, when the students have finished, the Best Selves can be secured to their desks, or another prominent display in the classroom that can be easily referenced. An example of this project can be seen in Figure 4.1.

When a student's behavior begins to slide away from their Best Self, the teacher can ask them to reference their drawing, reflect on their behavior, and make a plan to return to their Best Self. The goal would be to support enough of those conversations that students can begin to self-reflect and self-adjust their behaviors.

Another activity option would be to connect the classroom's Yoga practices with an existing SEL curriculum. I support and would recommend investigating Yale's RULER curriculum, Breathe for Change's SEL*F curriculum, and Educalme's curriculum. All are aligned with a system of standards, provides useful tools for educators, and already have varying levels of connections to mindfulness.

10.2   *Guided Meditations*
People who have never meditated before often find it very difficult to sit through a mindfulness activity or meditation. This symptom is also aggravated when the person suffers from anxiety, depression, or unprocessed trauma. Unfortunately, these are the people who would benefit from Yoga practices the most, and yet they are the least likely to try. One way to help coax someone

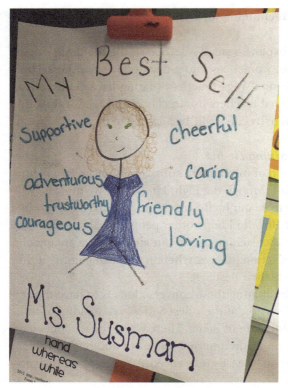

FIGURE 4.1 Have students write positive attributes of their best selves to reference throughout the school day.
Note: Lower scores on ACT eRS subscales indicates fewer problems noted by teachers, and less reported test-anxiety. Higher scores on TEA-Ch selective attention scores indicates an increase in ability to selectively pay attention.

into building comfort is through the use of guided meditation. There are several apps that can provide guidance such as Headspace, Calm, and GoNoodle. Sometimes, though, it helps to have a real person, with a real voice guiding you through. As a teacher, I often appreciate being able to lead my own meditations because I can adapt to what my students need in the moment. If I see wiggling, I can talk about stilling the body. If I see rapid breathing, I can invite them into a breathing exercise. Just as we adapt our lesson plans to fit our children's changing needs in the moment, we should adapt our Yoga instruction and cues to fit them as well.

Below are several scripts that can be used by a teacher in any classroom to help guide students through meditation. Be sure to allow for lots of pauses in between phrases to allow the students time to process and be still on their own.

10.2.1   Beach Meditation
What does your favorite beach look like? Imagine you are walking on it in your bare feet. Feel the warm sand between your toes. Lay down and feel the sun warm your body. Listen to the waves as they crash against the beach. Walk to the water and feel the coolness wash over your feet.

10.2.2   Space Meditation
Everything floats in space, even you. What do your arms feel like without gravity? What about your legs? Do you feel relaxed? Look at all of the stars and planets around you while you float through space.

10.2.3   Gratitude Count
Take three breaths. For every breath you take, think of something in your life that you are thankful for. Maybe it is your mommy or daddy. Maybe it is your friend or your favorite snack. Think of your three things. Now, let's take three breaths. Inhale. What are you thankful for? Exhale as you think "thank you." Breathe in as you think of something else. Breathe out and say "thank you" in your head. Breathe in one last time, really focusing on that last thing you are grateful for. Sigh out and think "thank you."

10.2.4   Rainbow Meditation
Breathe and see red. Feel your body relax. Breathe and see orange. What emotions are you feeling? Breathe and see yellow. Tell your thoughts to be quiet. Breathe and see green. Feel calm. Breathe and see blue. Fill your heart with love. Breathe and see purple. Say thank you to yourself for being so amazing. Breathe and see the rainbow. Isn't it beautiful? Breathe and open your eyes. Let's get ready to learn.

10.2.5   Loving Kindness
Imagine someone you love with all of your heart. See their face and their smile. Maybe you feel their hug or their hand in your hand. As you breathe, tell them the words "May you be safe. May you be healthy. May you be happy. May you be at ease." Now, imagine someone who you don't really know; someone you don't have strong feelings for. Maybe it is a stranger, or someone you pass every day without saying hi to. As you breathe, tell them the words "May you be safe. May you be healthy. May you be happy. May you be at ease." Now, imagine

someone who you fight with a lot. Someone who makes you feel uncomfortable or unpleasant. As you breathe, tell them the words "May you be safe. May you be healthy. May you be happy. May you be at ease." Now, imagine yourself. Maybe you visualize yourself in the present moment, or maybe you visualize an image of yourself from the past. As you breathe, tell yourself the words "May I be safe. May I be healthy. May I be happy. May I be at ease." Lastly, imagine the whole world – every person that is around you. As you breathe, tell them the words "May you be safe. May you be healthy. May you be happy. May you be at ease."

10.3 *Guided Asana Flows*

Much like with meditation, it is a lot easier for students to access the benefits of Yoga when given a certain degree of guidance. It is especially important during physical practices because there is a possibility with injury. If you are unfamiliar with a pose, please do not attempt to cue a student into it. Ensure that you know how to safely guide students in and out of each posture before trying. It is better to skip a challenging pose than end up with someone hurting themselves. Students are the only ones who truly know their own bodies. They should never put themselves into a position that causes them pain.

To ensure that only those with a basic understanding of each pose guides others through the postures, I will only be putting a list of very basic cues to give. Please build your own Asana practice and vocabulary before guiding others.

Additionally, when in a school setting, I recommend avoiding using the traditional Sanskrit names of the postures. English (or whatever language is spoken in the classroom) will allow more accessibility to the postures for all students and learners. I usually refer to the physical movement as "yoga" with my students because that term is more familiar to them than "asana."

10.3.1 Half Sun Salutation

- Begin in Mountain Pose, with feet firmly planted on the ground. Connect with your breath.
- Inhale and sweep your arms up above your head into Extended Mountain Pose.
- Exhale to forward fold, letting your arms comfortably drape towards the floor.
- Inhale into a flat back, finding halfway life with your hands on your thighs or calves.
- Exhale back into forward fold.

- Inhale and slowly roll your spine back up to Mountain Pose, one vertebrae at a time. Let your head by the last thing you lift.
- Ground your feet and reconnect with your breath, while your hands hang by your side or in prayer position at your heart.
- Repeat 3–5 times.

10.3.2   Full Sun Salutation
- Begin in Mountain Pose, with feet firmly planted on the ground. Connect with your breath.
- Inhale and sweep your arms up above your head into Extended Mountain Pose.
- Exhale to forward fold, letting your arms comfortably drape towards the floor.
- Inhale into a flat back, finding halfway life with your hands on your thighs or calves.
- Exhale back into forward fold.
- Inhale and place hands flat on the floor.
- Exhale to step back one foot and then the other.
- Inhale in Plank Pose.
- *Option for a Vinyasa Flow here.*
- Exhale into Downward Facing Dog. Stay for three rounds of breath.
- Exhale and walk towards the top of the mat.
- Inhale and slowly roll your spine back up to Mountain Pose, one vertebrae at a time. Let your head by the last thing you lift.
- Ground your feet and reconnect with your breath, while your hands hang by your side or in prayer position at your heart.
- Repeat 3–5 times.

10.3.3   Cat-Cow Flow
- Begin on your hands and knees, with a flat, neutral back.
- Inhale to drop your tummy, open your heart, and look forward – finding Cow Pose.
- Exhale to arch your back and bring your head down – finding Cat Pose.
- Move at your own pace for 5 breath cycles.

10.4   *Breathing Exercises*
Breathing is one of my favorite things to teach. There is no right or wrong way to do it because it is something every living being inherently knows how to do. Practitioners can feel the benefits of breathwork right away, and it can be used

as a coping skill at any moment. I could be in a meeting with my colleagues and my dead, begin to feel anxious, and decide to practice a breath exercise to regulate myself without anyone knowing. I especially love breathwork for little kids because it is very fun to turn into a game, and it can help them calm down during one of many crying sessions during a day.

10.4.1 Birthday Candle Breathing

Have the student hold a finger out in front of them. Cue them to take a deep breath in, and then exhale onto their finger as if they are blowing out a birthday candle. To turn into a game, which I usually use when trying to calm a crying child, I will hold my finger in front of them while giving these cues. After each breath, I will move my finger a little further away and keep seeing if the child can breathe so I can feel it on my finger.

10.4.2 Bee Breathing

Take a big inhale. Then, let the exhale come out with a buzzing sound like a bee. This activity also works well as Snake Breathing, where the exhale is let out of a hiss sound.

10.4.3 Heart Breathing

Sit with your hands making a heart shape in your lap. As you exhale, let your hands collapse into two fists. When you inhale, let your hands slowly grow back into the heart shape Figure 4.2.

FIGURE 4.2
On an inhale, bring the hands into a heart position. On an exhale, close the hands into fists.

10.4.4   Box Breathing

This exercise is very simple. Inhale for a count of four. Hold your breath for a count of four. Exhale for a count of four. Hold your breath for a count of four. When working with younger students, it helps to draw a square and trace it with your fingers. Inhale when tracing one line. Hold while tracing the next. Exhale for the next line, and then hold your breath for the last line. An example of this can be seen in Figure 4.3.

FIGURE 4.3
Trace the box with your finger, while following the labeled breathing pattern.

References

Arbeau, D. C. (2016). Take a breath: Yoga and meditation in the developmental classroom. *NADE Digest, 8*(1), 35–38.

Butzer, B., Day, D., Adam, P., Ryan, C., Coulombe, S., Davies, B., Weidknecht, K., Ebert, M., & Flynn, L., & Khalsa, S. B. S. (2015). Effects of a classroom-based yoga intervention on cortisol and behavior in second- and third-grade students: A pilot study. *Journal of Evidence-Based Complementary & Alternative Medicine, 20*(1), 41–49.

Ganpat, T. S., Romarao, H., & Selvi, V. (2013). Efficacy of yoga for mental performance in university students. *Indian Journal of Psychiatry, 55*(4), 349–352.

Harper, J. C. (2010). Teaching yoga in urban elementary schools. *International Journal of Yoga Journal, 20*(1), 99–109.

McFarlin, D. F., Perlman, D. M., Salomons, T. V., & Davidson R. J. (2012). *Meditation expertise changes experience of pain*. Center for Healthy Minds. https://centerhealthyminds.org/news/meditation-expertise-changes-experience-of-pain

Nankin, I., & Fenchel, M. (2019). *Breathe for change: 200-hour wellness & yoga training for educators*. Breathe for Change.

Napoli, M., Krech, P. R., & Holley, L. C. (2008). Mindfulness training for elementary school students. *Journal of Applied School of Psychology, 21*(1), 99–125.

Peck, H. L., Kehle, T. J., & Bray, M. A., & Theodore, L. A. (2005). Yoga as an intervention for children with attention problems. *School Psychology Review, 34*(3), 415–424.

Reva, V., Pavlov, S. V., Loktev, K. V., Korenyok, V. V., & Aftanas, L. I. (2014). Influence of long-term sahaja yoga meditation practice on emotional processing in the brain: An ERP study. *Neuroscience, 281*, 195–201. doi:10.1016/j.neuroscience.2014.09.053

Ruiz, R. (2014, July 7). How childhood trauma could be mistaken for ADHD. *The Atlantic*. https://www.theatlantic.com/health/archive/2014/07/how-childhood-trauma-could-be-mistaken-for-adhd/373328/

Shapiro, S., Lyons, K., Miller, R., Butler, B., Vieten, C., & Zelazo, P. (2015). Contemplation in the classroom: A new direction for improving childhood education. *Educational Psychology Review, 27*(1), 1–30.

Streeter, C. C., Jensen, J. E., Perlmutter, R. M., Cabral, H. J., Tian, H., Terhune, D. B., Ciraulo, D. A., & Renshaw, P. F. (2007). Yoga asana sessions increase brain GABA levels: A pilot study. *The Journal of Alternative and Complementary Medicine, 13*(4), 419–426.

Toscano, L., & Clemente, F. (2013). Dogs, cats, and kids: Integrating yoga into elementary physical education. *Strategies: A Journal for Physical and Sport Educators, 21*(4), 15–18.

Tummers, N. (2013). Yoga for your students. *Strategies: A Journal for Physical and Sport Educators, 19*(2), 35–37.

Van Der Kolk, B. (2014). *The body keeps the score: Brain, mind, and body in the healing of trauma*. Penguin Books.

YJ Editors. (2016, May 20). Can yoga save our schools, one teacher at a time? *Yoga Journal*. https://www.yogajournal.com/lifestyle/can-yoga-save-our-schools-one-teacher-at-a-time

CHAPTER 5

The Fine Arts and Teaching Efficacy
Creativity and Decision-Making

Kathleen M. Palladino

Abstract

The purpose of this study was to examine ways in which a background in the fine arts may impact teachers' selection of instructional practices and overall sense of self-efficacy. Various types of strategies selected by the participants were analyzed in order to consider why certain decisions were made and how these decisions impacted teachers' overall pedagogy. The study provided key ways in which the fine arts could guide best practices to support students facing trauma in their lives and provided educators with a variety of fine art strategies to support their students. The researcher utilized a qualitative approach for data collection. Methods included personal, informal interviews with teachers, direct observations, analysis of lesson plans, and open-ended surveys. Key findings related to research suggest that a fine arts background does influence the teachers' sense of self-efficacy in the selection of instructional strategies. In addition, results indicated how teachers' ways of fostering creativity of students, while developing critical thinking skills, was influenced by their background in the fine arts. These results provided ways in which the fine arts could aid educators in developing nurturing, creative environments in which every child may develop healthily and safely.

Keywords

fine arts – creativity – self-efficacy – school climates – decision-making – dispositions – educational theories – human development

1   Introduction

Early childhood is a time when the mind is developing. Children are filled with a natural sense of curiosity and a need to explore their world. Teachers, along with families, play a critical role in children's overall growth and development (Childress, 2014). In the classroom, it is the role of the educator to create a welcoming, intellectually engaging, and safe environment that is individualized to meet the various needs of her students. The educator focuses on learning goals targeting the whole child physically, cognitively, emotionally, and socially, while also considering ways in which tools and instructional decisions could impact children's engagement and overall motivation. Oftentimes, educational decisions are made following specific educational theories and take into account a number of factors, including the effects of trauma on a child.

Students are often faced with difficult challenges throughout their lives and are impacted by a number of factors within their homes, communities, and schools (Erikson, 1959). Some of these challenges include loss of loved ones, community violence, bullying, and more (National Child Traumatic Stress Network [NCTSN], 2019a); these are only a small handful of examples of trauma in a child's life that heavily impact a child's development. Educational theories support that when a child's emotional, physical, and cognitive development are negatively impacted from a young age, the child may show negative behaviors as they develop (Erikson, 1959; Piaget, 1970). Trauma is ever present in our society and inhibits students from healthily developing fundamental skills, such as emotional intelligence, critical thinking skills, as well as basic academic skills (National Association for the Education of Young Children [NAEYC], 2018). The impact of the child's environment is imperative to development, as Erikson (1959) supports. Teachers often must find ways of supporting children affected by trauma within their classroom. They must take into account the child's personal needs – physically, cognitively, emotionally, as well as academically – and must be able to simultaneously develop a nurturing classroom environment that allows the child to flourish and feel comfortable. These environments are, then, trauma-informed classrooms.

As Parker (2006) notes, integrating developmentally appropriate practices is one way teachers can go about creating trauma-informed classrooms. According to the National Association for the Education of Young Children (NAEYC), developmentally appropriate practices emphasize educating the whole child, rather than only academic skills (NAEYC, 2018). Parker (2006) notes that effective teachers utilize developmentally appropriate strategies in addition to maintaining an atmosphere where learning, in every regard, is paramount (p. 65). Utilizing a variety of approaches and strategies, particularly those in the fine arts, can be a means of implementing developmentally appropriate practices while keeping the child engaged and motivated (Frydenberg, 2012). Through the fine arts, educators can teach children a number of ways to manage emotions, problem solve, and build on academic skills; they also allow for self-expression and creation of identity (NAEYC, 2018). Teachers who utilize the fine arts may be considered more efficacious in some ways and may be more creative. According to Cremin (2009), teachers that are more "creative" in the development of educational spaces may have specific dispositions or backgrounds. Because teachers have a variety of strategies and approaches at their disposal when considering developmentally appropriate practices for instruction, it is imperative to consider what impacts decision making processes and ways in which creative thought could impact practice.

The need for creative classrooms in today's society is ever growing. Academic curriculums are becoming more rigorous, pushing for children to critically think more often. Communities are being effected by a number of different social issues, including violence, low socio-economic status, and more. Students are often caught in the cross hairs and asked to maintain a high academic standard despite the ongoing challenges they may face. Children often have difficulty problem-solving and brainstorming solutions to problems in their personal lives and in their communities. A creative early childhood classroom can help a child to build divergent thinking and develop in a nurturing environment. Creative classrooms focus on developing the whole child and provide frequent opportunities for self-expression. They also encourage respect, trust, collaboration, and more foundational concepts outlined by the National Association for the Education of Young Children (NAEYC). Foundational concepts and skills include emotional intelligence, sense of identity, and more (NAEYC, 2018). Children will often face challenges that will inhibit the successful acquisition of these skills. Educational theories act as a blueprint to understanding why certain behaviors are occurring and can help an educator to select practices that will best target the student's needs. Use of fine art strategies and approaches may be one way of addressing these issues while allowing the child to develop in a safe, nurturing environment.

2   An Extended Review of Educational Theories

Theoretical frameworks, serving as blueprints for educational practices, are one of the many references a teacher may use when planning developmentally appropriate experiences for their students (Parker, 2006). The writings of Piaget (1970), Erikson (1959), and Vygotsky (1925/1972) are often consulted by teachers interested in gaining additional knowledge related to philosophies that may impact the development of cognitive and social-emotional skills in children. Parker (2006) explained how instructional decisions are made by considering multiple factors, such as individual student needs, age of the children, and the stage in which they fall under Piaget's, Erikson's, and Vygotsky's theories.

Educators will frequently look to Piaget's theory for cognition, Erikson for socio-emotional development, and Vygotsky for play and creative development. Piaget (1970) provided various stages of cognition he believed all children would go through as they grow. His stages of cognitive development determine specific ages in which children begin to think abstractly, can interpret concrete information, and can interpret sensory information. According to Piaget (1970), pinpointing specific stages of development may impact the selection of experiences an educator will choose, the tools and materials used, and the amount of scaffolding needed to understand academic concepts. Erikson's (1959) theory is frequently referred to for social-emotional development, i.e., how a child interacts with others in their environment. Vygotsky's (1925/1972) readings are often utilized as guidance related to a child's play and how it relates to development. He developed stages of play and a theory of creativity which early childhood educators, in particular, use as a tool to move children through the stages of play and increase their critical thinking skills. His theory combines cognition with imagination and play. It will often guide the educator to choose strategies and materials that both allow children to interact with one another and allow each child to become creative in the way they engage with ideas. The combination of these theories partly informs instructional choices and allows the educator to select developmentally appropriate approaches and strategies.

2.1   Piaget

Jean Piaget (1970) studied cognitive development of the mind and concluded that we progress through a series of four stages as we grow (Piaget, 1970). His first two stages, the Sensorimotor and Preoperational Stages, most directly impact early childhood educators. The sensorimotor stage begins at birth. Infants begin to explore their world using their senses. An educator who is working with infants may provide opportunities that provide a large number of sensory experiences to students.

During the Preoperational stage, many children are beginning school in the U.S. This is generally a difficult transition period for children, as they are acclimating to a new, more structured environment compared to their home. They begin to interact with other children in a school setting and begin to discover other ways of thinking about situations. Students will generally show signs of "egocentrism" (Piaget, 1970), which means that students naturally have difficulty understanding the perspectives of others. Teachers may find that children have difficulty sharing or understanding that there are consequences to their actions. It is important to bear in mind that children in this stage cannot think abstractly yet. Concrete ideas, use of symbols, pretend play, and more, are paramount to helping children understand different perspectives and possibilities of solving problems.

If a teacher were to observe a child who, for example, was not sharing, and wanted to help the class understand the concept he or she may use the fine arts as a good place to start. The teacher may sing songs with the children that introduce the concept, and perspectives on why it is good to share, for example. The teacher may also look to a different theorist to understand why a particular challenge may be occurring.

2.2   *Erikson*

Erik Erikson (1959) is another common theorist that early childhood educators look to when considering developmentally appropriate practices. He created a stage theory, similar to Piaget, where we move through various stages throughout our life and acquire different attributes. His first four stages are crucial to early childhood, as they are the foundations of a stable relationship with adults and independence. Children in the first stage create secure attachments with adults, which Erikson (1959) describes as trust that someone else will provide for a child's needs. In the second stage, children build determination and begin to make simple choices for themselves (Boeree, 2006). The third stage results in courage and confidence. By this stage, children are interacting with one another in school and beginning to develop their own identities (Boeree, 2006, p. 9); if a child perceives that they are not appreciated by other children, they may react negatively. The fourth stage results in competence and successful development of age/grade appropriate skills. The remainder of his stages includes themes of love, fidelity, and accomplishment, etc.; and often occurs from middle school throughout adulthood (Erikson, 1959).

Students should be developing both emotional and social awareness as they grow older, but if something is prohibiting the child from properly developing, the teacher must address it. Erikson (1959) notes that a child reacts to his/her environment while developing. If a child is raised in a nurturing environment, the child will most likely exhibit nurturing behaviors. However, if there is difficulty in the child's environment, at home or at school, the child may react negatively and fail to acquire the proper skill in each of Erikson's stages. The fine arts can be a good outlet for students to express their difficulties in an appropriate manner and may help them to manage their emotions.

2.3   *Vygotsky's Theory of Creativity*

Vygotsky (1925/1972) created a stage theory of creative development. He began his work as a college literature professor in Russia during the early twentieth century, noticing that his students interpreted texts in different ways (West,

1999, p. 49). He based his studies initially on different forms of literature, but then expanded his studies to include the different mediums of the fine arts, theater, dance, visual art, and music. In his article, "The Psychology of Art," he explores the basic principles of what constitutes art and the innate feature of creativity. His main theory, in the words of D.W. West (1999), was this: "Each work of art, then, consists of a dialectic relationship between 'content' (or 'material') and the 'form' (or 'technique'); it is the conflict between these two elements which makes a work of art aesthetic, which gives it its status as 'art" (West, 1999, p. 51). In other words, art can be created in a number of ways and can express a variety of things, including emotions. When we perceive art, we do not respond to the form only, but to the content and its emotional appeal (Vygotsky, 1925/1972). Vygotsky also believed that we are all born with creativity; it must be consistently developed, however, in order for us to be considered "creative" as adults (Vygotsky, 1925/1972). He also noted that our experiences contribute to the way in which our creativity is hindered or developed. Vygotsky used these principles and applied them to pedagogy in order to create his theory.

His stage theory consists of four different stages that track the use of imagination and play throughout development. In the first stage, children are the most imaginative and are learning language to express their thoughts through play and various interactions with adults. At this stage, children need the support of adults to build language skills and to help them better interact with their peers (Vygotsky, 1925/1972). As they interact with one another more often, they begin to move through different stages of play, culminating in social play. At the second stage, children do not need the assistance of adults in order to play. Play, and imagination in turn, is now second nature to the child. Problem-solving and the ability to devise various solutions to problems also take root in this stage (Vygotsky, 1925/1972). The third and fourth stages occur from adolescence to adulthood. Here, we come to recognize that both imagination and creative thought are needed, and we look for outlets to express our creativity.

Vygotsky favors the participation of the teacher as a guide in this theory. Educators are needed to not only guide the child's play throughout the early years, but to develop their expressive and receptive language skills and plan activities that are developmentally appropriate and enriching (Vygotsky, 1935/1986). If the early learning environment is enriching, positive, and favors student-centered exploration, the child will learn to be imaginative and carry that imagination through adulthood. The child will also incorporate that imagination into his thinking and will be able to consider more carefully solutions to various problems that occur in his natural environment (Vygotsky 1935, 1986). Educators may be inclined to utilize imaginative play in order to illustrate different concepts, build critical thinking skills, and help the child to express themselves in different ways.

3   Dispositions and Teaching Philosophies

Theoretical frameworks are helpful for educators to use as references to guide their thinking, but do not provide a step-by-step way of discerning which approaches and strategies will benefit the class; they leave room for use of different approaches and strategies within them. As Parker (2006) describes, teaching practice is influenced by a number of factors, some external, like the student's behaviors and academic needs, and some internal, such as the educator's personal teaching philosophies, culture, beliefs, dispositions, etc. (Parker, 2006, p. 65). It is possible that two teachers who take different approaches to teaching may go about meeting a child's needs in different ways.

Educators will frequently consider their own philosophies and approaches to teaching. When considering different approaches, we cannot say that one is better than another. As long as the students are learning and growing in a nurturing environment and the teachers are willing to adjust their practices to meet the needs of their students, the approach is of little matter (Sawyer, 2004). In other words, educators may take different approaches as long as the desired outcome is achieved. Teachers will often reflect upon their own backgrounds and experiences as children. For example, an educator may take a particular approach to teaching because he/she was exposed to it as a student. They may also call upon their various skill sets, such as acting or sports, for example, and utilize their additional skills to target particular concepts (Sawyer, 2004).

The willingness of teachers to utilize different approaches and strategies to meet the needs of their students is known as teaching efficacy (Bandura, 1977). As Sawyer (2004) describes, teachers who are more efficacious and self-reflective on their practices have better outcomes when working with students (p. 322).

4   Human Development and Creativity

When considering the different possible approaches and strategies that efficacious teachers can utilize to promote creativity, the role of the fine arts must be considered. Ideas related to the fine arts can encourage creativity in students and teachers, as different parts of the brain are utilized to help make abstract concepts more concrete (Nadal, 2013). The arts leave room for use of evidence-based strategies while encouraging self-expression, appreciation for those involved, and divergent thinking (Oxlee, 1996). Oxlee (1996) writes that the creative process can be defined as "open, divergent thinking, involving new associations, relationships and analogies, applied to both problem formulation and solving" (p. 135). In other words, when children are actively engaged in a creative activity, they are constantly thinking and making neural connections. These connections act as building blocks for further activities that will begin to grow stronger if engaged often. Teachers who engage in the creative process may, therefore, be considered more efficacious. They are constantly considering new ways of meeting students' needs. They are encouraging their students to critically think about concepts and engage with them in a developmentally appropriate manner. They may also be utilizing their backgrounds or additional skill sets in the process. Utilizing an overall arts-based approach, therefore, may contribute to more efficacious teachers and produce more desirable outcomes in students.

4.1 *Human Development and the Brain*

Educators place emphasis on developing the whole child during the early years of life. We focus on academics, socio-emotional growth, cognitive development, as well as physical development. Perhaps the two most difficult areas for teachers to directly target are social and emotional development. There are several factors that educators must consider before making instructional decisions. Chief among these factors are neurological development and the effect that different experiences will have on the brain.

The early years are described as the period where the brain is consistently developing at a rapid rate. Students are utilizing different parts of their brains, making neural connections, creating memories and associations, developing receptive and expressive language skills, and much more (Haartsen et al., 2016). Brain development begins at birth; the experiences that a student has at home, therefore, will impact the child in many ways. According to Haartsen, Jones, and Johnson (2016), children's brains are developing in all areas. Their emotional houses, both hemispheres of the brain, their frontal lobes and more, are growing with exposure to each new experience that occurs. If a child is raised in a nurturing environment, as Erikson (1959) describes, he/she will develop necessary skills that will serve as a foundation for educators to build upon in school. However, if a child is not raised in a nurturing environment or is facing trauma of some sort, one or more areas of the brain may be impacted over time.

Perhaps the most difficult problem that children face, regardless of the environment in which they are placed, is problem-solving. This ability aids students in every facet – academically, physically, emotionally, and socially. Creativity, specifically divergent thinking, is a vital part of problem solving that educators target in a number of ways. Divergent thinking is best defined as the ability to brainstorm different ways of solving problems.

4.2 *Creativity*

Some researchers will argue that creativity, and subsequently divergent thinking, is innate, while others will argue that it can be developed over time. Researchers who argue that creativity is developed often use human brain development as their support. The brain develops over time and different parts of the brain are strengthened, depending upon the experiences to which the child is exposed. In other words, it is the teachers and parents who create a creative child. Those who argue that creativity is innate subscribe to the idea that children are naturally curious and will explore and make meaning out of their world naturally. Both Piaget's (1970) and Erikson's (1959) theories support this idea. Educators often subscribe to one side or the other when making instructional decisions.

Creativity, interestingly enough, is not something that can be measured directly. It is an idea, not a product, according to Oxlee (1996). Researchers often measure creativity in terms of the product produced and the guidelines given (Oxlee, 1996, p. 137). Therefore, researchers may say that teachers who utilize art-based approaches may be considered more creative because they ask more of their students. Others may say that teachers who use art-based approaches are not creative, because the products may not have specific guidelines; teachers may ask students to use specific tools but may not ask for a specific product. They may allow the child to explore materials/experiences and engage in divergent thinking.

There is little conclusive data to prove that teachers who use the arts are more or less creative than those who do not. However, when considering how to build students' executive functioning skills, the arts are often used in practice. Art-based approaches and strategies are common in preschool classrooms, according to Frydenberg (2012). The fine arts have the ability to make abstract concepts concrete, according to Nadal (2013). Piaget (1970) proposes that young children often have difficulty understanding abstract concepts. The arts also reach more than one area of the brain at a time, which neurologists have said is a benefit to children's overall brain development (Haartsen et al., 2016). They also encourage appreciation for others, self-expression, and collaboration, which are the foundations that the NAEYC depicts for early childhood programs (NAEYC, 2018). Erikson (1959) proposes that children are a product of their environment and the experiences to which they are exposed; the fine arts can promote a positive, rich environment. All of the following reasons make utilizing art-based approaches desirable to early childhood educators. Educators have the ability to utilize different areas of the fine arts, such as drama, visual art, dance, or music, and they can choose between utilizing specific strategies to target a singular concept or utilizing an overall approach to learning. Regardless, educators always have the ability to differentiate based on the needs of their students. The positive effects the fine arts can have on their students' creativity and thinking processes are another component that make the fine arts appealing to early educators.

In today's society, there is a stronger need for more creative classrooms and more efficacious teachers. Children face challenges at young ages, some that can be detrimental to their development. The fine arts can serve as outlets for educators to not only address some of the challenges their students may be facing, but to help them navigate their emotions and brainstorm solutions.

5   Current School Climates and the Need for Creative Classrooms

The need for creative classrooms in today's society is ever-growing. Academic curriculums are becoming more rigorous, pushing for children to critically think more often. Communities are being affected by a number of different social issues, including violence, low socio-economic status, and more. Students are often caught in the cross hairs and asked to maintain a high academic standard, despite the ongoing challenges they may face. Children often have difficulty problem solving and brainstorming solutions to problems in their personal lives and in their communities. A creative early childhood classroom can help a child to build divergent thinking and develop in a nurturing environment. Creative classrooms focus on developing the whole child and provide frequent opportunities for self-expression. They also encourage respect, trust, collaboration, and more foundational concepts outlined by the National Association for Education of Young Children (NAEYC). Foundational concepts and skills include emotional intelligence, sense of identity, and more (NAEYC, 2018). Children will often face challenges that will inhibit the successful acquisition of these skills.

Perhaps the most difficult challenges for children to cope with are those that are socio-emotional. Creative classrooms can address common challenges such as loss of a loved one, bullying, and community violence. The fine arts can serve as a means for teachers to help their students cope with their emotions, validate their feelings in a positive, safe environment, and address community issues that may have an overall impact on the child's development.

Loss of a loved one can impact a young child in multiple ways. According to Erikson (1959), children begin to make secure attachments from birth and rely on other adults in their life to provide for them. If a main caregiver for the child passes away, the child may feel lonely and may not be provided with adequate care. Cognitively, an infant may have difficulty processing sensory information and a pre-school aged child may not be able to understand the concept of loss (Piaget, 1970). Loss, according to the National Child Traumatic Stress Network (2019a), can have detrimental effects on the child's overall development if not addressed in a timely manner.

Educators who are seeing these effects may utilize visual art in order to help the child make sense of their emotions, validate their feelings, and help the child to react in a more positive way (Frydenberg, 2012). Creating visuals, according to Frydenberg (2012), helps the child use their "logical processing" skills (p. 63) as well as "develop imagination, empathy, creativity [spontaneity], and commitment" (p. 63). Successful educators will allow the child to explore materials, such as paint, colors, artistic tools and mediums, for example, and encourage them to express their feelings. They will often engage the child and talk to them about why they are making their artistic choices. The goal is to encourage exploration in every facet of learning and put a name to the child's emotions. Once the emotions are identified and the child's emotions are validated, the educator can then begin to utilize different strategies to alter a child's 'negative' behaviors.

Negative behaviors in an academic setting may be the result of loss, but they are often the child's response to something larger that is occurring in their environment (NCTSN, 2019b). Bullying and community violence are two social issues that can occur in a child's natural environment. Both can encompass a number of different, individual problems, but there is no denying that the effects of these issues have the potential to impair a child's development (NCTSN, 2019b). In the early years, community violence may impact the child more than we think. Children spend much of their first years at home and in the community (NAEYC, 2018), and if the community is not safe and encourages negative behaviors, the child will come to school with the thought that those behaviors are the norm (NCTSN, 2019c). This poses a challenge for teachers to not only modify the child's negative behaviors, but to change the way the child thinks about his behaviors.

Community violence is best defined as "an intentional attempt to hurt one or more people and includes homicides, sexual assaults, robberies, and weapon attacks" (Center for Mental Health Services (CMHS), Substance Abuse and Mental Health Services Administration (SAMHSA), U.S. Department of Health and Human Services, 2019) While the term is a broad umbrella for various social issues, children who are exposed to community violence will often show behaviors that suggest a lack of trust in authority figures (Lunenburg, 2010). Educators may be wary of utilizing community resources, so as not to further expose students to a negative environment (Lunenburg, 2010, p. 3). As educators, we always seek to expose our students to positive, nurturing environments where the students will feel comfortable. We want our students to feel safe and we, ultimately, want them to trust that we will provide for them. The fine arts, specifically music and dance, can help educators to create a relaxing, trusting, and collaborative environment in which students can interact.

According to Frydenberg (2012):

> Learning through dance in a social situation provides a unique tool for creative self-expression, and promotes a wide range of outcomes as follows: opportunities for the bodily communication of feelings and thoughts, relationship building, co-sharing of problems with important others through bodily kinesthetic exploration, opportunities for the uncovering of otherwise hidden issues, critical thinking and problem-solving, aesthetic decision making, etc. Dance brings together and energizes the connection between body, mind and spirit, providing a creative outlet for the emotions and for the self. (p. 90)

Educators who utilize dance and music, therefore, help students to see that their classroom is their 'safe space' where they can trust in their teachers and peers to provide for them, and help them to cope with difficult issues that may be troubling them. Dance physically allows for the child to express themselves while music helps the child to relax and become aware of their reactions. By helping the students to relax and clear their minds, we can then begin to integrate behavior management strategies and work towards brainstorming solutions to the problems within their communities.

Bullying is another issue that is common within school walls. In early childhood, children are beginning to develop their identities, according to the NAEYC, and they often have difficulty understanding the concept of uniqueness (Piaget, 1970). Preschool-aged students in particular may exhibit egocentrism, according to Piaget (1970), which means that children view their world from their perspective only. Children who bully may become physical with other children; they may also purposefully isolate others in an effort to make them feel different (Center for Mental Health Services (CMHS), Substance Abuse and Mental Health Services Administration (SAMHSA), U.S. Department of Health and Human Services , 2019). Those who are bullied may react emotionally, feeling hopeless and helpless, or they may become physical and defensive.

Educators who are viewing this situation may be inclined to intervene immediately with the students involved, using other strategies. Drama can serve as a method of addressing the issue with the whole group (Frydenberg, 2012). Educators may have students act out a situation in which a child is being bullied, and have students consider how each party feels in the situation. She can guide students to ultimately understand that each person is unique and deserves respect. She may ask students to display a particular skill that they feel is an asset to them, express interests and find others in their class who have similar interests, etc. The educator may also model proper behaviors that she wishes students to utilize (Frydenberg, 2012). Drama physically and cognitively engages the students and helps them to become aware of their actions. They also become aware of their emotions and how to react to them. It allows for abstract concepts, such as respect, to become visual and/or physical, which is considered developmentally appropriate based on Piaget's (1970) and Erikson's (1959) theories.

6   Dispositions and Backgrounds of Creative Teachers

When considering approaches and strategies that are developmentally appropriate for students, teachers will frequently consider their own backgrounds and strategies that they found helpful as children. They frequently reference theoretical frameworks for guidance and utilize strategies within their teaching philosophies. Some may be willing to utilize strategies outside of their comfort zone, a mark of an efficacious teacher. Creative teachers may possess specific dispositions and backgrounds in order to successfully allow their students to develop. Background will be defined as two or more years of professional training in a fine arts field or receipt of a higher education degree in a fine art field.

All teachers should encourage students to believe that they will reach their goals; they should set high expectations for their students. Teachers provide encouragement, in addition to the tools/strategies necessary to reach goals. While they encourage their students to reach their high expectations, they place high expectations for themselves in developing their practices in order to better serve their students. Teachers should always be willing to learn and adapt their practices in order to help their students succeed. Teachers who achieve this, then, may be considered efficacious and may be more creative in the decision-making process. Creative teachers may subscribe to using an art-based approach, as it allows for exploration, creativity, collaboration, and encouragement. Art-based approaches also encourage divergent thinking and encourage development of both logic and creativity.

Creative educators possess specific dispositions and sets of skills that prove useful in the classroom. Generally, these teachers may enjoy exploring new approaches or strategies, encourage their own professional development by seeking other opinions, and engage in both divergent thinking and self-reflection on their current practices. According to Cremin (2009), creative teachers are "confident, enthusiastic, and committed" (p. 67). They frequently keep in mind their personal strengths and backgrounds, look to theoretical frameworks to inform their practices, and display a willingness to develop their craft. They consider their personal strengths in relation to evidence-based pedagogical practices and the school's philosophy of education (Cremin, 2009). Creative teachers frequently tend to collaborate with other teachers and adapt their practices based on input from other colleagues; they may question different approaches and strategies before making instructional decisions. Creative educators not only model these dispositions, but they foster them in their students. By modeling confidence, enthusiasm, and commitment, the students learn what is expected of them and they often feel like they can take ownership of their learning (Cremin, 2009, p. 72). Cremin (2009) notes that modeling these dispositions leads to the creation of a nurturing environment where ideas are valued, creative thinking and exploration is encouraged, and making individual connections is highly supported.

When considering instructional decision-making in relation to creativity and the fine arts, there are multiple factors that can affect the way a teacher instructs her students. Some factors may be: the individual needs of her students, the need for a positive learning environment, personal teaching philosophy, the philosophy of the school, developmental levels, theoretical frameworks for developmentally appropriate practices, a teacher's own background in the fine arts, the need for creative thought, curriculums used in the schools, and much more (Parker, 2006; Oxlee, 1996; Cremin, 2009). In addition to making these instructional choices, educators must be efficacious and collaborate with one another, draw on their own backgrounds, consider their students' needs, and model the dispositions of creative educators for their students and colleagues (Bandura, 1977; Cremin, 2009). The successful combination of all of the factors listed above, in tandem with the usage of fine art strategies and student-centered approaches, will ultimately allow educators to encourage creativity in their students, produce a positive learning environment, and allow the child to healthily develop in all major domains.

7 Methods

7.1 *Overview*

The purpose of this study was to examine ways in which a background in the fine arts may impact teachers' creative selection of instructional practices and overall sense of self-efficacy in encouraging creativity in students. In addition, the various types of strategies selected by the participants were analyzed in order to consider why certain decisions were made and how these decisions may impact a teacher's overall pedagogy.

The researcher utilized a qualitative approach for data collection. Methods included personal, informal interviews with teachers, direct observations, analysis of lesson plans, and open-ended surveys. These methods allowed the researcher to identify specific ways in which the teachers' backgrounds in the fine arts were useful throughout the instruction process.

7.2 *Setting*

The study took place at an early childhood center located on the campus of a liberal arts college in Staten Island. The institution is a private center, offering two programs, half-day and full-day, for children between the ages of 2–5 years. In total, there are four different classrooms, each with a senior teacher and a minimum of two teaching assistants. On average, there are a maximum of 20 students per class. Each classroom is separated by program and age. At the time of this study, the institution followed a play-based curriculum and chose not to align with New York State Common Core Standards for Preschool. There were four full-time teachers on staff, with 8 graduate students acting as teaching assistants. On average, there were two graduate students assigned to each classroom. Some classes included private SEITS for individual students. SEITS are Special Education Itinerate Teachers assigned to specific students with special needs under the provisions of an Individualized Education Plan. In this setting, there were no students who spoke English as a second language or students formally classified as gifted students.

The researcher observed all four classrooms over the two programs offered. She observed the classes over a two day, consecutive period for roughly two hours each day. The age, time, and specific needs of the students in each class were noted during observations.

This site was selected by the researcher since she had been a graduate student working with the two full-day program groups, and currently maintains a strong relationship with both the educators and director of the center. In addition, the center was selected, in part, because of its play-based curriculum and the flexibility that such a curriculum provides to encourage creative thought.

There are multiple opportunities for student-discovery, creativity, and varied instructional strategies throughout the school day. Opportunities to engage with the arts are also a key element valued at this institution.

7.3 Participants

Participants in this study included four early childhood teachers who had strong backgrounds in the fine arts. Each teacher had either a higher education degree/certification in a fine art field or a minimum of two years of training in a fine art field. Each field of the fine arts-visual art, theater, dance, or music, was represented in this study. Some educators had training in multiple areas of the arts. Each teacher had been working at the center for at least four years and believed heavily in student-centered learning and the benefits of play/exploration of materials.

7.4 Design

A qualitative study was conducted using a variety of methods. Data collection consisted of direct observations of participating educators, informal interviews with participants, analysis of lesson plans coinciding with the observation period, and open-ended, self-reflective surveys. The variables noted included the reasoning behind particular instructional decisions during planning and implementation of lessons, specific fine art strategies and/or skills implemented during instruction, student reactions to these strategies/skills, and the creativity of educators when considering the individual, holistic needs of students, as well as the overall class needs. Data was analyzed by looking at themes and patterns in collected materials.

7.5 Materials

- Email to director of participating center. Before the researcher conducted her study, an email expressing the interest of utilizing the center for data collection and outlining the purpose of the study was sent to the director of the participating early childhood center.
- Emails to participants. After consent from the director of the center was obtained, and before the study was conducted, an email explaining the purpose of the study and overall procedure of the study was sent to possible participating teachers.
- Consent forms. Each interested participant received and signed a consent form outlining the purpose of the study, terms of participation, and privacy policy. The teachers were notified that if they chose to withdraw from the study at any time, their data would be destroyed and not counted in the study.

- Interview questions and note sheet. The researcher briefly interviewed participants, using a set of targeted interview questions as a guide. Notes were written on blank pieces of loose leaf with the participants' identifying letter at the top of the page.
- Observation and analysis forms. The researcher created two observation forms to help in analyzing lesson plans and organizing observations. The first sheet, was utilized during direct observations. Here, the researcher noted any fine art strategies implemented throughout the observation period, and noted student reactions before and after strategy implementation. The second sheet allowed the researcher to note particular areas within lesson plans that may have accounted for use of fine art strategies/ skills and creativity.
- Open-ended, self-reflective surveys. At the end of the observation period, participants were sent open-ended surveys via email. These surveys were self-reflective in nature, designed to help educators reflect on their practice and instructional decisions, their use or lack of creativity when making instructional choices, and their ability to adapt their strategies and/or approaches to best suit the needs of their students.

7.6 Procedures

The study was conducted over the course of eight days. Over the course of these eight days, two-days of consecutive observations of each classroom were conducted, lesson plans that aligned with these observations were collected, and participants received the survey via email upon completion of observations. Each educator was given one week from receipt to complete the survey.

Once IRB approval was received, the researcher reached out to each full-time teacher directly via email and asked for participation. As each teacher expressed their willingness to participate, the researcher sent a consent form via email to sign in order to ensure participation and informed consent. This consent form outlined the purpose of the study, what was expected from each participant, and outlined the privacy policy utilized in the study. Once all consent forms had been received by the researcher and filed on a password protected laptop in a private folder on her desktop, the researcher began her study.

First, she set-up observation and interview days that best suited each teacher. These observation days consisted of two consecutive days, and lasted approximately two hours per day. Two hours gave the researcher enough time to observe circle time, which is the main lesson for the day, and some playtime. This gave the researcher an idea of the overall classroom environment and routine. This also allowed the teacher a broader opportunity to use her background at different points during the day. In addition, the researcher observed not only planned strategies outlined in lesson plans, but the teacher's ability to adapt these strategies on demand, based on the students' needs for the day. A majority of the teachers observed were constantly adapting their practices during circle time, in order to ensure that everyone understood the lesson. These adaptations served as a mark of their self-efficacy and creativity as an educator.

The researcher observed both programs offered at the center. She observed the classrooms at different times of the day, 2 morning sessions and 2 afternoon sessions overall, based upon the daily schedules of each class and the flow for each program. For the full-day program, she observed Teacher C in the afternoon so as to observe circle time during their routine and outdoor play, and Teacher D in the morning so as to observe circle time during their normal routine and indoor play. She focused primarily on the ways teachers intervened or facilitated play during playtime and their ability to adapt on demand during circle time. For the half-day program, she observed the morning session with Teacher B and the afternoon session with Teacher A. This was, in part, because of the ages and comfortability of the children with new adults and changes in routine. The researcher wanted the students to be comfortable, and to follow their normal routine as closely as possible in order to avoid any confusion or additional pressure placed on the students and teachers.

In many cases, before beginning observations, the researcher conducted her informal interviews with the participants on their lunch breaks or in the morning before pick-up. Interviews lasted for an average of ten minutes and informal notes were taken on loose leaf with the identifying letter of each teacher at the top of the page. The main purpose of the interviews was to gain more insight into the educator's teaching philosophy, background/teaching experience, and more. These interviews then informed the researcher's observations and analysis of data collected. Teachers were also in the process of collaborating with one another at these times, which helped the researcher to gain more insight into their efficaciousness.

During each observation, the researcher noted any fine art strategies implemented, and overall student reactions, before and after strategy implementation. She also collected lesson plans and noted specific areas that allowed for fine art strategies, student exploration, or creativity. Interview responses were taken into account when analyzing data.

Upon the completion of each observation, participants were sent via email an open-ended, self-reflective survey to complete. The purpose of this survey was to allow teachers the opportunity to reflect on their own practice, specifically why they make instructional decisions and how their fine art background may influence their practices. Participants were given one week to complete the survey upon receipt and return to the researcher via email. All data was then downloaded and saved onto the researcher's personal, private laptop in a private folder and any identifying information was removed and replaced accordingly with an identifying letter.

7.7   Reliability and Validity

Two experts in the fields of Early Childhood Education and the Fine Arts have provided feedback on the design and materials used throughout the study.

7.8   Results

Table 5.1 displays the fine art backgrounds of the four participants. Each educator was given an identifying letter. The fine art field in which they have had training is noted. Some participants had backgrounds in multiple fields of the fine arts.

TABLE 5.1   Background of participants

Participant	Background/Fine art field(s)	Years of training in fine art field
Teacher A	Visual art	3 years +
Teacher B	Dance	~20 years +
Teacher C	Visual art; Music	~4 years; ~4 years
Teacher D	Music; Visual Art; Theater	2 years; ~20 years +; 5 years +

Table 5.2 displays specific fine art strategies that were utilized by the four participants observed. The intended purpose of these strategies, in addition to the effect of these strategies on the students, is noted. Strategies that were listed in lesson plans are noted with "P" and some that were implemented on demand are noted as "OD." Institutional practices are denoted with underlines.

Table 5.3 outlines common themes within various sections of lesson plans from all four participants. These sections indicated how teachers planned to incorporate their background(s) or specific fine art strategies, and illustrated their purpose for incorporating specific strategies into instruction.

Table 5.4 displays common themes within the surveys across all four participants. Each question was designed to assess a particular element of the

TABLE 5.2 Reflection on fine art strategies observed during the study

Fine art field	Strategy(s)	Intended purpose	Overall effect on students
Music	*Piggyback songs* (P/OD)	To focus students during transitions and help remember academic content during circle time	Students were more focused during transition times and were listening more closely to directions given; academic knowledge was better absorbed and assessed during subsequent lessons.
	Letter puppet songs (P)	Activate prior academic knowledge and acquire new vocabulary; student engagement	Students were actively engaged and listening to the songs. Students remembered some new vocabulary terms in subsequent lessons.
Theater	*Character voices/vocal intonations* (OD)	To differentiate between characters in a story; student engagement	Students were able to verbally identify characters in a story and were actively listening and/or mimicking the character voices.
	Props (P)	To enhance a lesson/story and make abstract concepts concrete; student exploration	Students were physically engaging with props after lesson time and exploring new ways of using the props (with guidance from the teacher).

(*cont.*)

TABLE 5.2 Reflection on fine art strategies observed during the study (*cont.*)

Fine art field	Strategy(s)	Intended purpose	Overall effect on students
Visual Arts	"Free" art (OD)	To develop emotional intelligence; to help the child to focus and relax; develops fine/gross motor skills	Students were verbally and visually identifying their emotions and elaborating on them (with teacher guidance). Students were practicing tripodal grip, directional movements, and more.
	"Group draw" (P)	To reinforce academic content; student engagement	Students were verbally identifying main academic concepts from previous lessons and asking relevant questions to the lesson.
	Structured art projects (P)	To reinforce academic content; develop fine and gross motor skills; student engagement; develop executive functioning skills	Students were waiting patiently for instructions and often had to complete multiple steps of projects under guidance from a teacher. They engaged with the creative process by selecting their own colors and materials and were expected to practice fine and gross motor skills throughout the project.
Dance	Planned routines (P)	To develop executive functioning skills (working memory); build gross motor skills and physical development	Students were focused and remembered combinations. Students were communicating with one another about the sequence of basic movements.
	Following the instructor's lead (OD)	To develop executive functions (attention and working memory)	Students maintained focus on the instructor and tried their best to copy basic movements and patterns.

TABLE 5.3   An analysis of common themes among lesson plans collected

Lesson plan section	Common themes among participants
Materials	Common Materials included open-ended art materials, such as blank paper, a variety of paints/crayons, various sizes of paint brushes, and a selection of writing utensils. Academic materials included developmentally appropriate children's books, mystery boxes containing academic materials or objects to enhance the lesson, and letter puppets.
Procedures	All teachers included at least 1 fine art strategy in their procedures. All teachers included modeling and prompting (according to the students' needs/age). Many teachers brought in additional strategies during instruction to further understanding of the lesson's concept(s).
Assessments criteria (Goals)	Criteria was developmentally appropriate for various age groups. All teachers followed Bloom's Taxonomy and incorporated the central focus of the lesson. Criteria allowed for student exploration and choice, but met the academic content/central focus.

participant's self-efficacy, creativity, or integration of their fine art background during instruction. The question, as well as the purpose, is noted in addition to common themes from participants. Some specific comments from teachers are noted by their designated identifying letter.

8   Analysis and Conclusions

The purpose of this study was to examine ways in which a background in the fine arts may impact teachers' creative selection of instructional practices and overall sense of self-efficacy in encouraging creativity in their students. In addition, various types of strategies selected were analyzed in order to consider why certain decisions are made and how these decisions may impact a teacher's overall pedagogy. Variables of interest included factors that impacted

THE FINE ARTS AND TEACHING EFFICACY 139

TABLE 5-4 An analysis of common themes among open-ended surveys given

Question	Purpose	Common themes among responses
Do you feel that you collaborate with other teachers in your grade level? In what ways do you collaborate (i.e., share ideas, offer advice, offer support, etc.)? About how often do you collaborate, plan, or share materials with your colleagues over the course of a week?	To assess the participant's self-efficacy, specifically their ability to collaborate with other teachers and their ability to adapt materials to suit the needs of their students.	All participants noted that they collaborate with one another, about 3–4 times per week on average. Participants share resources, ideas, strategies, and provide support for one another in and out of the classroom. Participants feel like mentors to annual graduate assistants and provide support for them, as well.
Do you feel you model creative behaviors for your students (i.e., thinking aloud, showing enthusiasm, collaboration, communication, etc.)? Please elaborate on ways you do or do not model these behaviors/skills and ways you can improve your practice.	To assess whether or not participants feel they possess and model dispositions of creative teachers for their students.	All participants felt they do model creative behaviors for students. Participants noted they encourage student input in activities, use props/voices, and offer a variety of materials in their classrooms for student exploration and expression.
With respect to student creativity and originality, how do you know if a child is successfully creative/original? By what standards, rules, guidelines, etc. do you measure creativity of students in your classroom?	To gain an understanding of how teachers measure student creativity and by what guidelines they measure student growth.	Participants DO NOT align Common Core Standards to their activities. All noted developmental milestones, individual student growth, opportunities to communicate/interact with one another, as well as any IFSP/IEP goals as factors that help them to assess student growth and creativity.

(cont.)

TABLE 5.4 An analysis of common themes among open-ended surveys given (cont.)

Question	Purpose	Common themes among responses
When choosing instructional materials, tools, activities, etc., what factors do you often take into account? How often, if at all, do you utilize the fine arts in your instruction (planning & implementation)? If you do utilize fine art strategies, what specific strategies do you use? What is the purpose/goal of these strategies (i.e., build problem solving skills, improve communication, identify emotions, etc.)? When do you utilize these strategies most often (i.e., during the lesson, small group work, facilitated play, transition periods, etc.)?	To gain insight into what factors primarily influence instructional decision making and when and for what purpose fine art strategies are utilized most often.	Participants noted developmentally appropriate academic content, age, ease of access and variety of materials, and the personal needs of students are chief factors in decision making. Teacher D – noted that "materials and activities should allow children to process, interpret, and reinterpret information." Participants believed that learning should be student-centered. Participants use fine art strategies throughout the day – most often during lessons/small group work, transitions, and play.
In what ways does your background in the fine arts influence your teaching? Are you more inclined to utilize art-based approaches or strategies knowing that you have a background in the arts, as opposed to other strategies that do not utilize your strengths?	To understand how teachers' backgrounds in the fine arts influence their decision-making.	Participants noted that their backgrounds help them to adapt instruction during implementation of their lessons and influence their planning by choosing developmentally appropriate strategies for conveying information. Participants also note that they utilize a combination of fine art strategies and various other developmentally appropriate strategies, rather than relying solely on the fine arts.

(cont.)

TABLE 5-4 An analysis of common themes among open-ended surveys given (*cont.*)

Question	Purpose	Common themes among responses
With regards to the lessons that were implemented over your designated three-day observation period, in what ways would you alter your instruction and why?	To allow participants the opportunity to self-reflect on their lessons and means of adapting them for future instruction.	All participants said that they would adapt their lesson in the future. Teacher B – noted that she would have incorporated more movement in her lesson. All teachers noted that they would have liked to have spent more time on student interests, rather than academic content. All participants noted that they may have chosen a different strategy/technique to better suit students with special needs.

decision-making, the types of fine art strategies being utilized most often, and how the background of participants influenced their decision-making. Table 5.1 provides a clear illustration of the participants' backgrounds.

Teacher A is a teacher in the half-day program, serving two sessions of children between the ages of 1.7 years and 2 years. She stated in her interview that she had a background in visual art but did not hold a higher education degree in art. However, she frequently takes painting and drawing classes at a local Staten Island community center in order to maintain her artistic skills. She has been attending these classes for over three years. She enjoys painting with the children and uses the visual arts as a means of developing fine motor skills with her students. For her, using visual art also allows for a personal interaction between the students and the teachers and allows the children a valued opportunity for self-expression. She will vary the style of art that she creates with her students, "free art" versus a more defined, specific outcome, based upon the skills and knowledge that she wants the children to experience.

Teacher B is also a teacher in the half-day program, serving two sessions of children between the ages of 2 years and 3 years. This educator has a higher education degree in dance and is currently a dance teacher at a local studio. As an educator, she finds herself frequently wanting to dance with her students, often dancing to build gross motor skills, maintain attention and increase listening skills, and to have a strong personal interaction with her students. Her role as a mentor to her dance students, she says, carries over to her classroom. It positively impacts her ability to provide emotional support to students, be a nurturing but strict educator, and to individualize her instructional practices to meet her students' needs.

Teacher C is an educator in the full-day program, serving children between the ages of 2.5 and 3.5 years. She does not hold a degree in the fine arts, but she frequently takes art classes and music lessons with her daughters at a local community center near her home. She has been involved in these classes for over four years. While her daughters opt to sing, she chooses to play musical instruments. She enjoys her time on Saturdays drawing with her daughters and making music with them. She will frequently engage her students with musical concepts, like rhythm, and play musical games in order to hold their attention, build listening skills, and incorporate academic concepts. She will frequently allow her students to draw pictures and describe their work as part of the daily activities. She will also engage in "group drawing," as she calls it, in order to assess student knowledge and allow the whole group to participate in a shared experience. During the researcher's observations, this "group drawing" was observed in addition to other fine art strategies.

Teacher D has a background in multiple areas of the fine arts, but did not pursue a higher education degree in any fine art field. Her experiences primarily make up her background in the theater, music, and visual art. Before choosing to become an educator, this teacher worked as a performer in a historic district of Staten Island for more than five years, often performing in reenactments during educational events or tours of the historic area. As a performer, she was animated and enjoyed immersing herself into the history she was presenting – both by reading books and engaging with the period attire, social norms, setting, and more. These experiences carried over into her classroom, as she frequently uses theatrical skills and elements to paint a better picture of academic content for her students. She also believes in engaging her students with music; she audited a semi-annual class given by the music department at a local liberal arts college, relating music to the field of early childhood education for two years in total, auditing 4 classes overall. Her experience with visual art stems from her college years, as she frequently engaged with her friends in painting and ceramics classes. She continues to do so today, taking painting classes on a once-weekly basis. Over the years, she has acquired different techniques and art styles to which she chooses to expose her students. Students are always creating new pieces of art using a variety of techniques. The combination of her backgrounds in theater, music, and art allow her students opportunities to become immersed in academic concepts, create unique pieces of art that allow them to express themselves while targeting academic concepts, and engage with strengthening their listening skills, organization skills, and attention spans.

The background of these teachers (Table 5.1) was seen throughout the observation period. Multiple teachers engaged with strategies from their fine art field that were developmentally appropriate and engaging for all students. The purpose for selection of these strategies varied, based upon what the educator wanted the child's outcome to be, but the presence of their backgrounds was evident throughout instruction. Many relied upon their professional background and personal exposure to the fine arts in conjunction with other developmentally appropriate strategies.

Table 5.2 illustrates that all four participants used a selection of strategies from each area of the fine arts in their lessons. Some participants utilized a combination of strategies shown, in order to achieve a specific outcome. For some educators, the outcome intended was the acquisition of academic content knowledge, in addition to student engagement. For others, the goal was for children to explore materials and create new meaning from them. Regardless of the intended outcome, students were consistently focused and engaged during implementation of each of these strategies. They were also developing skills simultaneously and thinking critically.

Common strategies among all four educators included piggyback songs, use of character voices/vocal intonations, and structured art projects. These strategies had the ability to focus students, develop executive functioning skills, and convey academic content and language. These strategies were developmentally appropriate for all students at the institution. In this case, these strategies were institutional practices that were implemented the exact same way in all four classrooms. The implementation of piggyback songs like the "circle time song" and "flag song" were always sung at the same time before the lesson in each classroom; the only thing that separated one class from another were the names of the students.

In this institution, a common requirement is the inclusion of structured art projects during small group work. These projects acted as assessments for students and markers of development for educators. During these projects, students were engaging with their academic content, in addition to practicing critical thinking skills and making choices. While the intended outcome and overall construction of the projects remained constant for all students, students were given the opportunities to choose their colors, papers, paint, and more, in order to create a unique project. The main focus during these projects was the thinking process that occurred, rather than the product produced. Teachers were engaging the child in discussion during the child's work time, and were encouraging him to defend their work; this served as a means of helping their students to develop critical thinking skills. Non-mandated strategies were incorporated in each classroom, in addition to the institutional strategies, and served multiple purposes.

Some strategies, as noted in Table 5.2, were planned, while some were brought in on demand in order to better meet the student's needs. Planned strategies, such as "group draw," and basic planned dance routines, were integrated in order to meet different needs. "Group draw" and the puppet songs were implemented in order to assess students' academic content knowledge. In the case of the "group draw," Teacher C wanted to assess children's understanding of the parts of a plant and what a plant needs to grow. While she engaged the students in an entertaining way, they were recalling previous knowledge, matching colors to create a realistic picture, and were communicating with one another; some were asking questions. She was actively assessing their knowledge and obtaining whether or not they understood her lesson. While not knowing it, however, she incorporated socio-emotional skills and executive functioning skills, and expanded children's vocabulary and interests.

Strategies that were implemented on demand varied in nature and appeared differently in each classroom. "Free art" varied in appearance and purpose (Table 5.2), and incorporated a variety of materials with which students could engage. In three classrooms, "free art" was accompanied by discussion between the teacher and the child. The main purpose in these discussions was to help the child build emotional intelligence skills, identifying their emotions, specifically. The children were often able to identify their emotions, but could not express why they were feeling them; the teacher, through prompting and modeling, helped the child to critically think and consider the "why" more deeply. In general, the visual arts and music seem to be more prevalent than strategies in theater or dance. All areas of the fine arts engage students and hold attention, but the visual arts and music appeared to fulfill multiple purposes, reaching multiple areas of development simultaneously.

An analysis of main sections of lesson plans, outlined in Table 5.3, highlights the planned strategies, goals of these strategies, and materials that allowed for student creativity. Participants offered a variety of open-ended materials for students to explore during small group time, and often included visuals during lesson time to build understanding. The goals participants had for students were developmentally appropriate, directly related to academic content knowledge, and did not mention other areas of development. A common goal among all participants was for children to explore the materials provided; many students engaged actively and created unique interpretations of the materials. Each teacher included at least one planned fine art strategy in their lesson plan, and many needed to incorporate other strategies, on demand, in order to best help their students understand the lesson.

Table 5.4 outlines each teacher's self-reflections on their efficacy, their creativity, and specific dispositions that they possess. It also denotes how, if at all, teachers incorporate their backgrounds in the fine arts during instruction. In the first two sections of the table, participants felt that they were efficacious. They collaborated often, typically at least 3 to 4 times a week, and adapted their practices based on different factors. They also felt that they modeled creative behaviors, such as "confidence, commitment, and enthusiasm" (Cremin, 2009). Many wrote that they model positive communication and thought for their students, in order to develop their critical thinking skills.

With regards to student creativity, participants noted that when assessing student creativity, they do not use academic standards as their sole guide. Rather, they utilize developmental milestones and each student's personal needs as primary means of assessing creativity. They follow the needs of the child and look for individual growth, confidence, and commitment to their work. When considering main factors that influenced their instruction, participants conveyed that student's personal needs, developmentally appropriate practices, and opportunities for student exploration were prevalent. Participants noted that their background does influence their decision-making, but often is not the primary factor involved in their instruction. Participants noted that they used their background to help students transition, understand and remember content, as well as develop executive functioning skills. They do not feel that they are more inclined to use their training because they have it. Rather, they use it because they believe it will best serve their students. All participants used a combination of fine art strategies, as well as other developmentally appropriate strategies, to meet student needs. The data shows that they do not rely only on their background, but use student needs and developmentally appropriate practices as their main factors in decision-making. All participants said that they would adapt their lessons and would focus more heavily on student interests, rather than academic content.

An analysis of the tables above indicate that participants are efficacious and creative, but do not rely only on their background when making instructional decisions. The data presented supports the need for more creative classrooms in today's society. Participants were able to successfully convey academic knowledge and content as well as offer the child crucial opportunities for self-expression and creativity-foundational concepts that are laid out by the National Association for the Education of Young Children (NAEYC, 2018). Participants successfully created an active, engaging, and nurturing environment in which skills such as respect, trust, and collaboration could be developed. Children were given the freedom to explore their emotions through visual art and music and were able to understand emotions of others through stories and drama. Most of all, students felt valued, loved, and supported in a safe, welcoming, and intellectually engaging environment. If educators can successfully create these creative environments for students, regardless of the socio-economic status or community issues their children may be facing, students will ultimately succeed. They will be encouraged to critically think and develop their creativity, a theory in which Vygotsky heavily believed (1925/1972), and will feel individually valued as a member of their classroom. All students deserve this opportunity; utilizing the fine arts and becoming more efficacious are only some ways of reaching a larger, more difficult goal to attain in today's society.

References

Bandura, A. (1977). Self-efficacy: Toward a unifying theory of behavioral change. *Psychological Review*, *84*(2), 191–215.

Boeree, D. C. (2006). *Erik Erikson (1904–1994): Personality theories* (pp. 1–17). Shippensburg University, Psychology Department.

Childress, S. A. (2014). Collaboration & teamwork with families and professionals. In S. A. Raver (Ed.), *Family-centered early intervention* (pp. 31–52). Brookes Publishing.

Cremin, T. (2009). Creative teachers & creative teaching. In A. Wilson (Ed.), *Creativity in primary education* (2nd ed., pp. 63–78). Learning Matters Ltd.

Erikson, E. (1959). Identity & the life cycle. *Psychological Issues*, *1*(1), 1–52.

Frydenberg, E. (2012). *Developing everyday coping skills in the early years: Proactive strategies for supporting social & emotional development.* Continuum International Publishing Group.

Haartsen, R. (2016). Human brain development over the early years. *Current Opinions in Behavioral Sciences*, *10*, 149–154.

Lunenburg, F. C. (2010). School violence in American schools. *Focus on Colleges, States, and Universities*, *4*(1), 1–6.

Nadal, M. (2013). The experience of art: Insights from neuroimaging. In S. Finger, D. W. Zaidel, F. Boller, & J. Bogousslavsky (Eds.), *The fine arts, neurology, and neuroscience: New discoveries and changing landscapes* (Progress in Brain Research, Vol. 204, pp. 135–158). Elsevier.

National Association for the Education of Young Children. (2018, January 1). *Accreditation tips and tools.* https://www.naeyc.org/accreditation/early-learning/standards

National Child Traumatic Stress Network (NCTSN). (2019a, January 25). *Bullying: Effects.* https://www.nctsn.org/what-is-child-trauma/trauma-types/bullying/effects

National Child Traumatic Stress Network (NCTSN). (2019b, January 25). *Community violence: Effects.* https://www.nctsn.org/what-is-child-trauma/trauma-types/community-violence

National Child Traumatic Stress Network (NCTSN). (2019c, January 25). *Traumatic grief: Effects.* https://www.nctsn.org/what-is-child-trauma/trauma-types/traumatic-grief/effects

Oxlee, J. (1996, June 24). *Analysis in the creativity in the practice & teaching of the visual arts, with reference to the current work of art students at GSCE level and above* [Doctoral thesis]. University of Newcastle upon Tyne, School of Education. https://theses.ncl.ac.uk/jspui/handle/10443/339

Parker, A. (2006). Developmentally appropriate practices in kindergarten: Factors shaping teacher's beliefs and practices. *Journal of Research in Childhood Education*, *21*(1), 65–78.

Piaget, J. (2003). Part I: Cognitive development in children – Piaget development & learning. *Journal of Research in Science Teaching*, *40*(S1), 1–11.

Sawyer, S. E. (2004, March). Primary-grade teachers' self-efficacy beliefs, attitudes toward teaching, & discipline and teaching practice priorities in relation to the "responsive classroom" approach. *The Elementary School Journal*, *104*(4), 321–341.

Simatwa, E. M. (2010, July). Piaget's theory of intellectual development & its implication for instructional management at pre-secondary school level. *Education Research and Reviews*, 5(7), 366–371.

Vygotsky, L. S. (1972). The psychology of art. *Journal of Aesthetics & Art Criticism*, 30(4), 564–566. (Original work published 1925)

Vygotsky, L. (1986). *Thought & language* (A. Kozulin, Trans.). The Massachusetts Institute of Technology. (Original work published 1935)

West, D. W. (1999). Lev Vygotsky's psychology of art and literature. *Changing English*, 6(1), 47–55.

CHAPTER 6

The Impact of Social Support on First Year Teacher Development

Eman Metwally

Abstract

It is an educator's responsibility to care for and meet the needs of her respective students; however, a first year teacher's experience, can be overwhelming without the proper guidance and support. In order to provide a nurturing and positive environment for students, educators need to be validated as professionals in the workplace (Charner-Laird, Kirkpatrick, Szczesiul, Watson, & Gordon, 2016). A lack of support impacts the ways in which teachers instruct and connect with students in the classroom. Without a proper support system in place to instruct teachers on how to tackle challenges, a teacher's development as an educator is hindered. Doubt and burnout are common stressors that prevent teachers from effectively supporting their students and can impact teacher attrition rates. Lack of resources, whether it is lack of mentorship, collegiate support, or management support, can impact a teacher's career development.

Keywords

practices – mentoring – first-year teacher – reflection – interpersonal skills – intrapersonal skills – growth

1   Benefit of Support Systems

Froschauer and Bigelow (2012) explored the implications of support systems for first year teachers and concluded that lack of support, such as being in a building full of teachers with no one reaching out to make sure that the teacher has adapted to his/her new environment, may correlate to a lack of teacher efficacy in fully supporting their students.

According to Johnson (2010), first year teachers experience challenges such as adjusting to the school life while getting to know their students. The adjustment to a new set of colleagues, school policies, instructional responsibilities, and set of students and families can certainly be difficult to manage for starting teachers. It is difficult to address rising challenges when a school does not have a clear structure of support and resources available to address the individual experiences of new teachers. This lack of support could create additional challenges impacting teachers' professional identity, especially when seeking to establish themselves as effective new teachers. Teachers who are not grounded in their work environment, or do not have the support of colleagues and school staff, will feel unappreciated and lack validation as educational professionals, which in turn will impact they the way they connect and relate to their students (Charner-Laird et al., 2016). According to Dias-Lacy and Guirguis (2017), it is important to ensure that teachers have a well-rounded view of their students, as they serve as mentors that need to create not only trusting relationships, but establish nurturing environments for their students.

The first year experience for starting teachers is filled with feelings of stress, self-doubt and ongoing challenges. Therefore, the need to offer support for first year teachers is critical to ensure their success. A first year teacher becomes responsible for the development of instruction, class management, setting motivation, and finding ways to help students reach their potential (Thompson, 2013). Therefore, first year teachers may feel challenged, stressed, and doubtful in an effort to establish said goals. Feelings of self-doubt and an eagerness to connect with others, may create stressors impacting pedagogical practices and teachers' sense of efficacy. Typically, a new teacher's main goal is to show professional efficacy and be able to establish effective partnerships with a variety of stakeholders. According to Froschauer and Bigelow (2012), "when you see a purpose in what you do, feel confident, and like what you do, it shows" (p. 62). Many teachers enter the field of education with a passion to accomplish specific goals to support children's progress in education; however, teachers find their efforts hindered by their inability to tackle new challenges due to a lack of support. Feelings of doubt and burnout can easily occur when there is a lack of social support or resources that can aid first year teachers through this new transition and process. When first year teachers are faced with feelings of self-doubt, they may find they are unable to effectively support students and this may impact teacher attrition rates.

2 Group Dynamics

Positive group dynamics is essential for first year teachers, as it allows for validation of individual practice, and creates bonds between coworkers that are based on common experiences and trials (Haynes, 2012). Interacting with other co-workers allows for new teachers to fully adapt to their environment. Inclusion in group dynamics is essential because it allows for the initiation of dialogue where ideas become exchangeable (Haynes, 2012).

The role of group dynamics on teachers' success during the first year experience is essential to consider when thinking about ways to help teachers succeed. Group dynamics is defined as "an entity comprised of individuals who come together for a common purpose and whose behavior in the group are guided by a set of shared values and norms" (Haynes, 2012, p. 6). According to Haynes (2012), groups are formed when:

> … we are very happy and we form groups as we grieve our pain. We may be organized in groups to provide information, to build community, or to contribute hope. We are social creatures who use language and the sharing of ourselves to move forward with our interests and with our goals. (p. 6)

This exemplifies the importance of group dynamics as it allows for a group to bond based on common themes and goals. When a positive group is formed it becomes a support system to those in the group and encourages inclusivity and collaboration. In a school setting, a group dynamic is beneficial in that it allows for first year teachers to be able to express feelings about challenges and new experiences they are facing. In addition, a group support system may be a catalyst for dialogue between teachers to listen to each other and provide feedback (Haynes, 2012). Successful group dynamics allows for first year teachers to relate to their colleagues, feel supported as new grads, and allows for peer to peer review and validation of each other's work.

When establishing partnerships between new colleagues, many variables need to be considered. It is critical to pay particular attention to a mentor's and mentee's prior experiences and emotions, as these aspects may impact the success of a group dynamic (Portner, 2008).

3   Mentorship

Mentorship consists of a long-term relationship focused on supporting the growth and development of the mentee. Mentorship programs in relation to education and teachers are often seen through the lens of an induction program (Dias-Lacy & Guirguis, 2017). An induction program pairs a new teacher with a senior teacher. Through this pairing, an exchange of ideas and access to pedagogical practices is facilitated. Mentorship gives teachers more insight to strategies and techniques in the workplace in real time. It also allows a mentor to help a mentee navigate the workplace quicker and therefore easily adapt to their work environment. A mentee is able to receive feedback from her mentor about her practice. Constructive criticism from the mentor is essential for teachers to be able to better their practice. A mentee is therefore able to track her growth, reinforcing strengths and focusing on weaknesses.

The relationship between a mentor and mentee allows for an exchange of ideas and knowledge (Dias-Lacy & Guirguis, 2017). This partnership often provides first year teachers with opportunities to listen to new perspectives and better understand their strengths and ways in which they can work to better themselves as educators. The mentor may also give insight on how the new first year teacher can overcome hurdles they may encounter in their first year on the job (Dias-Lacy & Guirguis, 2017). In a report by the Scottish Social Services Council (2014), different models of mentorship and ways in which they can be implemented are explained. The report discusses four models that can be adapted when thinking about mentoring, that include "one to one peer mentoring," "group peer mentoring," "two by two," and "team peer mentoring" (Scottish Social Services Council, 2014, p. 16). One to one mentoring includes the first year teacher paired with a mentor. This mentor will guide the first year teacher, providing support. Group mentoring can include a group of first year teachers, the mentees, along with one experienced mentor. This allows for the group of first year teachers to share and bond over their first year challenges, and ask for advice, while coming up with strategies together to tackle any problems they may face. "Two by two" mentoring is described as having two mentors, alongside two mentees. The mentors can include a more experienced mentor with a new mentor, and mentees have the choice of asking for one-on-one sessions with either mentor. This is useful for the first year teachers, as they are exposed to a range of "skills and knowledge" (Scottish Social Services Council, 2014, p. 17). Team mentoring can include both mentors inside and outside of the workplace working closely with the first year teachers. With each mentorship model, an action plan is created that clearly expresses goals, evaluates outcomes, and defines the role of the mentor vs. mentee in this experience (Scottish Social Services Council, 2014). Through the creation of an action plan, a successful mentorship can ensue.

Mentorship programs can be implemented in a variety of ways in order to effectively meet the needs of teachers. Limited, or lack of specific mentorship programs at a school, may create a barrier for new teachers seeking to secure a mentor for guidance and support. It is important to acknowledge that while schools strive for successful mentorships, challenges may arise between a mentor and a mentee that can hinder success. When a mentor and first year teachers are unable to identify a clear purpose to their meetings, a poor foundation is created that does not foster a mentee/mentor relationship (Washington, 2017). Role identification is lost if a mentor fails to effectively offer support, feedback, and evaluate outcomes, and if a mentee fails to be receptive to his/her mentor's influence. A mentor and mentee need to offer flexibility and a willingness to work together and create an individualized action plan for their mentorship group. When mentors and first year teachers are paired together and there is a mismatch of personalities, and goals/expectations are not aligned, a mentorship will not be successful (Scottish Social Services Council, 2014).

4 Professional Development

Job-embedded professional development offers an opportunity for there to be a "direct connection" between the teacher's classroom practices and the feedback he or she receives (Croft et al., 2010, p. 1). Job-embedded professional development, or JEPD, impacts teacher learning by offering feedback that improves teachers' instructional practices. Croft et al. (2010) gives an example on how a mentor may work with a beginning teacher utilizing JEPD:

A mentor conferences with a beginning teacher during the planning of and after observing a lesson. She supports the teacher in describing the strengths and weaknesses in his instructional planning and implementation, prompting him to incorporate changes in his instruction the following day (Croft et al., 2010, p. 3).

This strategy ensures that beginning teachers are supported during the course of their day, and are able to connect to the content they are teaching. JEPD gives an opportunity to those teachers to also create conversation centering around their own teaching. Once the teacher receives feedback, he or she is then able to better tailor his or her lessons accordingly. Examples of job-embedded professional development formats include "Critical Friends Groups," "Mentoring," and "Implementing Individual Professional Growth/Learning Plans" (Croft et al., 2010, p. 6). Critical Friends Group is a JEPD that allows teachers to meet for the purpose of giving each other feedback based on the work they present. Teachers also have the opportunity, during this time, to discuss any difficulties they may be facing in class, whether it is about a specific subject matter, or ways to meet student needs. Mentoring, especially designed for first year teachers, may cross over as instructional coaching as well as peer support. Teachers will usually collaborate with those teaching the same subject content, and will take turns observing each other during class time. Implementing Individual Professional Growth/Learning Plans targets areas in which teachers need to develop more and grow. Teachers engage with instructional leaders, administration, or professional learning community members to develop professional learning goals and decide which professional developments to engage in as well (Croft et al., 2010).

First year teachers could greatly benefit from JEPD, as it provides opportunity for further learning and growth. JEPD may provide teachers with a structure that allows for them to reflect on their own practices, acquire new knowledge, as well as perspectives from others, and support in the implementation of existing and new ideas (Croft et al., 2010).

It is critical for principals to offer first year teachers opportunities to engage in professional development concerning collaboration with others in the school. Jorish (2017) demonstrated examples of teachers' experiences when collaborating with others in a school. Many teachers reflect on how there were barriers to connecting with their colleagues, such as "lack of teachers' personality compatibility," lack of "openness and flexibility," or the need for constant "control" (Jorish, 2017, p. 36). Jorish (2017) describes professional development as if it was a "fertilizer" that fosters "positive external, interpersonal, and intrapersonal factors that deepen inter-professional partnerships" (Jorish, 2017, p. 143). Many first year teachers relay that, as new teachers to the school, it can be difficult at times to approach more experienced faculty members, as they do not want to seem overbearing or are unsure of how to begin conversation. Professional development can support first year teachers by providing ways in which these teachers can deepen collaboration with others, as well as reflect and/or practice their own interpersonal skills. Teachers are able to engage in conversation about intrapersonal conditions by pinpointing any internal feelings or circumstances that may impact their practice with others as well as contemplating their colleagues' as well.

5   Administration

Administrative support becomes vital in tracking the progress of the mentee and ensuring the mentorship process is to the benefit of the oncoming teacher. Administrative support comes in the form of meeting with both the teacher and the mentor to discuss growth, and to first and foremost make sure the teacher's "dignity is preserved" (Brown, 2002, p. 3). Administrative staff can take part and create a schedule that is optimal for the mentor and mentee to meet, as well as provide a welcoming environment for both mentor and mentee. Administrative support lets teachers know their progress is being monitored to ensure their success.

Setting evaluations at the beginning of mentorship that outlines the mentee's progress can be shared by the mentor and the administration. Administration supervises how well the mentee is progressing through the program and can give support when needed, as well. To maximize the potential benefits of this relationship, all three parties must work together in a close unit to benefit the development of first year teachers. Administrators should put forth an "open door policy" that encourages trust and teamwork (Brown, 2002, p. 4).

Charner-Laird et al. (2016) relays how administration can provide a structure that allows for these first year teachers to reflect on their own practice and discuss their progress. They can utilize administration as a way in which they can ask for feedback, work on skills, and make stronger connections. It is critical that first year teachers utilize all these resources in place. It is also important for first year teachers to acknowledge their strengths and weaknesses, and utilize their own strengths to overcome challenges they may face.

6   Dispositions

Johnson (2010) explained how it is important for first year teachers to be eager to teach students, have an intellectual shared experience, and be committed to inspire others by being passionate and engaging in their own development as professionals.

Each teacher entering the workforce brings to the schools his/or her own unique qualities (Charner-Laird et al., 2016). According to Johnson (2010), the greatest asset a new teacher can bring to the school is the eagerness to learn and providing a positive outlook to all those under the teacher's guidance. Teachers make the life-long commitment to inspire others to find their voice and passion. They carry the responsibility of growth, not only for their students, but for themselves as educators, and should come with the understanding that this process takes time and effort. Teachers should come into their first year with the belief that hard work surpasses talent, as talent can not be manifested with tools and dedication. This belief should be passed down to a teacher's own students. Regardless of the student's capabilities, a teacher's passion should drive the education of her students, and of the teacher's own learning (Johnson, 2010). According to Johnson (2010), teaching is like "wading through a strong current" (Johnson, 2010, p. 57). Teachers must be willing to keep pushing through and have the intrinsic drive of wanting to become better each day for the sake of their students. Teachers, as educators, should be as naturally inquisitive as their students. First year teachers will have questions ranging from the set up of their classroom environment, to how best to support their students' learning styles (Feiman-Nemser, 2003).

A first year teacher may be skeptical in his or her capabilities of fully engaging with his or her students, and their families (Feiman-Nemser, 2003). Feelings of loneliness may arise despite being surrounded by a number of students. What strengthens the initial impression of a first-year teacher, and drives away moments of uncertainty, is the support of a first year teacher's colleagues (Charner-Laird et al., 2016). Consistent reflection with other teachers about their progress, challenges they face, and how to give more, is critical during a teacher's first year of teaching (Charner-Laird et al., 2016). A first year teacher comes to teach with the ideology of putting him or herself out there for the students, but must also be willing to ask for assistance from his or her peers, even if it is not given right away (Charner-Laird et al., 2016). Peer review is critical to building relationships with colleagues and strengthening interpersonal relationships. When first year teachers are supported, their potential to do great things and better serve their students is maximized. The teacher will become innovative, willing to grow along with his or her students.

The integration of a mentorship program that is cognizant of the needs of a first year teacher is a necessity. Senior teachers, or qualified mentors comfortable in their role as educators, should be able to impart their experience and knowledge onto beginners. Everyone who graduates has a fundamental foundation and the certifications necessary to become an educator. However, being able to relate to someone in their first year, in this case seasoned educators, assures first year teachers that what they are going through is part of a normal transition. Having a support system provides opportunities for discussion; it allows for inclusion and allows new teachers to understand that others have survived the challenges they are facing. Previous teachers who have served as an inspiration can be utilized as both an emotional and pedagogical support for first year teachers. Blogs, for example, emphasize past teacher experiences and struggles and are utilized as a source of connection between others that went through similar experiences. Connecting with colleagues, and knowing they are a resource present to support starting educators, is important in the career and personal development of first year teachers; overcoming challenges with the proper support systems in place is essential for a teacher's success. A case study was created to further examine mentorship, or the lack of mentorship, and the effect it had on teachers.

7 Case Study

A case study was done to examine the role of mentoring and to analyze how group dynamics, administration support, and access to professional development may impact a first year teacher's overall experience. Methods of data collection included self-reflection on the part of the researcher, as well as interviews with experts such as the Director of a mentorship program, as well as first-hand feedback from a teacher who has made it past her first year.

7.1 *The Director*

The Director of a mentorship program had twenty-five years of teacher/administrator experience and served many roles in the school system. She took on the role of a school principal, a special education administrator, and a reading specialist. She continues to take an active role in supporting first year teachers, meeting and guiding them through challenges by observing them in their classroom, and having them reflect on their practices.

7.2 *The Expert Teacher*

The expert teacher, who was interviewed, is an early childhood educator in her third year of teaching, and has her Bachelors in Finance and a minor in Education. She has volunteered her time in various charter schools, and has prior education experience abroad, as well as experience writing curriculum. She has served students with both very low socioeconomic backgrounds as well as students from high socioeconomic backgrounds. The researcher utilized this expert teacher to report on any challenges she may have had during her first year experience as a teacher and how she has adapted to her role now.

7.3 *The Researcher's Experience*

The researcher conducted her case study about her overall first year teaching experience in the school, and did not ascribe her experience to a certain classroom. Areas of interest that were examined included the dispositions of the first year teacher, challenges that a first year teacher may experience, the support systems in place, and the role of mentoring on alleviating some of the stressors associated with becoming a first year teacher. Data was analyzed by looking at themes and patterns of the three different participant experiences.

After this time, the researcher took the time to first research the specific dispositions associated with becoming a first year teacher. The researcher wanted to understand if there was something that she needed to do to better support her students, and herself, in the process. The researcher then researched all the different challenges that a first year teacher may face, and was interested to learn more about the systems in place in regards to supporting a teacher during her first year experience. She continued to research on whether these support systems had any impact on tackling those challenges, and what needs to be integrated to create a system that fosters a teacher's growth and development.

7.4 Results

Results of the data indicate how mentorship can play a significant role in teachers' sense of efficacy during the first year. Data indicates how "Dispositions, Mentorship, and Experiences," can significantly impact the effectiveness of mentorship programs.

Table 6.1 relays the specific dispositions with which all three participants started their first year teaching journey with, or what attributes they thought

TABLE 6.1 Dispositions

	Dispositions	Literature
Participant A Director of Mentorship program	The willingness to try to be a better educator Administrators encouraging attitude Key points: Perseverance Encouragement	It is important for administrators to foster trust and teamwork between teachers. Teachers should feel comfortable going to the administrator and asking questions or look for support (Brown, 2002, p. 4).
Participant B Expert teacher	Seeking out friends and a mentor to help coach you through your experience Seeking opportunities for feedback – involve all in the learning process Key points: Inquisitive Collaborative Interpersonal communication	Teachers should be naturally inquisitive, ask questions, and seek resources to support their students (Feiman-Nemser, 2003).
Participant C Researcher: First year teacher	Eager to learn Team approach Seeking resources to be able to provide students with what they need Key points: Driven Motivated Inquisitive	Teachers should be passionate about meeting the needs of their students. They should be positive, and eager to learn to better support themselves and their students (Johnson, 2010).

were most important. Johnson (2010) emphasized dispositions such as being passionate, inquisitive, and positive. It is important that a teacher utilize her dispositions as ways in which he or she can overcome struggles, and support the students in his/her classroom.

Table 6.2 provides information related to the different mentorship programs in place for the participants, and the components present in this mentor to mentee relationship. The researcher also analyzed key points discussed about mentorship, and teacher needs that may not have been addressed during the mentorship program. According to Dias-Lacy and Guirguis (2017), mentorship acts as a platform for first year teachers in supporting their growth and development. Research has made it clear that first year teachers are part of a program that is cognizant of their challenges. This stress and feelings of uncertainty are significantly reduced.

Table 6.3 reflects on the participants' overall experience as first year teachers. Key needs are discussed as well as ways that a mentorship program is able to support those first year teachers' growth and development.

7.5 *Participant A*

Based on Table 6.2 and participant A's description of her mentorship program, the researchers concluded that there were two main components to the mentorship program in place; the instructional aspect of teaching and the emotional piece. Participant A relays that many of her mentees describe this mentorship program as a "safe place." The participants of her program meet at this director's house to have a conversation. This group dynamic, according to the literature, allows for the participants to bond based on common themes and goals, encouraging both inclusivity and collaboration. Based on Participant A's responses, her mentorship program is built upon making connections initially. Participant A, when interviewed about her mentorship program, says that the program is "not a teacher-dominated program ... we are having a conversation ... about challenges, about theory." This fosters dialogue between teachers where they are able to help one another and support one another through challenges they may be facing, or applying theory to practice, which targets the instructional piece of the director's program. Some components of this mentorship program include discussing topics such as "parent involvement, diversity, multiple intelligences, emotional intelligence, and interpersonal/intrapersonal skills." According to Table 6.3, participant A's own experience was one accompanied with challenges as well as various learning experiences without a mentor in place. Securing a mentor meant having a champion that fought for the case of teachers, and supported them to become the best they can be.

TABLE 6.2   Mentorship

	Mentorship	Literature
Participant A Director of Mentorship Program	Conversations Discuss challenges/theory Observations in classrooms Addressing parent involvement, diversity, multiple intelligences, emotional intelligence, interpersonal/intrapersonal skills Key points: Building connections Emotional support Instructional support	Mentorship focuses on supporting the growth and development of a first year teacher (Dias-Lacy & Guirguis, 2017). Mentorship can be carried out through different models (Scottish Social Services Council 2014). Group mentoring includes an experienced mentor and a group of first year teachers. A dialogue is created around first year teacher challenges, and they are able to give each other advice and come up with strategies to tackle problems (Scottish Social Services Council, 2014, p. 17).
Participant B Expert Teacher	Mentor provides opportunity for goal setting, brainstorming curriculum, and observations of teaching practice. Assistant head of school providing Co-teaching and observations Key needs: Emotional support	An action plan is a critical component of a mentorship model. A successful action plan includes goals, outcomes, and clearly defines the role of a mentor and mentee (Scottish Social Services Council, 2014). The social-emotional well-being of a teacher is critical as emotion plays an important piece in the learning process as well as in the workplace (Druskat et al., 2013).
Participant C Researcher: First Year Teacher	No formal mentorship program in place Administrator will check in and ask how I am doing Administrator will ask about what I am doing with students Key needs: Support system	It is critical to provide a support system for first year teachers, as the first year experience is riddled with feelings of stress, challenges, and self-doubt (Thompson, 2013).

IMPACT OF SOCIAL SUPPORT ON FIRST YEAR TEACHER DEVELOPMENT 161

TABLE 6.3 Experience

	Experience in practice	Literature
Participant A	Unable to connect with coworkers	
	Lack of feedback from coworkers	Teachers during their first year
	Information overload without clear instruction	of teaching experience may be doubtful of their capabilities
	Reaching out to faculty elsewhere for support	(Feiman-Nemser, 2003). A first year teacher may feel lonely (Charner-Laird et al., 2016).
	Key needs:	
	Lack of mentorship contributes to teachers' feelings of failure	The support of a first year teacher's colleagues helps to
	Interpersonal/Intrapersonal	alleviate feelings of stress and loneliness (Charner-Laird et al., 2016).
Participant B	A challenging, learning experience	Securing a mentor to help
	Valuable constructive criticism	guide new teachers can be a
	Positive praise	challenge, unless a school has a system in place to facilitate
	Key points:	the process (Boyd et al., 2011).
	Mentorship program can meet the needs of first year teachers	
Participant C	Did not have a mentor at first	Mentors who take the time to
	Was able to secure a mentor years later	understand a teachers needs become an invaluable asset to
	Learned from perspective of mentor	new teachers, helping them to
	Mentor provided direction/insight/ resources provided	adapt and fully recognize and use their potential
	"She was there … She was my champion."	(Dias-Lacy & Guirguis, 2017).
	Key points:	
	A mentor can be a champion.	

7.6   *Participant B*

Participant B, according to Table 6.2, had a mentorship program available during her first year. Based on what the mentorship program provided for participant B, her pedagogical needs, such as goal setting, brainstorming curriculum, and observations of her teaching practice, were met. This is helpful in supporting a teacher to meet the needs of her students and modify instruction based on the feedback of the mentor. Based on this mentorship program, Participant B claims that her first year experience as a teacher was one that was challenging, but a learning experience nonetheless. Based on Participant B's experience, the researcher concluded that participant B had been offered a mentorship program that met her instructional needs, but was missing the personal connections with other coworkers which she intentionally sought out. Participant B was cognizant of this and she was able to reach out and connect with other teachers for emotional support as she stated during the interview, saying "My relationships with other teachers is my strongest support system. It is something I learned my first year – make friends!" These findings suggest that for a mentorship program to meet the needs of a mentee, both the pedagogical and emotional aspects of a teacher need to be addressed. Participant B was able to address both her needs because she sought out the emotional support, and was supported pedagogically through a mentor's feedback. Participant B reinforces this concept by mentioning two things that would be valuable for a teacher to have when providing the best education for children, feedback in terms of constructive criticism and positive praise. Feedback given to a first year teacher, as mentioned by participant B, has the ability to improve instructional practice and provide further opportunity for learning. Positive praise allows for a positive learning environment in which teacher and student can flourish successfully. As first year teachers come in at times skeptical of their ability to support their students, positive praise from supportive colleagues provides the emotional support that strengthens that first year teacher's intrinsic desire to push herself, despite the challenges he or she may face.

7.7   Participant C

The researcher is labeled as participant C and has provided insight on her experience as a first year teacher. She was hopeful, eager to apply her knowledge and provide what she can for her students. She starts her first year teaching experience without an official mentorship program in place, as stated in Table 6.2. Due to the experience mentioned in Table 6.3, the challenges participant C faces without a support system hinder her ability to view herself as a successful educator. Though participant C started her teaching career with strong interpersonal skills, willing to reach out for emotional support, she was unable to connect with her coworkers. Analyzing her experience as provided in Table 6.3, participant C continued feeling like an outsider, and this affected all aspects of her growth in the workplace. Her director may have acted as a support system, as stated in Table 6.2; he was encouraging, checking in at points to make sure participant C was enjoying her experience. Participant C was able to utilize this as a form of support; however, other factors in the workplace were not addressed, in contrast to participant B's experience. Participant C's experiences as a first year teacher did not fully allow participant C to feel confident in her ability to perform at her best. Table 6.1 depicts participants C's experience where she questions herself about her ability to provide a supportive environment for her students. Table 6.1 depicts that participant C reached out for a support system outside of the environment where she did not feel welcome. Based on the data provided, there seems to be a lack of both pedagogical and emotional support during participants' C's first year experience.

8 Inclusion vs. Exclusion

All three participants of this study offered a different perspective of the inclusion versus exclusion of mentorship in the workplace. In parallel contrast to one-another, Participant B and participant C had opposite experiences. Participant C lacked mentorship while Participant B was able to benefit from a mentorship program. However, their challenges as first year teachers are the same. This is further reinforced by Participant A, who validates that first year teachers go through struggles to adapt to the workplace. As a director, however, she is able to actively oversee how mentorship can impact struggling teachers.

The goal of this study was to provide insights on the impact of support systems and mentorship programs on a teacher's first year experience. It is important to note that each person learns differently, and while other teachers may have utilized different forms of support, first year teachers nonetheless will be able to relate and be influenced by how senior educators overcame their challenges. A teacher's personal and professional well-being is grounded by so many factors; however, it is important not to underestimate how relating to someone else with the same struggles can have an impact. This is why pairing a first year teacher with a mentor, with a good knowledge and experience base, can be monumental in a first year teacher's development.

Data from this study indicates how important it is for first year teachers to come in with specific dispositions as they transition into the new school environment. Charner-Laird et al. (2016), emphasize "hard work," and refers to a teacher's inclination to ask for resources, reflect with others, and be naturally inquisitive to support their students' learning styles. However, these attributes against all those challenges a 1st year teacher can face can lead to self-doubt. There is a need for a foundation to be in place, a mentorship program that meets both the emotional and pedagogical needs of first year teachers as indicated by the data, as well as an action plan that relays expectations and goals. Reflections throughout this process are critical, as they support a first year teacher's sense of well-being, as well as validating practices as an educator.

9 Theoretical Framework

The theoretical framework as given in Figure 6.1 can be utilized in schools, implementing a mentorship program that meets the needs of first year teachers.

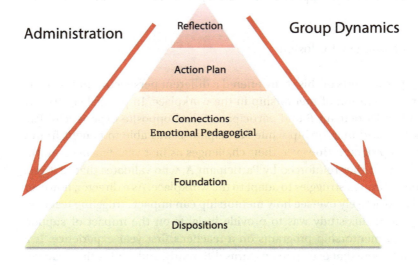

FIGURE 6.1   Pedagogical and emotional support for new teachers

10 Providing Pedagogical and Emotional Support

The theoretical framework is built upon the belief that for a true mentorship program to succeed, pedagogical support and emotional support should go hand in hand. Schonert-Reichl (2017) emphasized how teachers are the providers of a positive classroom, and are responsible for the social and emotional well-being of their students. Research continues to depict how teaching can be one of the most stressful "professions in the human service industry" due to the "physical and emotional responses that arise from a mismatch between a job's requirements and a worker's capabilities, resources, or needs" (Schonert-Reichl, 2017, p. 4). If teacher's well-being are not thought of in the process, the education system that is dependent on a teacher's capability to thrive and adapt will not be able to support its students. This is validated by the expert teacher, participant B, whom had been offered a mentorship program that met her instructional needs, but was missing the personal connections with other coworkers which she intentionally sought out. This is further reinforced by Participant C who, as depicted in Table 6.3, felt like an outsider. She continued to feel discouraged and lost confidence in her ability to perform and support her students because she felt unable to support herself.

11   Self-Awareness

The framework is developed in steps; starting with dispositions. As mentioned by Schonert-Reichl (2017), it's important for teachers to recognize their emotions. When teachers have a clear understanding of their emotions, and are self-aware, they are then able to address their needs appropriately and the needs of their students. They have the intrinsic drive to become better each day for the sake of their students, and are eager to support their students in any way they can. What makes them a teacher, ranging from passion, inquisitiveness, positivity, is grounded before they embark on the journey of being there for their students (Johnson, 2010).

12   Establishing a Support System

A teacher who has made a life-long commitment to help her students utilize their potential to become the best they can be, should then transition into a strong foundation in that school. The next tier in the theoretical framework depicts that there needs to be a support system in place in terms of a mentorship program ready to meet the needs of that teacher coming in. According to Dias-Lacy and Guirguis (2017), mentorship will act as a platform for first year teachers in supporting their growth and development. Research has made it clear that when first year teachers are part of a program that is cognizant of their challenges, stress and feelings of uncertainty are significantly reduced.

13   Making connections and Professional Development

The following tier is what makes this foundation strong. It is the connections that a first year teacher will make, both emotional and pedagogical, as they are both equally important parts of a mentorship program. This can happen in a group setting or 1-2-1 setting, and may include professional development and support both on the administrative and collegiate level. As previously mentioned by Haynes, 2012, when a first year teacher becomes part of a group that bonds on common themes and goals, the teacher feels encouraged to collaborate and share feelings about challenges he or she may face. A successful group dynamic will also allow for feedback and opportunity for improvement of instructional practices. Both these aspects of a support system allow for validation of the teacher, both personally and professionally, and addresses challenges that a first year teacher may face, such as adjusting to classroom life, coming up with appropriate instructional practices, meeting the needs of the students, and building interpersonal relationships with colleagues (Charner-Laird et al., 2016). Based on the interviews, when part was missing, the teacher failed in terms of trusting herself as an educator capable of addressing her students.

14 Creating an Action Plan

For these needs to be met, an action plan needs to be created and put into effect. As mentioned by Scottish Social Service Council, 2014, mentors and mentees should create an action plan that defines the role of each member, as well as expressing goals, and evaluating outcomes. An action plan is meant to detail what should be done and implemented to provide support for first year teachers. It emphasizes the importance of having a base in place for others to build on.

15 Reflection

The last step of this model is reflection. Reflection is consistent throughout each tier, as it is a necessary component of learning. First year teachers, though full of knowledge, are taking part in an experience that can be overwhelming and new in many ways. Reflection in terms of emotional intelligence is critical in understanding and expressing one's emotions, and understanding how they are relating to others (Druskat et al., 2013). First year teachers should continue to self-reflect on how they perform daily in the classroom, and reflect on challenges that they need to address, both in and out of the classroom (Bartolome, 2017). Administration, professional development, and colleagues should provide a structure that allows for these first year teachers to reflect on their own practice, about their progress, and what they may need, or how they are able to give more (Charner-Laird et al., 2016).

16 Future Research

Future researchers should investigate the role of gender and culture when it comes to mentorship, in order to identify specific strategies that may help first year teachers adapt to their school environment. A study analyzing the perspectives and experiences of female first year teachers, in comparison to males, during their first year teacher experience should be integrated. It may be interesting to research and analyze when there is a reversal of roles of teacher and mentor, and whether an impact can be seen.

17 Conclusion

Mentorship provides a foundation for teachers as they start their career. By building on the past experience of experts, creating interpersonal relationships within the workplace, and providing sufficient resources, a system is created to ensure the success of first year teachers. Mentorship allows for the necessary support to be provided, and available, for first year teachers, as they build on their careers to become educators.

References

Brown, K. L. (2002). Acclimating induction teachers to low-performing schools: Administrators' role. *Education, 123*(2), 422.

Charner-Laird, M., Szczesiul, S., Kirkpatrick, C., Watson, D., & Gordon, P. (2016). From collegial support to critical dialogue: Including new teachers' voices in collaborative work. *Professional Educator, 40*(2), 1–17.

Cohen, S., & Pressman, S. (2004). Stress-buffering hypothesis. In N. B. Anderson (Ed.), *Encyclopedia of health and behavior* (Vol. 1, pp. 696–697). Sage Publications, Inc. doi:10.4135/9781412952576.n200

Croft, A., Coggshall, J. G., Dolan, M., Powers, E., & National Comprehensive Center for Teacher Quality. (2010). *Job-embedded professional development: What it is, who is responsible, and how to get it done well.* National Comprehensive Center for Teacher Quality. https://eric.ed.gov/?q=ED520830&id=ED520830

Dias-Lacy, S. L., & Guirguis, R. V. (2017). Challenges for new teachers and ways of coping with them. *Journal of Education and Learning, 6*(3), 265–272.

Druskat, V. U., Mount, G., & Sala, F. (2013). *Linking emotional intelligence and performance at work: Current research evidence with individuals and groups.* Psychology Press.

Froschauer, L., & Bigelow, M. L. (2012). *Rise and shine : A practical guide for the beginning science teacher.* NSTA Press.

Guarasci, C. M. (2017). *When the going gets tough: New teachers perceptions of emotional intelligence skills and grit while participating in a support program* [Doctoral dissertation]. Columbia University Teachers College. Proquest Dissertations and Theses Global.

Haynes, N. (2012). *Group dynamics: Basics and pragmatics for practitioners.* University Press of America.

Jorisch, R. (2017). *Cultivating collaborative relationships: A case study of teacher collaboration and professional development* [Doctoral dissertation]. University of Maryland. https://drum.lib.umd.edu/bitstream/handle/1903/18583/Jorisch_umd_0117E_17393.pdf?sequence=1&isAllowed=y

Schonert-Reichl, K. A. (2017). Social and emotional learning and teachers. *Future of Children, 27*(1), 137–155. doi:10.1353/foc.2017.0007

Scottish Social Services Council. (2014). *Mentoring & tutoring: Partnership in learning.* http://www.stepintoleadership.info/assets/pdf/SSSC%20Mentoring%20guidance.pdf

Talley, P. (2017). *Through the lens of novice teachers: A lack of administrative support and its influence on self-efficacy and teacher retention issues* [Doctoral dissertation]. University of Southern Mississippi. https://aquila.usm.edu/cgi/viewcontent.cgi?article=2463&context=dissertations

CHAPTER 7

Collaboration across Disciplines to Treat Children Exposed to Adverse Childhood Experiences

Karen Prihoda

Abstract

Educators, medical professionals, and social workers are three critical groups of experts that work with children on a daily basis. These experts work with an array of children, including those exposed to Adverse Childhood Experiences (ACEs). It is the responsibility of the experts to best serve children exposed to ACEs. Collaboration among these experts has proven to be beneficial in helping a child to recover from the negative impacts of ACEs. However, there are challenges to the collaboration of experts when working with children exposed to ACEs. Experts have identified challenges to collaboration and suggest ways in which more effective partnerships can be created which ultimately best serve the child. Early intervention through a collaborative approach gives a child the best tools for recovery.

Keywords

collaboration – trauma – achievement – intervention – trust – connections – supports – community

1   Defining Adverse Childhood Experiences (ACEs)

Children are exposed to various experiences throughout their day to day lives, and unfortunately some of these experiences are adverse. One of the largest studies regarding ACEs, conducted by the Center for Disease Control (CDC), defines Adverse Childhood Experiences as "potentially traumatic events that occur in a child's life, from birth through age 17" (Feletti et al., 1998, pp. 245–258). The CDC recognizes violence and abuse, as well as witnessing violence, as factors of ACEs. In addition, environmental factors that threaten the safety, stability, or appropriate bonding with a caregiver are factors of ACEs (Feletti et al., 1998). The ten factors of Adverse Childhood Experiences, as defined by the CDC, are: "physical, emotional and sexual abuse; physical and emotional neglect; witnessing domestic violence, living with someone with mental illness, living with someone with substance abuse, having a family member incarcerated, and having parents separated or divorced" (CDC, 2016, para. 1). ACEs were formally recognized in the literature in 1998 by Felitti et al. (1998). Upon its initial recognition, it was viewed as a much more general concept without much analysis until 2014 when it was more distinctly defined. Kalmakis and Chandler (2014) explained how Adverse Childhood Experiences could vary based on the severity, as well as the recurrence, of these adverse experiences. Kalamankis and Chandler (2014) defined the term Adverse Childhood Experience as, "childhood events, varying in severity and often chronic, occurring within a child's family or social environment that cause harm or distress, thereby disrupting the child's physical or psychological health and development" (pp. 1489–1501). The definition provided by Kalmakis and Chandler acknowledges the varying severity of the ACEs that can have a substantial impact on the outcome of ACEs. In this definition the stressor, environment and outcomes are acknowledged.

2   Physical, Emotional, and Sexual Abuse

The CDC found, through its 1998 study at Kaiser-Permanente, that ACEs can be a determining factor for social, emotional, physical and cognitive impairments. These impairments are gateways to higher health risk behaviors, violence, disease, disability, and early death (Felitti et al., 1998, pp. 245–258). ACEs, in many cases, can lead to negative social, emotional, cognitive, and physical outcomes over the course of an individual's lifetime (Boulier & Blair, 2018). The effects of ACEs may take different forms and can impair each individual differently.

Childhood sexual abuse (CSA) affects between 7% and 37% of children across the globe, which is comparable with data in North America (Finkelhor, 1994). As a result, between 40% and 60% of CSA survivors develop mental health difficulties (Collin-Vézina, Hébert, & Brabant, 2007, p. 22; Ensink et al., 2017; Hébert et al., 2006). CSA is a risk factor for negative developmental outcomes (Fergusson, McLeod, & Horwood, 2013; Stoltenborgh, Bakermans-Kranenberg, Alink, & van Ijzendoorn, 2011). CSA can have a negative impact on factors such as regulatory processing, cognitive functioning, and interpersonal functioning. Research by Perez-Fuentes et al., (2013) has found that 70–75% of CSA survivors experience mental health problems in their lives (Perez-Fuentes et al., 2013; Trickett, Noll, & Putnam, 2011). Approximately 25–30% of survivors do not experience mental health problems. This notion points to the idea that protective factors can help limit the ill effects of CSA (Aspelmeier, Elliott, & Smith, 2007; Limke, Showers, & Zeigler-Hill, 2010; Roche, Runtz, & Hunter, 1999). Therefore, it is important for experts that interact with children to work to develop these protective factors so that the children exposed to ACEs can overcome the adversity.

3 Physical and Emotional Neglect

The traumas that children exposed to ACEs may experience can manifest in a variety of ways. Physical, emotional, and sexual abuse are all forms of child abuse that have negative impacts on a child's life. Southall et al. (1997) define child abuse as, "an act by the caregiver to intentionally do harm to the child" (pp. 735–760). The abuse that a child may be exposed to may come physically, verbally, or sexually, and it may come as a result of substance abuse by the parent, domestic violence, mental health issues of the parent or neglect (Austin et al., 2016). Fuchshuber et al. (2018) identified the relationship between early traumatic experience, like physical and emotional neglect, and the occurrence of mental health issues later in life. Fuchshuber et al. (2018) found that early traumas are often the root cause of mental health issues (Fuchshuber et al., 2018). Traumas that are experienced earlier in life can affect that individual as an adult (Briere, 2015). Briere (2015) described this impact as potentially significant. Briere et al. (2016) noted that early trauma can affect an individual by impairing his or her ability to differentiate current stimuli being experienced from traumatic memories or experiences that were traumatic in childhood (Briere et al., 2016). Childhood traumas can have a lasting effect through adulthood. Physical and emotional neglect are two forms of trauma that may affect a child adversely, but they are not the only traumatic events that may cause adverse effects in children.

4 Parental Incarceration

Children having a parent who is incarcerated is not extremely rare in the United States. In 2007, of the incarcerated parents, 809,900 of them had children who were minors (Glaze & Maruschak, 2008; Graham & Harris, 2013). The number of children under the age of 18 that had an incarcerated parent was 2.7 million in 2008 (Johnson & Easterling, 2015). That number will continue to grow as the number of individuals incarcerated in the United States continues to grow. The National Resource Center on Children and Families of

Incarcerated (2014) reported that the number of children who have, at some point during their childhood, had a parent incarcerated is around 10 million children (Nation Resource Center on Child and Families of Incarcerated, 2014). These numbers, according to Pew Charitable Trusts (2010), correlate to 1 in 28 children in the United States having an incarcerated parent and 1 in 14 having an incarcerated parent at some point in their life (Murphey & Cooper, 2015).

The impact of having an incarcerated parent can have negative implications for their child. Turney (2018) found that children who have an incarcerated parent experience 5 times as many ACEs than their peers who do not have an incarcerated parent (Turney, 2018). Since incarceration disrupts a close relationship; it can not only cause traumatic stress for the child, but also result in inadequate care for the child. Both traumatic stress and inadequate care can result in a negative impact or delay in the child's development (Nesmith & Ruhland, 2008). The child of an incarcerated parent may experience stress, a lack of supervision, an increase in household responsibilities, and socioeconomic strain (Robertson, 2007). The results of these factors can cause the child to regress emotionally, mentally, physically and academically.

Children that have an incarcerated parent are affected socially, as well. Children can be associated with the actions of their parent and may be considered at risk by their peers and teachers (Dallaire et al., 2010). Dallaire et al. (2010) found that teachers of students with an incarcerated parent often set low expectations for those students. In addition, the level of competency of those students was, in part, based on the knowledge of having a parent incarcerated (Dallaire et al., 2010). The stigma associated with having a parent incarcerated can often be reflected in the child's life. The child may not feel accepted by peers, teachers, and support staff, which results in a disconnect in academics (Nichols & Loper, 2012). Children will often remove themselves from the classroom environment and make few meaningful relationships with peers in the classroom (Saunders, 2018).

The Professional Counselor (9:3) reports that while the effects of parental incarceration are negative, they often do not last throughout the child's academic career (Cho, 2009). While the effects do not last forever, they do make themselves known in the child's academic performance. For instance, struggles in academics, as well as an increase in dropout rate, are more evident in children who have one or more parent incarcerated (Dallaire et al., 2010). Most children are able to build resilience to this ACE, but in some cases they do not (Shillingford & Edwards, 2008). Therefore, it is important to identify this ACE and treat it so that the number of children that overcome this ACE continues to rise. Parental incarceration is just one of the ACEs that affects children negatively. Another factor that can cause trauma for a child is parental separation or divorce.

5 Parental Separation or Divorce

Parental divorce and separation may have negative impacts on both the child and the parent, as a result of stress (Rappaport, 2013). However, research by Hetherington (1979), revealed that when a child is not exposed to additional stressors, aside from the separation or divorce, the child is much more likely to be able to cope (Hetherington, 1979). The research by Hetheringhton is not to say that children will remain completely unaffected by the divorce. Rather, as research by Rappaport (2013) suggested a child will, initially, demonstrate more emotional and behavioral problems than children from non-divorced families, even if those children come from high conflict households (Rappaport, 2013, pp. 353–377). High conflict households are defined by Weeks and Treat (2001) as having, "chronic quality and high degree of emotional reactivity, blaming and vilification" (Weeks & Treat, 2001, p. 173). Anderson (2010) explained high conflict households as somewhere between "normal" conflict and domestic violence (Anderson, 2010). The emotional or behavioral reactions displayed by children of a divorce are a result of the initial stress experienced by the child (Amato, 2010). As the child continues to work through the stressor, their challenges will continue to diminish. Additionally, children of divorce cope better than children of non-divorced, high conflict households (Hetherington, 1979). Research points to the idea that the impact of divorce on a child will have negative impacts on the child's functioning, initially. However, these negative impacts will be short-term, rarely causing long-term physiological challenges (Amato, 2010). This research highlights the importance of identifying divorce or separation as an ACE, because without the identification of the ACE, the root and length of the child's negative behavior may lead to an improper diagnosis.

6 Outcomes of ACEs

The outcomes of adverse childhood experiences (ACEs) are negative in nature. Children exposed to ACEs in childhood become more likely to develop substance abuse issues and are more likely to become addicted. Research by Zimmerman and Posick (2016) have attributed this to emotional disturbance caused by the trauma, which in turn increases the occurrence of risk-taking behavior. Research by Elton et al. (2015) investigated the connection between those exposed to child abuse and cocaine addiction. Similarly alcohol has been found to serve the same purpose as cocaine for child abuse survivors, a coping machanism. Alcohol and substances can have a numbing effect, therefore, children that are exposed to trauma are more likely to experiment with them because it is a form of self-medication to minimize the stress caused by childhood trauma (Smith et al., 2015). Further research in the study completed by Smith et al. (2015) outlines the higher frequency of individuals that were affected by childhood trauma to have addictive traits because the substance or alcohol proved to be a method of coping.

7   Who Are the Children Affected by ACEs

The 10 factors associated with ACEs are more prevalent in areas with higher rates of poverty. Research has shown that low income children are exposed to this type of adversity much more than their more affluent counterparts (Wade et al., 2014). The Kaiser Permanente study, which was the largest study investigating ACEs, consisted of 54% female and 46% male participants. Additionally, 74.8% of the participants in the study were white, 4.5% black, 7.2% Asian, 11.2% Hispanic, and 2.3% other. The Kaiser Permanente Health System study found that 64% of the more than 17,000 patients in the study had been exposed to at least one ACE, and close to 13% of participants in the study had been exposed to four or more ACEs (CDC, 2013). These rates of early childhood trauma are even higher in areas with high rates of poverty and higher criminal populations (Christensen et al., 2005; Eckenrode, Smith, McCarthy, & Dineen, 2014; Larkin, Felitti, & Anda, 2014; Levenson, Willis, & Prescott, 2014; Wallace, Conner, & Dass-Brailsford, 2011). The high frequency of ACEs among impoverished populations makes the necessity for identification of ACEs, and appropriate interventions for children affected by ACEs, much more necessary within these communities.

Children who are affected by ACEs are also threatened with the risk of lower academic achievement. The groups most affected by this are non-Hispanic Black and Hispanic populations (Centers for Disease Control and Prevention, 2010; Duncan & Magnuson, 2005). Lopez and Bhat (2007) present that "African American children were nearly nine times more likely to have a parent in prison than Caucasian children. Hispanic children were three times more likely than Caucasian children to have a parent in prison" (p. 141). Children being subject to the incarceration of one or more parent are considered to have experienced an ACE. Further statistics gathered by Morsy and Rothstein (2016) found that 10% of African-American children, below the age of 18, had an incarcerated parent. In addition, they found that 25% of African-American children will experience a parent being incarcerated at some point in their lives.

Children that are raised in poverty are at a higher risk of being exposed to ACEs (Tomer, 2014). In addition, Duncan and Magnuson (2005) have found that children raised in poverty are also at higher risk for lower academic achievement. A need for increased awareness of ACEs treatment is needed among professionals that work with children in areas of higher poverty because they are more prone to ACEs exposure.

The prevalence of traumas in the life of children was investigated by The National Child Traumatic Stress Network. They found that of their 1,699 patients, the average number of traumas those children were exposed to was 2.9 traumas. The traumas most commonly reported, within this group of children, were emotional abuse, loss, impaired caregiver, and domestic violence (Blodgett and Lanigan). Additionally, 75% of the patients investigated experienced multiple traumatic events or continued exposure to the stressor. Research by Spinazzola et al. (2002) also found that the most common outcomes of these traumatic exposures were dysregulation, limited attention and concentration, negative self-image, limited impulse control, and aggression. The common outcomes of traumatic exposure that were identified by Spinazzola et al. (2002) are areas which could potentially affect a child's performance in the classroom.

The prevalence of abuse in the life of a child is greatly impacted by the environmental factors around that child, including the family and household where the child lives, as well as the demographics (Klossner and Hatfield, 2010). Research by Keane et al. (2015) demonstrated how children most likely to be exposed to ACEs are those who grow up in situations of poverty, have improper socialization with the caregiver, lack of familial supports, or grow up with a parent with mental health problems or substance abuse (Keane et al., 2015). A child is more at risk to be exposed to ACEs depending on the socioeconomic status of their family, as well as the stability and parenting abilities of the child's parent or caregiver. A study by Zimmerman and Posick (2016) found that children exposed to these negative factors were subject to an increase in the risk of indirect violence. Indirect violence consists of violence between parents or violence between family members, not directly involving the child (Zimmerman & Posick, 2016).

Another group of individuals that is prone to a higher rate of ACEs is children with disabilities. Austin et al. (2016) conducted research that found that children with disabilties are 3 times more likely to be exposed to sexual abuse than a child without a disbility. Sexual abuse is the most common ACE that children with disabilites are exposed to throughout their childhood (Austin el al., 2016). As a result, children with disabilities who have experienced ACEs have higher risks of maladaptive behaviors such as smoking and a higher risk of contracting HIV (Austin et al., 2016).

8 Impacts of ACEs in the Classroom

Adverse Childhood Experiences can have a negative impact on brain development. Research has shown that brain development can be altered from birth through adolescence when adversity is experienced in the forms of maltreatment within the family and psychosocial deprivation (Bick & Nelson, 2016). As a result, the child may be affected in a negative way both emotionally and cognitively. These changes to brain development will inevitably affect a child's ability to engage and work within a classroom setting. Research conducted by McLaughlin et al. (2013) found that trauma can impact the cognitive, academic, social, emotional and behavioral functioning of a child (McLaughlin et al., 2013). However, there is hope that early intervention can reduce and reverse these ill effects. The possibility for change makes it crucial that educators, medical professionals, and social workers are educated and willing to collaborate to help children exposed to ACEs, because the effects do not need to remain permanent throughout the child's life.

Research has looked at the correlation between ACEs and factors that indicate success in school. These factors include: school absenteeism, school engagement, school performance and grade repetition (Bethell et al., 2014). Research conducted by Christopher Blodgett of Washington State University, Spokane, and Jane D. Lanigan of Washington State University, Vancouver, suggests that the higher prevalence of exposure to ACEs exponentially increased children's risk to have poor school attendance, behavioral issues, and failure to meet grade level standards in mathematics, reading, or writing (Blodgett & Lanigan, 2018). Additionally, children with higher exposure to ACEs are more likely to have behavioral issues, mental health disorders, special health care needs, as well as a higher risk of obesity (Bethell et al., 2014; Burke et al., 2011). Through this research, a positive correlation between ACE exposure and learning and behavioral problems was found. Further research has determined that exposure to one or more ACEs has been found to negatively affect a child's reading ability (Delaney-Black et al., 2002; Duplechain et al., 2008). Some of the academic implications of exposure to ACEs have been identified, therefore, it must be determined how experts that interact with children can collaborate to best serve the children affected by ACEs. This research begs the question: What can be done by medical professionals, educators, and social workers to limit the ill effects of ACEs in relation to academic success?

9 What Can Be Done to Combat ACEs

Children who are exposed to trauma can develop post-traumatic stress disorder. Additionally, children who are involved in an accident or disaster can also develop post-traumatic stress disorder. However, the recovery process for children exposed to trauma can last up to 10 years, which is significantly longer than children involved in accidents or exposed to disasters (Gospodarevskaya, 2013).

Unfortunately, each and every child cannot be protected from all adverse childhood experiences; however, identification and interventions are the best way to assist a child who has experienced one or more adverse childhood experiences (Walkley & Cox, 2013). If a child is exposed to an adverse childhood experience, developmental, emotional and other negative outcomes are not guaranteed. Through the use of combative interventions like safe, nurturing relationships, and family and community supports, a child's risk of the harmful effects of exposure to ACEs (Brown & Shillington, 2017; Hamby et al., 2018) can be reduced. A child who faces one or more ACE needs consistency across disciplines to help him or her after exposure to ACEs. If a child can receive multiple systems of support through people such as medical professionals, social workers, and educators, he or she will be much more likely to be able to overcome the adversity (Blodgett and Lanigan). The importance then falls on getting these groups of people to collaborate in the best interest of the child.

Child care can have a large impact on recovery following exposure to ACEs. Mortenson and Blair (2019) have found that children who benefit the most from quality child care – that is, child care from a sensitive and responsive teacher, are children most at risk from ACEs. This research shows that the effects of an educator have the potential to lessen the negative effects of ACEs so that a child may begin to heal. The provision of quality child care proves to be a crucial factor in helping children affected by ACEs.

Research has found that social workers and those that work with children on a day to day basis can be beneficial to the overall health of the individual affected by an adverse experience if they incorporate trauma-informed care, TIC, into their practice. TIC is an approach to working with those affected by ACEs that looks at the frequency, as well as the impact of adversity, on an individual's psychosocial functioning throughout his or her lifetime. This approach attempts to understand the individual affected by the ACE on a deeper level, in order to understand the impact of the adversity he or she has experienced (Substance Abuse and Mental Health Services Administration [SAMHSA], 2014a). The focus of TIC is not to outwardly look into the trauma of the past, but to look at the current issues that may affect an individual and relate it to the previous traumas that the individual has experienced (Brown, Baker, & Wilcox, 2012). Key attributes that social workers must have when exercising trauma-informed care is carrying themselves with respect and compassion so that the individual with whom they are working can continue to build upon their own self determination, in order to rebuild a healthy social lifestyle. A healthy lifestyle includes one in which an individual possesses interpersonal skills and coping strategies throughout everyday life. Social workers are trained to look at individuals through a trauma-informed lens to understand why individuals may have poor coping strategies and maladaptive behaviors. Adversity and trauma in an individual's early life are often root causes for negative behaviors as the individual ages. Social workers often are able to look at individuals who have been exposed to ACEs and understand their behaviors and form new coping strategies with the survivor of the trauma (National Association of Social Workers, 2015). The interventions performed by social workers in accordance with TIC are aimed to help minimize the effects of trauma experienced early in life. TIC is used to individualize the experience of the person affected by an ACE so that their experiences are respected and they are able to connect with others so that their recovery seems possible to themselves (Bloom & Farragher, 2013; Harris & Fallot, 2001; SAMHSA, 2013). The benefits of TIC are often only achieved through social workers and counselors. This type of care could be beneficial and reach more survivors of ACEs if it was practiced by all individuals working with children exposed to ACEs. A sense of fluidity among social workers, medical professionals and educators would allow children to receive this beneficial support in multiple aspects of their lives which would magnify the benefits of TIC.

10 Programs and Practices

A review of the literature indicates how steps have been taken to explore ways that social workers and schools can work together to help serve children affected by ACEs. Wediko Children's Services (2019) offers a perspective into possibilities of ways that social workers can work with educators, including administrators and teachers, so that student achievement, despite adverse childhood experiences, can still be achieved (Pataky et al., 2019). The nonprofit group works using a mix of therapies including: relational, attachment, psychodynamic, cognitive behavioral and family systems therapy (Pataky et al., 2019).

It is essential to explore best practices in order to help mitigate the negative effects of ACEs on individuals. Felitti (2012) identified the notion of making the individual who has experienced this adverse experience feel heard, as well as validating their feelings about their experiences. Discussion can often be the first step in aiding the individuals affected. Felitti (2012) notes that providing validation for individuals affected by ACEs is not necessarily complicated. It can be as simple as asking a question in a manner to make the patient feel validated. Using discussion techniques to make the individual feel validated helps to build resilience to support the individual to overcome the negative impacts of ACEs. Finding ways to build resilience is critical in helping a child overcome ACEs. Ultimately, resilience is the key to an individual overcoming ACEs.

11   Resilience

Resiliency is a unique ability that can be developed by individuals and aid children exposed to ACEs to adapt to their environment after their trauma. Through the development of protective factors, children are able to develop more resilience (Luthar, 1991, p. 13; Pizzolongo & Hunter, 2011, p. 23). Through research, the "core protective systems" that are linked to the adaptation of a person previously exposed to one or more ACEs are: a sense of belonging with caring competent people, as well as a protective community, individual capacities, and attachment to a nurturing caregiver (Masten et al., 1990, pp. 425–444). Through implementation and continual growth in these areas, the impact of ACEs will continue to diminish (Masten et al., 1990). Educators who work with young children exposed to ACEs can have a large impact in helping students to develop these attributes and overcoming the negative impacts of exposure to ACEs.

Research has found that children exposed to ACEs are much more at risk of repeating a grade in school, and they also lack resilience. For instance, these children are less able to stay calm when faced with a challenge in school which leads to a lack of success in the classroom (Bethel et al., 2014). An important step for all experts who work with children is to become educated in ACEs and the ways in which they can reinforce behaviors to promote resilience for the child exposed to ACEs. Experts that have received training in trauma have found that they have reported they are more aware and more able to respond to those affected by ACEs. Experts are more readily able to help children affected by ACEs if they receive education to help them deal with those affected by trauma (Wagenhals, 2017). Knowing how to deal with those affected by trauma helps experts develop a new level of respect and compassion for children exposed to ACEs.

12   Challenges to ACEs Treatment

There is often a stigma among medical professionals in asking both children in trauma and adults about a history in trauma, many doctors, nurses and other healthcare professionals lack confidence in approaching the subject (Edwards et al., 2007; Felitti, 2012; Glowa et al., 2016; Kalmakis et al., 2016). The stigma is associated with a lack of familiarity with these mental health issues. Since these questions may be associated with the mental health field, other medical experts struggle to know their place in this area (Felitti, 2012; Kalmakis et al., 2016). Research by Feletti (2010) shows that despite this discomfort among clinicians, patients respond well to screening of ACEs by their primary care physicians. If the healthcare provider is able to show a grasp on the topic and confidence in discussing it, patients are often able to breathe a sigh of relief in being able to discuss their exposure to ACEs (Felitti, 2010). Research has found that an increase in education about ACEs also increases confidence in ACE screening (Glowa et al., 2016).

A limitation in the eyes of medical professionals, in regards to ACE screening, is a lack of time in the office setting. However, studies by Glowa et al. (2016), Kalmakis et al. (2016), and Weinreb et al. (2010), have shown that ACE screening can be incorporated in the limited time of an office visit (Glowa et al., 2016; Kalmakis et al., 2016; Weinreb et al., 2010). The study by Glowa et al. found that the length of office visits were increased by performing ACE screening, but not by more than 5 minutes if the score of the ACE questionnaire was 4 or lower. Meanwhile if the score was higher than 4, the office visit still did not exceed a time of 15 minutes longer than a normal visit (Glowa et al., 2016). The data gathered from the Glowa et al. study aligns with data gathered from Kaiser Permanente, the largest study of looking into ACEs exposure, in which it took patients less than two minutes to retell their childhood traumas, if any, to their healthcare provider. This research found that it was helpful for the healthcare provider to learn about the patients' past experiences and to determine how to proceed from there (Felitti, 2012). A level of transparency is important between medical professionals and patients because it is impossible to give someone the best treatment available without knowing the causes of their ailments. This idea holds true in the classroom, as well. An educator cannot serve his or her students to the highest degree possible without knowing the previous experiences that the child has had, especially one or more ACEs. Therefore, a level of collaboration among professionals is essential in knowing how to work with a child who has been exposed to trauma.

First-hand experiences point to a positive outlook on ACE screenings during medical visits. An example of a patient who looked favorably on ACE screenings took part in the Felitti et al. study. She wrote,

> The shame, guilt, and pain for the abuse and molestations in childhood, and being raped, was so great that I had to come forward or die. If your questionnaire had been put in front of me, it would have shown me that people existed in the medical profession who knew about the sad things that happen to some people. (Felitti, 2014, p. 26)

Individuals who have suffered an ACE often feel they need to suppress their feelings about their experience. However, having these experiences in the open and discussed helps these survivors know they are not alone. That is why all experts who deal with children need access to trauma education so that they are able to identify and help treat children who are exposed to ACEs.

13 ACEs Treatment Programs

There are approaches that are useful in treating individuals impacted by ACEs. Through utilizing neuroplasticity, individuals can begin to heal the brain and body as a whole. Neuroplasticity is the brain's ability to change. Using neuroplasticity aids an individual in building resiliency, which is crucial in overcoming ACEs. While no single intervention can reverse the negative impacts of ACEs, there are ways that the ill effects can be lessened (Litken, n.d.). There must be a strong support system for those affected by ACEs. This foundation includes supportive families and trauma-informed communities and schools. Communities include everyone who works with children – medical professionals and social workers, included. Being prepared to work with children exposed to ACEs is a group effort and there are programs that allow groups to work together to serve this population (Early Childhood Education Unified Agenda, 2016). There are successful programs available to help children recover from ACEs, some programs even combine expert care from different sectors. Proven programs should be used as a guide that can be followed across the country to help children recover from ACEs.

Initiatives have been started in order to best serve those affected by ACEs. The National Council for Behavioral Health and the Kaiser Family Foundation created an initiative in 2015, in which 14 health-care centers from across the United States gathered to develop best practices in how medical professionals deliver primary care. The focus of the initiative was to mitigate the negative effects of trauma so that patients can begin to heal instead of enduring the lifelong effects of trauma (National Council for Behavioral Health). Collaboration among health care professionals helps create an environment that encourages treating those negatively impacted by ACEs.

A program known as Home Visiting through The Nurse-Family Partnership serves as a preventive measure against ACEs. The partnership pays home visits and services to mothers from their pregnancy through their child's infancy (Braverman et al., 2014). The visits and services are designed to support both the family structure, as well as the economic stability of the family. Both are factors that can contribute to ACEs in the child's lifetime. In addition, the services offer health education that is designed to reduce prenatal smoking and alcohol use. Research by Mercy and Saul (2009) has found, by observing randomized controlled trials, that the services offered through The Nurse-Family Partnership promoted a decrease in abuse and an increase is cognitive and social-emotional functioning of the children. Preventative measures are useful in limiting ACEs before they occur.

In Washington, the Family Policy Council used the Behavioral Risk Factor Surveillance System (BRFSS) ACEs data to determine which communities were most at risk of experiencing ACEs. The network was composed of 42 medical professionals, social service providers, and educators. Together these experts worked with families to help children heal from ACE exposure (Litken, n.d.). This collaboration is the start of what is needed to fully mitigate the negative impacts of ACEs on children across the United States.

14 Study

A study was conducted to investigate the perceptions of medical professionals, educators and social workers when collaborating to serve individuals affected by Adverse Childhood Experiences (ACEs). This study investigated how medical professionals, social workers, and educators can use their individual skill sets in order to best serve populations affected by ACEs. This study sought to identify a means to increase collaboration among these groups of experts. Without collaboration individuals affected by ACEs do not receive a holistic recovery experience and may not overcome the impact ACEs. The participants in this study included educators, social workers, and medical professionals that work intimately with children, including those exposed to ACEs. The questions that drove the study were: What challenges do medical professionals, educators, and social workers face when collaborating to help children affected by ACEs? How can collaborators work together in order to best serve a child affected by an ACE? What is being done to help the collaboration among doctors, educators, and social workers to attend to the needs of children exposed to one or more ACE? The researcher utilized a study that was qualitative in nature in order to collect data related to experts' experiences working with children exposed to ACEs. Methods of data collection included an open-ended survey and one-on-one interviews with experts. The goal was to analyze ways in which collaboration among experts can be increased and best used to treat children exposed to ACEs.

Table 7.1 identifies participants' perceptions and experiences of the short- and long-term impacts that children may face when they are exposed to ACEs. The table consists of data collected from educators, social workers, and medical professionals that work with children exposed to ACEs. The short-term effects and impacts consist of both psychological and physical impacts. The experts were asked to list the short- and long-terms effects that they see while working with children exposed to ACEs.

14.1   *Social Workers*

There were 5 social workers that participated in the study. Themes that were found throughout their responses to the short-term impacts of ACEs were: trust issues with both peers and adults, as well as academic and behavioral issues. The trust issues described presented themselves in the form of difficulty forming relationships with others, such as the inability to make friends, interact with peers, and the inability to trust adults. 4 of the 5 social workers that participated identified difficulty developing trust, forming meaningful relationships, or both, as a short-term impact of ACEs. Through the social worker perspective, long-term impacts manifested themselves in the form of mental health issues, drug addiction, substance abuse and lack of productive employment. There is a correlation between short- and long-term impacts of ACEs on children. The impacts that children face immediately following ACE exposure can lead to long-term effects. For instance, the short-term effects of trust issues, difficulty forming relationships, and behavioral problems are gateways to the long-term effects that these children will face into adulthood.

14.2   *Educators*

Participants with a background in education indicated, through their responses, that common themes related to the short-term impacts of ACEs were: trouble focusing, building relationships, low self esteem and being easily triggered. All of these short-term effects negatively impact children in the classroom. The short-term effects correlate with the long-term effects of ACEs. The long-term effects, as identified by educators, were seen in the form of unemployment, addiction, trouble in the community, low work ethic, relationship problems, and lacking necessary tools to succeed in life. The educators that participated in this study identified short-term impacts that directly affect a child in the classroom. The short-term impacts of ACEs, identified by educators, directly

TABLE 7.1 Impacts of ACEs social-emotional and physical health

	Short-term impacts	Long-term impacts
Social workers	– Nightmares, bed wetting, inability to make friends. – Difficulties in forming relationships – Anxiety, trouble forming relationships – both are short and long-term – Some short-term effects are academic issues, behavioral issues and trust issues – A few would be nightmares, school problems, behavioral acting out, difficulties in peer interactions, and lack of trust in adults	– Social isolation, depression, anxiety – Learning to problem solve with violence, mental and substance abuse issues – Mental health issues – I see addiction issues, relationship issues, domestic violence and incarceration as some of the long-term effects – I see peer problems, and problems forming positive relationships throughout adulthood. Increased levels of incarceration, substance abuse, and often an inability to maintain positive and productive employment
Educators	– Low self-esteem, apathetic, attention seeking – Lack of support in home and outside of home – These children cannot focus on their daily activities and are easily distracted by minor upsets. They suffer from triggers and become frustrated with their current situation.	– Unemployment, Drug or Alcohol Abuse, Mental Hospitalization – Long-term effects are getting into more trouble with the community and in school and not doing well educationally. – They build weak learning and work ethics. They do not have strong personal and professional relationships due to lack of the necessary tools.
Medical professionals	– Acting out, trust issues and comfort – They can be quiet and withdrawn – Each individual is different – Psychological stress, anxiety, depression, anger, physical ailments, like GI distress	– Drug use, suicide, self-mutilation, aggression – I don't have that experience – A variety of poor outcomes including chronic health conditions, depression, drug, and alcohol dependence – Substance abuse, psychological disorders, chronic diseases, like hypertension

lead to many of the long-term impacts of ACEs. Short-term impacts often manifest in the long-term impacts because of a lack of intervention.

14.2.1 Medical Professionals

Participants working in the medical field, a total of 5, indicated how that the most common short-term impacts, as identified by these medical professionals were: trust issues, negative behaviors, depression, and physical ailments. The long-term impacts focused on drug and alcohol use, self-harm, chronic conditions, psychological disorders, and depression. One of the medical professionals, an emergency room nurse, openly admitted that she did not have experience in working with the long-term impacts of ACEs. This alludes to the fact that because of the fast-paced work environment, there is an inability to check-in on patients after their ER trip. The medical professionals focused on the physical and psychological impacts of ACEs, which is understandable because the focus of medical professionals is on the physical and mental health of individuals.

14.2.2 Analysis

All three groups of experts identified similar ailments that result from exposure to ACEs. Both social workers and medical professionals identified the lack of trust and inability to form meaningful relationships as a short-term impact of ACE exposure. This sentiment was seen in responses from educators, as well, in the identification of children being withdrawn or apathetic following ACE exposure. From the research, it is clear that some symptoms may be more apparent based on which expert is working with the child exposed to ACEs. For instance, social workers were able to identify symptoms such as nightmares and bedwetting which were not symptoms identified by educators or medical professionals. Meanwhile, educators identified that children exposed to ACEs are often easily distracted and easily triggered in the classroom. Finally, medical professionals were able to recognize the physical ailments that are a result of ACE exposure, like gastrointestinal distress. While there were commonalities in the short-term impacts identified by the experts, there were also impacts that were related closely to the area of expertise that could not necessarily have been identified by the expert in a different field of study. This promotes the notion that collaboration among these experts could be beneficial in order to avoid these short-term impacts from manifesting into the long-term impacts identified by the experts.

Long-term impacts identified by the three groups of experts were: unemployment, substance abuse and addiction, mental health issues, violence, trouble within the community and chronic illness. While all three groups of experts identified mental health issues, unemployment, and substance abuse as common long-terms impacts. Social workers also recognized domestic violence and medical professionals recognized self harm and chronic illness, as well. Again, this data reinforces the notion that some impacts are only seen in specific areas of expertise which leads to the importance of collaboration among experts.

15 Collaboration of Experts

15.1 Perceptions of Collaboration

Table 7.2 illustrates the responses of experts in terms of the extent, strengths and barriers of collaboration with other experts. When asked whether collaboration among experts is beneficial. The responses were an overwhelming yes. Some benefits of collaboration, described by the experts were: "a collaborative plan that addresses the full needs of a child is so important" (social worker); "teamwork and working with a common goal for the child is the best practice" (educator); "people in other fields may offer other outlets of help that we aren't aware of" (educator); and "the patient often benefits from a plan that utilizes multiple angles so that no aspect of potential treatment/interventions gets lost in the mix" (medical professional). While the benefits of collaboration were clearly stated by the experts, the extent of their collaboration told a different story. One social worker who participated noted that she is only involved in formulating a plan, but after that she is not involved in collaborating with educators or medical professionals. The educators that discussed their collaboration with other experts both noted that they work with a child study team that consists of school psychologists, counselors, parents and teachers to create short- and long-term goals for the child. Both educators mention the importance of creating these goals, as they help create a plan for the child moving forward. Collaboration here is seen as immensely beneficial and necessary for helping the child. The medical professionals that participated noted that their collaboration with other experts is minimal. One ER nurse mentioned that she has referred cases to a social worker in the past, but following this there is no follow up. This lack of collaboration leads to the next section of Table 7.2: barriers.

15.2 Barriers to Collaboration

A common theme in terms of barriers to collaboration among experts was parental and familial consent to treatment. Experts from all three areas noted that parents can be a barrier when they do not accept that their child needs treatment for ACE exposure. Another common theme identified by both social

TABLE 7.2 Collaboration of experts

	Extent	Strengths	Barriers
Social workers	– I get involved only in formulating a plan for the adoptive parents going forward in accepting a child into their family for adoption. – Teachers and psychiatrists and medical doctors; Ensuring appropriate medication and difficulty with academics i.e. best way for teaching. – When I first started working as a Social Worker a number of years ago, we routinely had team meetings with school, medical, child study team, family and mental health professionals.	– Absolutely. A collaborative plan that addresses the full needs of the child is so important. The teacher needs to know what is happening in the home so that they are able to know when the child is having an especially hard time, the therapist needs to know how the child is doing academically – and the caregivers need to be consulted in all areas. – Absolutely. I feel this approach was very valuable in providing case work services. – Collaboration among providers is key for a treatment plan. Deviation could negatively affect the outcome.	– Most of the time it is most effective. If not, it is usually due to other professionals being overwhelmed and a lack of time and resources for a child. – At the current time I'm working with adults. – Their parents are major barriers. – Consent from parents.

(cont.)

TABLE 7.2 Collaboration of experts (cont.)

	Extent	Strengths	Barriers
Educators	– I am a teacher and work with guidance as well as the school psychologist. Students need to have a child study team as well as IRST meetings that help with short- and long-term goals. Creating long-term and short-term goals for the students to have a better outcome in the classroom. Also making modifications and accommodations for that child. – As a classroom teacher, I have collaborated with the counselor and the child's parent(s) or guardians in helping to create a strategy and plan; During school time and scheduled meetings, we have created daily goals and yearly plans.	– Yes! Teamwork and working with a common goal for the child is the best practice. It takes a village. – Yes. I feel the more involved can help if they know the student well. – Yes. People in other fields may offer other outlets of help that we aren't aware of.	– Health Care and insurance is one of the only factors. – Sometimes parents or other family members refuse help. – Some families are not as open to accepting the help their children need, especially if they feel attacked or judged. If these children don't have consistent access to their counselors or the skills that they need to practice, they will not progress. – I don't have the necessary experience and accessibility to the cases.

(cont.)

TABLE 7.2　Collaboration of experts (cont.)

	Extent	Strengths	Barriers
Medical professionals	– As a nurse practitioner I interact with all aspects of a child's life. Social workers, physicians, parents and educators. I think we need to be more involved with public policy. – Mostly limited to daily report/patient rounding and sharing of information. – It's minimal … I have relationships with people in the mental health field that could be useful. However, more relationships should be established. – In the ER, we would refer to social work but not sure of the follow up.	– Yes! There needs to be a collaborative approach between medical, education, social services, etc. to address the issues. Addressing the social determinants of health and ACE's can lead to healthy communities. – Professionals tend to focus on their specialty and the patient often benefits from a plan that utilizes multiple angles so that no aspect of potential treatment/intervention gets lost in the mix. – Yes! Interprofessional relationships are key to providing children the continuity of care that is needed to address their needs appropriately. – Collaboration between different specialties gives different perspectives.	– Access to care, insurance issues, time constraints, available services, compliance. – The availability of time sometimes prevents access to these individuals – especially timely access/response. – Time is a huge factor. If patients/children feel rushed, they will be less likely to open up about their experiences. – Time constraints during health visits and uncertainty of availability resources. – Some professionals communicate better than others; professionals not being available or interested. – Finding the cooperation of the patent to get the child help. – ER visits are short-term and may only be one instance.

workers and medical professionals was time constraints. One impact of time constraints is that professionals may feel overwhelmed and therefore cannot best serve the child. Another impact of time constraints is that if a child feels rushed "they will be less likely to open up about their experiences." Both of these impacts of time constraints limit a child from receiving the best care possible. Finding a way to lessen time constraints and have more accessible resources are the highest areas of need identified to increase collaboration among experts.

15.3   Interventions and Strategies

Table 7.3 provides information related to the interventions and strategies that experts have found useful in their practice and what the target or focus of this intervention or strategy was.

15.3.1   Social Workers

One social worker mentioned that treatment facilities can either be extremely beneficial for children exposed to ACEs and lead to "real healing" or they can worsen a child's situation. This social worker attributed healing to: "emphasis on developing warm, nurturing and caring situations where the children are heard and validated," but also mentioned that there must be consequences for adverse behavior. She argued that children need an environment where they can learn that they are cared for and where they can begin to develop trust in the adults around them. She says this will help them to develop trust, regulate emotions and ultimately begin to heal. Another social worker who is also a foster parent herself attributes "love, attention, and beliv[ing] them" as key strategies to help children exposed to ACEs. Key themes from the social workers' responses were: trust, consistency, and validation. When these themes are carried out, children are able to heal based on the development of relationships, positive environments, and being able to regulate emotions.

15.3.2   Educators

The educators that participated in the survey identified the following as key interventions for children exposed to ACEs: safe spaces, 1–1 supports, redirecting bad behavior, gaining trust, building confidence, and developing coping skills. Two educators mentioned that developing strong coping skills helps to combat triggers or unexpected negative situations. In order to develop these skills, gaining trust and building confidence is essential. Another educator noted the importance of having safe spaces where students can reflect and self-regulate if necessary. This same educator mentions, "Letting them make good choices and redirecting bad behavior" as a key to helping children recover and avoid the negative short and long impacts of ACEs.

TABLE 7.3 Interventions

	Interventions/strategies	Target/focus
Social workers	– I have seen a number of treatment facilities that are able to structure themselves in such a way that they can work with a child in a way that leads to real healing. I have also seen facilities that worsened a child's situation. It requires management that puts the emphasis on developing a warm, nurturing and caring situation where the children are heard and validated. Consequences for adverse behavior are important, but programs that emphasize these types of consequences without being able to develop the type of environment where children can learn that they are cared about and can begin to develop trust in the adults around them will not be successful. Believe their story, listen to them, provide a warm, nurturing and caring environment so that the child can begin to develop trust, learn to regulate their emotions and begin to heal. – In the past I have. At my agency we have a few programs working with children exposed to ACEs and I believe they experience some success as these contracts have been ongoing. – Love, attention, believe them. – Everyone is different; therefore modalities will differ. However ongoing consistency and in-vivo for trauma is beneficial when ready to discuss that exposure.	– Healing – Develop trust – Regulate emotions – Consequences for adverse behaviors – Love – Attention – Consistency – Warm, nurturing environments
Educators	– They need a safe space where they can go if they are feeling any type of emotional response to an ACE; with lots of 1-1 support and accommodations for the students. Letting them make good choices and redirecting bad behavior. – Yes. Each student has different needs and requires a different approach. – Gaining their trust will help them build their confidence and eventually build new skills to help them cope in case of triggers and unexpected negative situations. These students prefer calm and quiet environments. Whenever they need time to reflect or more time to complete their assignments, they succeed and gain more confidence. – Yes. Students that have worked closely with the school counselor have found continuous success and have build strong skills to cope with their situations.	– Safe space – 1-1 support – Redirect bad behaviors – Trust – Build confidence – Coping skills

(*cont.*)

TABLE 7.3 Interventions (*cont.*)

	Interventions/strategies	Target/focus
Medical professionals	– Early identification and intervention. We need to use screening tools to identify these issues and then do something about it; screening first and then intervention. We don't even know what some children are going through. We assume if a child seems "ok" and functioning there isn't anything wrong; Teaching preschool teachers the issues that ACE's presents so they can deal with their own experiences and to identify those issues that the children they are working with face. There needs to be more awareness of the issue and how it impacts life. – Serving as a positive role model and/or helping children to see the value that psychotherapy could provide by discussing it in a positive light. – Individualized approaches are key. I believe it would be crucial to develop a relationship with each child, to determine the best approach. – I need to become more familiar with community resources that are available to refer patients to. – Consistent support. – When a parent is willing to engage in services. – Helping to coordinate services and finding available successful programs. – Trusting relationship; I believe interventions need to be individualized. – Recognizing they exposure quickly.	– Screening – Early intervention – Increasing awareness – Encouraging positive role models – Creating individualized experience – Trust coordination

15.3.3 Medical Professionals

The medical professionals emphasized the importance of screening, early intervention, and an increased awareness of ACEs. Themes that were discussed by the experts included: trust, consistency, and coordination. In order to implement these interventions, medical professionals suggested encouraging positive role models and creating individualized experiences for each child based on his or her needs. The medical professionals that participated emphasized the importance of early intervention that is individualized, but also made note that coordination with other experts is not always available nor is it consistent. This data suggests an area of need in regards to collaboration among experts to offer consistent support across disciplines.

15.4 *Analysis*

A common theme that was mentioned by all three groups of experts was trust. In order to begin the healing process for children exposed to ACEs each group suggested that trust be a major focus of the child's treatment. The theme of consistency was also recognized by the experts. There is a need for consistent treatment across disciplines to help negate the negative short and long-term impacts of ACEs.

16 Discussion

The current study made it apparent that the short-term impacts of ACEs often lead to the long-term impacts affecting individuals throughout their lifetimes. Therefore, the necessity for early intervention is clear. This notion is supported by the responses of medical professionals in the study that claim that early intervention and screening give children the best chance at a successful recovery and could possibly establish forms of collaboration during early stages of ACEs treatment among experts. In response to the question, "In your opinion, how would you be able to best serve children exposed to ACEs?", a pediatric nurse practitioner responded that early intervention is how she would best serve a child exposed to ACEs. By limiting the negative outcomes associated with ACEs to only short-term impacts, a child will not be plagued by long-term impacts for the duration of his or her life.

    A specific need that was identified by all three groups of experts was building trust and meaningful relationships for children affected by ACEs. Therefore, a major focus must be placed on finding ways to effectively help children build trust with others, as well as meaningful relationships so that more negative impacts do not develop from this. The lack of trust of adults and peers can affect children in the classroom, as well as in the community. One educator identified that "getting into more trouble with the community and in school" is a long-term impact of ACEs that she has witnessed in her career. She also mentions that this can lead to "not doing well educationally." These results support the conducted by Crouch et al. (2019), which found the relationship between exposure to four or more ACEs positively correlated to challenges individuals may have in school. The study found that having experienced four or more ACEs had a strong association with experiences of the three challenges to school success that were studied: school absenteeism, lack of school engagement, and repeated grade (Crouch et al., 2019, pp. 899–907). There clearly is a relationship between ACEs and school success. The current study found that the inability to form trust and meaningful relationships can lead to problems in school. Therefore, the need for early intervention in the area of trust and relationship building is extremely important for children impacted by ACEs so that the short-term impacts, inability to form trust and meaningful relationships, do not lead to the long-term impacts of trouble in the community and school.

The current study highlighted the different perspectives that came from the different areas of expertise. While medical professionals, educators, and social workers identified some of the same short and long-term impacts of ACEs, each also offered many different responses than the others. In addition, the groups of experts identified different interventions that they believed would best serve a child impacted by ACEs. The experts all identified that each child's experience is unique and he or she must be treated as an individual; however, it is critical to find the intervention that is most effective. The experts agree that the best chance of helping a child recover from ACEs is by collaborating with different groups of experts because of the unique perspectives each group can offer.

Major challenges to collaboration that were identified from the study included: time, resources, parental consent, insurance, and knowledge. Since the challenges to collaboration of experts have been identified by the experts themselves, the next step is identifying possible solutions to create these meaningful partnerships. A pediatric nurse practitioner stated that "There needs to be more awareness of the issue and how it impacts life ... so they can deal with their own experiences and to identify those issues that the children they are working with face." This lack of knowledge is a fundamental issue regarding collaboration among experts, because there simply is not enough awareness of ACEs among the experts that work with children exposed to ACEs. The need for more awareness about ACEs has been identified, now an increase in communication among experts must take place so that, as one educator described it, all experts are able to "work with a common goal for the child." The benefits of collaboration are echoed by all groups of experts, but the form that this collaboration will take must still be developed. Therefore, further research should be conducted to determine how experts feel this collaboration should take place.

17   Suggestions for Practice

After review of the literature and completion of the current study, the researcher has created Figure 7.1 to illustrate suggestions to best serve children exposed to ACEs. Figure 7.1 illustrates the short and long-term effects of ACEs on a child, as well as challenges to the collaboration of experts. The figure is divided into three sections to separate the responses of social workers, medical professionals, and educators. The "child" is the center of this figure because the "child" is the subject that is trying to be helped through this study and further research. The layer beyond the child is the short-term effects of ACEs. The effects are separated based on which group of experts reported them. These are the immediate impacts a child experiences as a result of ACE exposure. The next layer represents the challenges to collaboration of experts. These challenges are also separated based on the group of experts that reported them. Finally, the outer layer represents the long-term effects of ACEs on a child. Challenges to collaboration have been identified in the current study. Many experts that participated in the current study identified communication as a primary means to combat these challenges. The goal for further research should include how this communication can most effectively be carried out among different groups of experts. If the challenges to collaboration can be overcome in the "orange layer" of Figure 7.1, the long-term effects in the "red layer" will never manifest in a child. It is imperative to keep the negative impacts of ACEs as short-term effects before they develop into long-term effects which can cause further damage in the life of an individual impacted by ACEs.

18   Further Research

Future studies should focus on what communication means for individual experts. It will be useful to study what the individual experts believe is the most effective form of communication when working with children exposed to ACEs, as well as when do these experts believe this communication should begin and for how long. The individual opinions of the experts on communication will be useful in furthering the treatment of children exposed to ACEs.

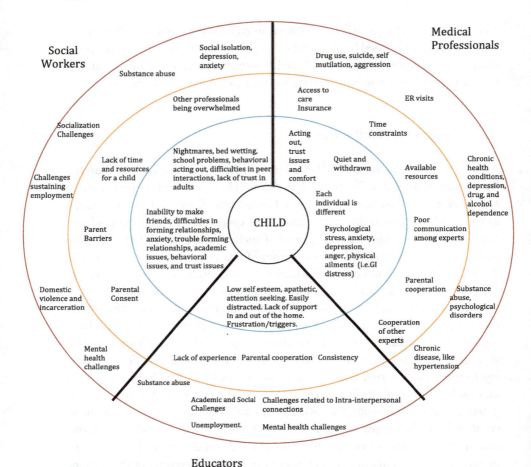

FIGURE 7.1 Effects of ACEs on a child (blue: short-term effects; orange: challenges to collaboration; red: long-term effects)

Through communication, experts can have the power to limit the negative effects of ACEs to short-term impacts instead of long-term impacts that will affect a child throughout his or her life.

19   Conclusion

Collaboration among experts is essential in helping to treat children exposed to ACEs. Developing effective partnerships is important to the health of individuals exposed to ACEs so that the negative impacts of ACEs can be mitigated before they become long-term impacts that will have lifelong effects on the individual. Experts must work together to overcome the challenges that prevent effective collaboration in order to best serve children exposed to ACEs.

References

Amato, P. R. (2010). *Research on divorce: Continuing trends and new developments. Journal of Marriage and Family, 72*(3), 650–666. https://doi.org/10.1111/j.1741-3737.2010.00723.x

Anderson, S. R., Anderson, S. A., Palmer, K. L., Mutchler, M. S., & Baker, L. K. (2010). Defining high conflict. *The American Journal of Family Therapy, 39*(1), 11–27. https://doi.org/10.1080/01926187.2010.530194

Aspelmeier, J. E., Elliott, A. N., & Smith, C. H. (2007). Childhood sexual abuse, attachment, and trauma symptoms in college females: The moderating role of attachment. *Child Abuse & Neglect, 31*(5), 549–566. https://doi.org/10.1016/j.chiabu.2006.12.002

Austin, A., Herrick, H., Proescholdbell, S., & Simmons, J. (2016). Disability and exposure to high levels of adverse childhood experiences: Effect on health and risk behavior. *North Carolina Medical Journal, 77*(1), 30–36.

Barile, J. P., Edwards, V. J., Dhingra, S. S., & Thompson, W. W. (2015). Associations among county-level social determinants of health, child maltreatment, and emotional support on health-related quality of life in adulthood. *Psychology of Violence, 5*(2), 183–191. doi:10.1037/a0038202

Bellis, M. A., Hughes, K., Ford, K., Hardcastle, K. A., Sharp, C. A., Wood, S., Homolova, L., & Davies, A. (2018). Adverse childhood experiences and sources of childhood resilience: A retrospective study of their combined relationships with child health and educational attendance. *BMC Public Health, 18*(1), 792. https://doi.org/10.1186/s12889-018-5699-8

Bethell, C. D., Gombojav, N., Solloway, M., & Wissow, L. (2016). Adverse childhood experiences, resilience and mindfulness-based approaches: Common denominator issues for children with emotional, mental, or behavioral problems. *Child and Adolescent Psychiatric Clinics, 25*(2), 139–156. https://doi.org/10.1016/j.chc.2015.12.001

Bethell, C. D., Newacheck, P., Hawes, E., & Halfon, N. (2014). Adverse childhood experiences: Assessing the impact on health and school engagement and the mitigating role of resilience. *Health Affairs, 33*(12), 2106–2115. https://doi.org/10.1377/hlthaff.2014.0914

Bick, J., & Nelson, C. A. (2016). Early adverse experiences and the developing brain. *Neuropsychopharmacology, 41*(1), 177–196. doi:10.1038/npp.2015.252

Blodgett, C., & Lanigan, J. D. (2018). The association between Adverse Childhood Experience (ACE) and school success in elementary school children. *School Psychology Quarterly, 33*(1), 137–146.

Bloom, S., & Farragher, B. (2013). *Restoring sanctuary: A new operating system for trauma-informed systems of care*. Oxford University Press.

Boullier, M., & Blair, M. (2018). Adverse childhood experiences. *Pediatrics and Child Health, 28*(3), 132–137. https://doi.org/10.1016/j.paed.2017.12.008

Braveman, P., Egerter, S., Arena, K., & Aslam, R. (2014). *Early childhood experiences shape health and well-being throughout life* [Issue Brief No 2]. Robert Wood Johnson Foundation (pp. 1–16). https://www.rwjf.org/en/library/research/2014/08/early-childhood-experiences-shape-health-and-well-being-througho.html

Briere, J. (2015). Pain and suffering: A synthesis of Buddhist and Western approaches to trauma. In V. M. Follette, J. Briere, D. Rozelle, J. Hopper, & D. I. Rome (Eds.), *Mindfulness-oriented interventions for trauma: Integrating contemplative practices* (pp. 11–30). Guilford.

Briere, J., Dietrich, A., & Semple, R. J. (2016). Dissociative complexity: Antecedents and clinical correlates of a new construct. *Psychological Trauma: Theory, Research, Practice, and Policy, 8*(5), 577–584. https://doi.org/10.1037/tra0000126

Brown, S. M., Baker, C. N., & Wilcox, P. (2012). Risking connection trauma training: A pathway toward trauma-informed care in child congregate care settings. *Psychological Trauma: Theory, Research, Practice, and Policy, 4*(5), 507–515. https://doi.org/10.1037/a0025269

Brown, S. M., & Shillington, A. M. (2017). Childhood adversity and the risk of substance use and delinquency: The role of protective adult relationships. *Child Abuse & Neglect, 63*, 211–221. https://doi.org/10.1016/j.chiabu.2016.11.006

Burke, N. J., Hellman, J. L., Scott, B. G., Weems, C. F., & Carrion, V. G. (2011). The impact of adverse childhood experiences on an urban pediatric population. *Child Abuse & Neglect, 35*(6), 408–413. https://doi.org/10.1016/j.chiabu.2011.02.006

Centers for Disease Control & Prevention. (2016). *Adverse childhood experiences*. https://www.cdc.gov/violenceprevention/childmaltreatment/consequences.html

Cho, R. M. (2009). Impact of maternal imprisonment on children's probability of grade retention. *Journal of Urban Economics, 65*(1), 11–23. doi:10.1016/j.jue.2008.09.004

Christensen, R. C., Hodgkins, C. C., Garces, L., Estlund, K. L., Miller, M. D., & Touchton, R. (2005). Homeless, mentally ill and addicted: The need for abuse and trauma services. *Journal of Health Care for the Poor and Underserved, 16*(4), 615–622.

Collin-Vézina, D., Daigneault, I., & Hébert, M. (2013). Lessons learned from child sexual abuse research: Prevalence, outcomes, and preventive strategies. *Child and Adolescent Psychiatry and Mental Health, 7*(1), 22. https://doi.org/10.1186/1753-2000-7-22

Crouch, E., Radcliff, E., Hung, P., & Bennett, K. (2019). Challenges to school success and the role of adverse childhood experiences. *Academic Pediatrics, 19*(8), 899–907. https://doi.org/10.1016/j.acap.2019.08.006

Dallaire, D. H., Ciccone, A., & Wilson, L. C. (2010). Teachers' experiences with and expectations of children with incarcerated parents. *Journal of Applied Developmental Psychology, 31*(4), 281–290. doi:10.1016/j.appdev.2010.04.001

Dallaire, D. H., Ciccone, A., & Wilson, L. C. (2012). The family drawings of at-risk children: Concurrent relations with contact with incarcerated parents, caregiver behavior, and stress. *Attachment & Human Development, 14*(2), 161–183. doi:10.1080/14616734.2012.661232

Delaney-Black, V., Covington, C., Ondersma, S. J., Nordstrom-Klee, B., Templin, T., Ager, J., Janisse, J., & Sokol, R. J. (2002). Violence exposure, trauma, and IQ and/or reading deficits among urban children. *Archives of Pediatrics & Adolescent Medicine, 156*(3), 280. https://doi.org/10.1001/archpedi.156.3.280

Division of Violence Prevention National Center for Injury Prevention and Control Centers for Disease Control and Prevention. (2019). *Preventing Adverse Childhood Experiences (ACEs): Leveraging the best available evidence.* Center for Disease Control. https://www.cdc.gov/violenceprevention/pdf/preventingACES.pdf

Duncan, G. J., & Magnuson, K. A. (2005). Can family socioeconomic resources account for racial and ethnic test score gaps? *The Future of Children, 15*(1), 35–54. https://doi.org/10.1353/foc.2005.0004

Duplechain, R., Reigner, R., & Packard, A. (2008). Striking differences: The impact of moderate and high trauma on reading achievement. *Reading Psychology, 29*(2), 117–136. https://doi.org/10.1080/02702710801963845

Eckenrode, J., Smith, E. G., McCarthy, M. E., & Dineen, M. (2014). Income inequality and child maltreatment in the United States. *Pediatrics, 133*(3), 454–461.

Elton, A., Smitherman, S., Young, J., & Kilts, C. D. (2015). Effects of childhood maltreatment on the neural correlates of stress- and drug cue-induced cocaine craving. *Addiction Biology, 20*(4), 820–831.

Ensink, K., Bégin, M., Normandin, L., Godbout, N., & Fonagy, P. (2017). Mentalization and dissociation in the context of trauma: Implications for child psychopathology. *Journal of Trauma & Dissociation, 18*(1), 11–30. https://doi.org/10.1080/15299732.2016.1172536

Felitti, V. J. (2004). Looking back, and forward. *The Permanente Journal, 8*(1), 3–5.

Felitti, V. J. (2009). Adverse childhood experiences and adult health. *Academic Pediatrics, 9*(3), 131–132. doi:10.1016/j.acap.2009.03.001

Felitti, V. J. (2012, October 28). *How we integrated ACE screening into the health appraisal center at Kaiser Permanente in San Diego.* ACEs Connection. http://www.acesconnection.com/blog/how-we-integrated-ace-screening-into-the-health-appraisal-center-at-kaiser-permanente-in-san-diego

Felitti, V. J., Anda, R. F., Nordenberg, D., Williamson, D. F., Spitz, A. M., Edwards, V., & Marks, J. S. (1998). Relationship of childhood abuse and household dysfunction to many of the leading causes of death in adults. *American Journal of Preventive Medicine, 14*(4), 245–258. doi:10.1016/S0749-3797(98)00017-8

Felitti, V. J., Jakstis, K., Pepper, V., & Ray, A. (2010). Obesity: Problem, solution, or both? *The Permanente Journal, 14*(1), 24–30. doi:10.7812/TPP/09-107

Fergusson, D. M., McLeod, G. F. H., & Horwood, L. J. (2013). Childhood sexual abuse and adult developmental outcomes: Findings from a 30-year longitudinal study in New Zealand. *Child Abuse & Neglect, 37*(9), 664–674. https://doi.org/10.1016/j.chiabu.2013.03.013

Finkelhor, D. (1994). The international epidemiology of child sexual abuse. *Child Abuse & Neglect, 18*(5), 409–417. http://dx.doi.org/10.1016/0145-2134(94)90026-4

Fuchshuber, J., Hiebler-Ragger, M., Kresse, A., Kapfhammer, H. P., & Unterrainer, H. F. (2018, July 18). Depressive symptoms and addictive behaviors in young adults after childhood trauma: The mediating role of personality organization and despair. *Frontiers in Psychiatry.* https://doi.org/10.3389/fpsyt.2018.00318

Glaze, L. E., & Maruschak, L. M. (2008). *Parents in prison and their minor children.* U.S Department of Justice – Bureau of Justice Statistics. https://www.bjs.gov/content/pub/pdf/pptmc.pdf

Glowa, P. T., Olson, A. L., & Johnson, D. J. (2016). Screening for adverse childhood experiences in a family medicine setting: A feasibility study. *Journal of the American Board of Family Medicine, 29*(3), 303–307. doi:10.3122/jabfm.2016.03.150310

Gospodarevskaya, E. (2013). Post-traumatic stress disorder and quality of life in sexually abused Australian children. *Journal of Child Sexual Abuse, 22*(3), 277–296.

Graham, J. A., & Harris, Y. R. (2013). Children of color and parental incarceration: Implications for research, theory, and practice. *Journal of Multicultural Counseling and Development, 41*(2), 66–81. doi:10.1002/j.2161-1912.2013.00028.x

Hamby, S., Grych, J., & Banyard, V. (2018). Resilience portfolios and poly-strengths: Identifying protective factors associated with thriving after adversity. *Psychology of Violence, 8*(2), 172–183. https://doi.org/10.1037/vio0000135

Harris, M. E., & Fallot, R. D. (2001). *Using trauma theory to design service systems.* Jossey-Bass.

Hébert, M., Tremblay, C., Parent, N., Daignault, I. V., & Piché, C. (2006). Correlates of behavioral outcomes in sexually abused children. *Journal of Family Violence, 21*(5), 287–299. https://doi.org/10.1007/s10896-006-9026-2

Hetherington, E. M. (1979). Divorce: A child's perspective. *American Psychologist, 34*(10), 851–858. https://doi.org/10.1037/0003066X.34.10.851

James, F. (2018). Long-term effects of child abuse: Lessons for Australian paediatric nurses. *Australian Journal of Advanced Nursing, 35*(4), 42–51.

Johnson, E. I., & Easterling, B. A. (2015). Coping with confinement: Adolescents' experiences with parental incarceration. *Journal of Adolescent Research, 30,* 244–267. doi:10.1177/0743558414558593

Kalmakis, K. A., & Chandler, G. E. (2014). Adverse childhood experiences: Towards a clear conceptual meaning. *Journal of Advanced Nursing, 70*(7), 1489–1501. doi:10.1111/jan.12329

Keane, C., Magee, C. A., & Lee, J. K. (2015). Childhood trauma and risky alcohol consumption: A study of Australian adults with low housing stability. *Drug and Alcohol Review, 34*(1), 18–26.

Klossner, N., & Hatfield, N. (2010). *Introductory maternity and pediatric nursing* (2nd ed.). Wolters Kluwer Health | Lippincott Williams and Wilkins.

Larkin, H., Felitti, V. J., & Anda, R. F. (2014). Social work and adverse childhood experiences research: Implications for practice and health policy. *Social Work in Public Health, 29*(1), 1–16.

Levenson, J. S. (2019). Trauma-informed social work practice. *Social Work, 62*(2), 105–113. doi:10.1093/sw/swx001

Levenson, J. S., Willis, G. M., & Prescott, D. S. (2014). Adverse childhood experiences in the lives of male sex offenders. *Sexual Abuse, 28*(4), 340–359. doi:10.1177/1079063214535819

Limke, A., Showers, C. J., & Zeigler-Hill, V. (2010). Emotional and sexual maltreatment: Anxious attachment mediates psychological adjustment. *Journal of Social and Clinical Psychology, 29*(3), 347–367. https://doi.org/10.1521/jscp.2010.29.3.347

Litken, M. (n.d.). *Health brief: ACEs for health systems and providers*. Health and Medicine Policy Research Group. https://www.hmprg.org/wp-content/themes/HMPRG/backup/ACEs/Health%20Policy%20Brief.pdf

Lopez, C., & Bhat, C. S. (2007). Supporting students with incarcerated parents in schools: A group intervention. *Journal for Specialists in Group Work, 32*(2), 139–153. doi:10.1080/01933920701227125

Luthar, S. S. (1991). Vulnerability and resilience: A study of high-risk adolescents. *Child Development, 62*(3), 600. https://doi.org/10.2307/1131134

Masten, A. S., Best, K. M., & Garmezy, N. (1990). Resilience and development: Contributions from the study of children who overcome adversity. *Development and Psychopathology, 2*(4), 425–444. https://doi.org/10.1017/S0954579400005812

McLaughlin, K. A., Koenen, K. C., Hill, E. D., Petukhova, M., Sampson, N. A., Zaslavsky, A. M., & Kessler, R. C. (2013). Trauma exposure and posttraumatic stress disorder in a national sample of adolescents. *Journal of the American Academy of Child & Adolescent Psychiatry, 52*(8), 815–830.e14. https://doi.org/10.1016/j.jaac.2013.05.011

Mercy, J. A., & Saul, J. (2009). Creating a healthier future through early interventions for children. *Journal of the American Medical Association, 301*(21), 2262–2264.

Morsy, L., & Rothstein, R. (2016, December 15). *Mass incarceration and children's outcomes: Criminal justice policy is education policy*. Economic Policy Institute. https://www.epi.org/publication/mass-incarceration-and-childrens-outcomes/

Mortensen, J. A., & Barnett, M. A. (2019). Intrusive parenting, teacher sensitivity, and negative emotionality on the development of emotion regulation in early head start toddlers. *Infant Behavior and Development, 55*, 10–21. https://doi.org/10.1016/j.infbeh.2019.01.004

Murphey, D., & Cooper, P. M. (2015). *Parents behind bars: What happens to their children?* ChildTrends.org. https://www.childtrends.org/wp-content/uploads/2015/10/2015-42ParentsBehindBars.pdf

Murphey, D., & Sacks, V. (2019). Supporting students with adverse childhood experiences: How educators and schools can help. *American Educator, 43*(2), 8–11.

National Association of Social Workers. (2015). *Trauma-informed primary care initiative.* The National Council for Behavioral Health. https://www.thenationalcouncil.org/trauma-informed-primary-care-initiative-learning-community/

National Resource Center on Children and Families of the Incarcerated. (2014). *Children and families of the incarcerated fact sheet.* Rutgers. https://nrccfi.camden.rutgers.edu/files/nrccfi-fact-sheet-2014.pdf

Nesmith, A., & Ruhland, E. (2008). Children of incarcerated parents: Challenges and resiliency, in their own words. *Children and Youth Services Review, 30*(10), 1119–1130. doi:10.1016/j.childyouth.2008.02.006

Nichols, E. B., & Loper, A. B. (2012). Incarceration in the household: Academic outcomes of adolescents with an incarcerated household member. *Journal of Youth and Adolescence, 41*(11), 1455–1471. doi:10.1007/s10964-012-9780-9

Pataky, M. G., Báez, J. C., & Renshaw, K. J. (2019). Making schools trauma informed: Using the ACE study and implementation science to screen for trauma. *Social Work in Mental Health, 17*(6), 639–661. https://doi.org/10.1080/15332985.2019.1625476

Pérez-Fuentes, G., Olfson, M., Villegas, L., Morcillo, C., Wang, S., & Blanco, C. (2013). Prevalence and correlates of child sexual abuse: A national study. *Comprehensive Psychiatry, 54*(1), 16–27. https://doi.org/10.1016/j.comppsych.2012.05.010

Pew Charitable Trusts. (2010). *Collateral costs: Incarceration's effect on economic mobility.* Economic Mobility Project. https://www.pewtrusts.org/~/media/legacy/uploadedfiles/pcs_assets/2010/collateralcosts1pdf.pdf

Pizzolongo, P., & Hunter, A. (2011). I am safe and secure: promoting resilience in young children. *Young Children, 66*(2), 67–69.

Rappaport, S. R. (2013). Deconstructing the impact of divorce on children. *Family Law Quarterly, 47*(3), 353–377.

Robertson, O. (2007). *The impact of parental imprisonment on children.* Quaker United Nations Office. https://www.quno.org/sites/default/files/resources/ENGLISH_The%20impact%20of%20parental%20imprisonment%20on%20children.pdf

Robles, A., Gjelsvik, A., Hirway, P., Vivier, P. M., & High, P. (2019). Adverse childhood experiences and protective factors with school engagement. *Pediatrics, 144*(2), e20182945. https://doi.org/10.1542/peds.2018-2945

Roche, D. N., Runtz, M. G., & Hunter, M. A. (1999). Adult attachment: A mediator between child sexual abuse and later psychological adjustment. *Journal of Interpersonal Violence, 14*(2), 184–207. https://doi.org/10.1177/088626099014002006

Saunders, V. (2018). What does your dad do for a living? Children of prisoners and their experiences of stigma. *Children and Youth Services Review, 90,* 21–27. doi:10.1016/j.childyouth.2018.05.012

Sciaraffa, M. A., Zeanah, P. D., & Zeanah, C. H. (2018). Understanding and promoting resilience in the context of adverse childhood experiences. *Early Childhood Education Journal, 46*(3), 343–353. https://doi.org/10.1007/s10643-017-0869-3

Shillingford, M. A., & Edwards, O. W. (2008). Professional school counselors using choice theory to meet the needs of children of prisoners. *Professional School Counseling, 12,* 62–65. doi:10.1177/2156759X0801200107

Southall, D. P., Plunkett, M. C. B., Banks, M. W., Falkov, A. F., & Samuels, M. P. (1997). Covert video recordings of life-threatening child abuse: Lessons for child protection. *Pediatrics, 100*(5), 735–760. https://doi.org/10.1542/peds.100.5.735

Spinazzola, J., Ford, J., van der Kolk, B., Blaustein, M., Brymer, M., Gardner, L., & Smith, S. (2002). *Complex trauma in children and adolescents.* The National Child Traumatic Stress Network. http://www.nctsnet.org

Stoltenborgh, M., Bakermans-Kranenburg, M., Alink, L., & van IJzendoorn, M. (2014). The prevalence of child maltreatment across the globe: Review of a series of meta-analyses. *Child Abuse Review, 24*(1), 37–50. doi:10.1002/car.2353

Substance Abuse and Mental Health Services Administration. (2014, July). *SAMHSA's concept of trauma and guidance for a trauma-informed approach.* SAMHSA's Trauma and Justice Strategic Initiative. https://ncsacw.samhsa.gov/userfiles/files/SAMHSA_Trauma.pdf

Trickett, P. K., Noll, J. G., & Putnam, F. W. (2011). The impact of sexual abuse on female development: Lessons from a multigenerational, longitudinal research study. *Development and Psychopathology, 23*(2), 453–476. https://doi.org/10.1017/S0954579411000174

Turney, K. (2018). Adverse childhood experiences among children of incarcerated parents. *Children and Youth Services Review, 89,* 218–225. doi:10.1016/j.childyouth.2018.04.033

Voices for Virginia's Children. (2016). *Early childhood education unified agenda.* http://vakids.org/wp-content/uploads/2015/09/2016-Early-Childhood-Education-Final.pdf

Wade, R., Shea, J. A., Rubin, D., & Wood, J. (2014). Adverse childhood experiences on low-income youth. *Pediatrics, 134*(1), e12–e21. doi:10.1542/peds.2013-2475

Wagenhals, L. D. (2017). *Enhancing trauma awareness.* Lakeside Educational Network. https://www.lgi.training/courses/enhancing-trauma-awareness/

Walkley, M., & Cox, T. L. (2013). Building trauma-informed schools and communities. *Children & Schools, 35*(2), 123–126. https://doi.org/10.1093/cs/cdt007

Wallace, B., Conner, L., & Dass-Brailsford, P. (2011). Integrated trauma treatment in correctional health care and community-based treatment upon reentry. *Journal of Corrections Health Care, 17*(4), 329–343.

Warren, J. M., Coker, G. L., & Collins, M. L. (2019). Children of incarcerated parents: Considerations for professional school counselors. *The Professional Counselor, 9*(3), 185–199. https://doi.org/10.15241/jmw.9.3.185

Zimmerman, G. M., & Posick, C. (2016). Risk factors for and behavioral consequences of direct versus indirect exposure to violence. *American Journal of Public Health, 106*(1), 178–188.

CHAPTER 8

A Call for Trauma-Informed Understanding at Colleges and Universities

Ange Concepcion and Kevin Nadolski

Abstract

As prevalence of trauma becomes more visible with incoming college students, faculty and administrators are called to identify students who may struggle and also have a history of trauma exposure. This chapter will present the need for a trauma-informed understanding for Generation Z undergraduates, review relevant literature, present findings of content analysis of websites from five institutions with intervention teams, and conclude with recommendations for faculty and administrators.

Keywords

higher education – trauma-informed – behavioral intervention team – Generation Z

1   Introduction

The lives and experiences of incoming college students, especially those from Generation Z, are relevant to how they are able to adjust and thrive on a college campus (Shalka, 2019a; Stolzenberg, 2018). As K-12 classrooms continue their preparations in trauma-informed understanding and approach, college faculty and administrators should also consider how they can implement a trauma-informed perspective to support college student development and success (Gutierrez & Gutierrez, 2019). While literature and research on the experience of undergraduate college students with trauma exposure are emerging (Artime et al., 2018; Banyard & Cantor, 2004; Frazier et al., 2009), trauma-informed approaches in response to sexual violence on college campuses have made the college student experience of trauma become more visible (Shalka, 2019a; Yoshimura & Campbell, 2016). While trauma from sexual violence is often considered in how to develop a trauma-informed approach, experiences of trauma are varied; consideration must be provided to the unique experience and identity development of trauma survivors in a holistic manner (Shalka, 2019a, 2019b).

Generation Z students, born in the mid 1990s to 2010, are characterized as resilient, realistic, pragmatic, more likely to protest than the five decades of students that preceded them, and driven to solve problems and improve intercultural understanding (Anotale, 2013; Eagan et al., 2015; Seemiller & Grace, 2019; Siegel, 2016). They are more likely to be active and directed in their learning, motivated to confront complex problems, and value direct communication (Dupont, 2015; Siegel, 2016; Wiedmer, 2015). Generation Z grew up in an environment with economic instability, violence, racial injustice, geopolitical conflict, and uncertainty about the future (Anotale, 2013; Seemiller & Grace, 2019; Siegel, 2016). Such conditions can create a vulnerability for these students' human development and socialization which can result in trauma, moving college and university leaders to claim a responsibility for academic and student life programs to include trauma-informed understanding and practice.

Seemiller and Grace (2019) report that 18% of Generation Z members struggle with mental and emotional health issues, based on self-reporting of college seniors. Along with high rates of anxiety, depression, and feelings of being overwhelmed and stressed, trauma and vicarious trauma challenge this cohort. Carello and Butler (2014) cite studies where 66–94% of present college-aged students have been exposed to at least one traumatic event. Trauma is dimensionalized as single-incident trauma and complex or interpersonal trauma. The former includes experiences that are frequently broadcast in the media, such as natural disasters and school shootings. The latter is a stress reaction to a protracted trauma throughout a person's child and adolescent development that resulted from serious and abusive treatments (Gubi et al., 2019). Vicarious trauma, largely the result of the 24/7 news cycle and ubiquity of media, occurs when one feels personally the trauma that is broadcast (Seemiller & Grace, 2019). Gutierrez and Gutierrez (2019) further categorize trauma into macro-traumatic events and micro-traumatic events. Sudden events like natural disasters, wherein many have little to no control over the event, are macro-traumatic. Individuals who experience an incident that can drastically impact their lives are considered micro-traumatic events.

The need for colleges and universities to integrate trauma-informed care (TIC) into their academic and student life programming is clear. In the wake of the September 11th, 2001 terrorist attack on the World Trade Center and school shootings, TIC grew out of the psychological counseling field and is emerging as an essential need for schools at the primary, secondary, and tertiary levels. In the educational context, TIC is often referred to as trauma-informed or trauma-sensitive schools (Gubi et al., 2019). Trauma-informed schools acknowledge, in a systematic manner, how trauma is a prevalent force that can impact students, families, educators, and school staff (Blitz et al., 2020). Furthermore, these schools incorporate a "comprehensive perspective on trauma that enacts trauma-informed practices throughout the entire school system" (Gubi et al., 2019, p. 178). A system-wide approach for higher education would extend from the classroom to all aspects of the college experience, from residence life and athletics to orientation programs and enrollment management. The values that ground TIC align with the mission of higher education in general. Safety, trustworthiness, choice, collaboration, and empowerment are critical to building a rich college experience; they also form the foundation of TIC as core values (Ford et al., 2009).

Prior to examining the relevant literature, a brief review of the cohort group presently completing or entering their undergraduate years will support the call for leaders in higher education to bring TIC to the various dimensions of student engagement. Though characterized as resilient, Generation Z is also referred to as a "worried generation" in light of the traumatic experiences its members have endured; their worries center around "fear of failure, money, and social issues" (Seemiller & Grace, 2019, p. 146). The authors also assert that these young people have been reared with "tight, hand-holding behaviors" by their parents (p. 145). While college and university leaders, faculty, and staff would not engage in professional relationships that would mirror this type of parenting, students expecting a similar sort of care and guidance may be set up for disappointment. Placed in a context where something provokes trauma, such as a professor or classmate announcing physical threats or a student on the verge of failing an exam, course, or out of college itself, undergraduate learners may seek, out of authentic need, a firm hand to hold as they negotiate trauma. Although it is unreasonable for the faculty or staff members to provide the same care as their parents, college and university personnel have a responsibility to educate young people effectively and form them appropriately in accord with the school's mission. If students are sensitive to trauma and susceptible to being sidetracked because of it, faculty and staff will need to learn how to accommodate their students and walk with them as they navigate this challenge. TIC is a resource to inform this professional competency.

Based on a content analysis of college and university resources on trauma informed services and behavioral intervention teams (BIT) or campus assessment, response, and education (CARE) teams, the authors support and propose a community-based, collaborative approach among stakeholders to support college students who have experienced trauma. This chapter will also consider national trends on incoming first-year students from the Higher Education Research Institute's (HERI) Cooperative Research Institutional Research

Program (CIRP) Freshman Survey, selected literature on trauma exposure and trauma-informed approaches at the university level, and notable practices. CIRP Freshman Survey contains responses from first-time, full-time students at colleges and universities. Since 1966, more than 15 million students at approximately 1,900 colleges and universities have completed, with the Freshman Survey as the longest-running survey offered.

2 Arriving on Campus – National Trends

Although college students' self-reported academic drives have increased between 1985–2017, mental health and emotional wellness have declined (Eagan et al., 2017; Stolzenberg, 2018). Some attribute this to isolation experienced through increased social media use and stress teens experience prior to their arrival on campus, with rates of sleep deprivation on the rise alongside depression and anxiety, in addition to trying to find their identity among peer groups and discovering how to navigate uncertainty of the job market (Nicholls, 2017; Twenge, 2017).

In highlighting the decline of students' overall physical health and lower emotional health, Stolzenberg (2018) suggests that faculty and staff should be trained to learn about how incoming students may be generationally different. For instance, 63.6% of incoming students in 1985 viewed their emotional health as above average; in 2017, this rating dropped to 47.4%. Stolzenberg (2018) adds that campus climate surveys may assist with identifying if there are subsets of the campus population that need support or services to improve emotional wellness. Aside from the aforementioned stressors, many students arrive to campus having already been exposed to at least one traumatic event (Frazier et al., 2009; Galatzer-Levy et al., 2012; Read et al., 2011).

HERI's Undergraduate 2016–2017 faculty survey asked respondents (n = 20,771) to consider how their role helps undergraduate students in their development. For instance, nearly three-quarters of faculty strongly agreed that they are responsible for encouraging students to write effectively. Conversely, about a quarter of faculty strongly agreed that they have a responsibility to provide for the emotional development of their students (Stolzenberg et al., 2019). While these reported attitudes are notable, this connotes that support for student emotional development should exist outside of the classroom. However, faculty are in an important position to establish a caring and encouraging environment for students that improves their quality of learning, self-efficacy, and belonging (Baier et al., 2019; Bohannon et al., 2019).

2.1 Transition to College

Before the start of the semester, first year students typically attend a one to two-day orientation. After orientation, some institutions have first year students attend a first-year seminar as a continued, fuller approach to orient them. Topics featured in first year seminars include purpose of a college education, expectations of class attendance, and general topics surrounding college life (Boylan, 1999). To ease the academic and social transitions, some colleges and universities may also implement different types of cohort models, also referred to as learning communities (Baier et al., 2019; Boylan, 1999; Han et al., 2018; Zhao & Kuh, 2004). Learning communities feature a cohort of students that are co-enrolled in at least two courses, typically from different disciplines, that have a common theme. The instructors work as a team to design their courses in a manner that allows students to link concepts between the courses (Boylan, 1999; Zhao & Kuh, 2004). Activities in learning communities are linked in and extend out of the classroom for students to construct knowledge and experience that is personally relevant to students (Zhao & Kuh, 2004).

Researchers have noted benefits for students enrolled in learning communities. Well-designed learning communities improve the learning environment, along with helping encourage and augment learning (Lenning & Ebbers, 1999). Lenning and Ebbers (1999) contend that collaborative learning among students results in better student retention, satisfaction, and grade point average. They further note that learning communities allow for a "better understanding of self and others, and a greater ability to bridge the gap between academic and social worlds" (p. 6).

Zhao and Kuh (2004) reviewed data from the National Survey of Student Engagement (NSSE) to determine if learning community participation is connected to student success. Their findings revealed that learning community participation is connected to improved academic performance, increases in attendance, engagement of educational and social activities, and favorable view of their college environment.

Han et al. (2018) explored the experience of 41 minority students who participated in a living and learning community. While students cited some negative experiences such as interpersonal issues and isolation, many mentioned benefits such as social connection and integration, a safe haven among peers, validation of cultural experiences, care from staff, support for self-growth, and cultural learning.

Baier et al. (2019) researched developmental courses designed as learning communities that featured support from peer mentors. Students in the developmental learning communities had higher grade point averages at the end of their first and second years than those that were not in a learning community. Their study supported previous findings on learning communities, emphasizing that collaborative work with students and creating a setting that supports engagement among peers, mentors, and faculty are beneficial.

3 Selected Literature on Trauma Prevalence and Trauma-Informed Approaches in Higher Education

A review of literature regarding trauma-informed understanding and practice reveal some of the most common traumatic events reported by college students. These traumatic events, whether experienced in childhood, adolescence, or in college, included unexpected death of a loved one, life threatening illness, accidents, physical abuse, witnessing family violence, unwanted sexual attention, and sexual assault (Banyard & Cantor, 2004; Boyraz & Waits, 2018; Frazier et al., 2009; Galatzer-Levy et al., 2012; Read et al., 2011; Shalka, 2019b; Vrana & Lauterbach, 1994; Yoshimura & Campbell, 2016). Consequences of experiencing traumatic events included post-traumatic stress disorder, suicide ideation and attempt, learning difficulties, sleeplessness, decreased energy, depression, anxiety, inability to concentrate, decreased self-esteem, difficulty maintaining relationships, and impact on identity formation (Banyard & Cantor, 2004; Shalka, 2019a; Slaninova & Stainerova, 2015; Yoshimura & Campbell, 2016).

Boyraz and Waits (2018) explored the wellness factor of college students who have experienced trauma, with an emphasis on their physical health. However, the authors provide a picture of the type of trauma these young adults carry in their emotional backpacks: interpersonal trauma (IPT), "events in which an individual is personally assaulted or violated by another human being that is either known or unknown to the trauma survivor" (Lily & Valdez, 2012, p. 140, as cited in Boyraz & Waits, 2018). This includes physical, sexual, and emotional abuse, as well as emotional neglect. A gap in the literature for trauma-exposed college appears to be for those who have experienced non-IPT, such as a house fire, serious illness, or natural disaster.

Nevertheless, a non-IPT population frequently overlooked when considering trauma-exposed students is military veterans. Matriculating into colleges and universities after completing their terms of military service, these veterans carry lasting trauma, with one study reporting 47% of student veterans have been treated for post-traumatic stress disorder (PTSD) (Artime et al., 2018). In an effort to meet the needs of these students, colleges and universities could seek to partner with governmental veteran affairs agencies to learn how to ease the transition from combat to the classroom.

Clustering around IPT, the research developed the consideration of trauma beyond psychological context. Shalka (2019a) addresses the multidimensionality of trauma, asserting that this painful experience impacts a person's relational, spiritual, physical, and cultural contexts of existence. Here, the interventions a college community provides to aid its trauma-exposed students will require a more holistic approach that extends beyond the counseling center.

For instance, Kuhl and Boyraz (2017) considered the reduced social support among trauma-exposed students, which is a great concern as social relationships can be beneficial to aiding those struggling with impact of trauma. One activity the researchers studied was the practice of mindfulness, "the ability to pay attention to the present moment in a nonjudgmental way" (p. 151), which was shown to increase students' compassion and empathy, which can facilitate social support.

Aware of this multidimensionality, colleges can make available different services for the various dimensions related of the trauma experience. The campus ministry department can lead the mindfulness practices; wellness centers could host massages and healthy-touch or art therapy activities; and student life offices might highlight the importance of social support in the aftermath of trauma in its orientation programming.

One area of campus life that requires immediate attention is alcohol and drug use awareness, for trauma-exposed students turn to these substances to cope with their challenges (Aarstad-Martin & Boyraz, 2017). This type of self-medication commonly complicates, instead of ameliorates, the distress resulting from trauma. Aarstad-Martin and Boyraz (2017) found that these students also misused prescriptions drugs at a high rate, a finding that parallels the rates of alcohol use. The health threat to this trend beckons focused attention from leaders in higher education.

In consideration of how many students arrive at college with a history of exposure to trauma, Banyard and Cantor's (2004) work focused on exploring factors that contribute to resilience among first-semester college students (n = 197) that have been exposed to traumatic events. This sample represented over half of the number of students that completed the questionnaire. Factors that contribute to resilience were the perceived high levels of social support, ability to make meaning from traumatic experiences, and the belief that they can control how to respond to life events. Banyard and Cantor (2004) noted that individuals who reported higher frequencies of cumulative trauma may have a more negative college transition or adjustment period and tended to be less resilient.

In a multi-institutional study, Frazier et al. (2009) assessed the prevalence of experiencing traumatic events and symptoms related to these as reported by undergraduate students. Majority of the sample (n = 1,528), or 85%, reported to have experienced a traumatic event during their lifetime before college. During a two-month period in college, 21% of the sample had experienced a traumatic event. The most common worst events reported by the students were death of a loved one, accident, other life-threatening event, violence in the family, and sexual assault. Those who identified sexual assault as their worst traumatic event had the highest probably post-traumatic stress disorder rate.

Focusing on trauma-informed approach in counseling, Yoshimura and Campbell (2016) provided reflections and suggestions based on tracking counseling services for survivors of sexual assault, relationship violence, and/ or stalking, over two academic years. The researchers note that many college counseling centers use a Solution Focused Brief Therapy (SFBT) model. SFBT model focuses on encouraging clients to identify future solution to their problems, rather than uncovering origins of a problem. Though this model is adaptable, cost-effective, and shows positive outcomes for emotional and behavioral change, SFBT's approach presents limitations for trauma survivors. Since SFBT is focused on generating future solutions, some counselors may overlook past issues of trauma and may retrigger trauma and others counselors may shy away from continuing treatment and refer the trauma survivor to external settings, leaving the trauma survivor feeling stigmatized (Yoshimura & Campbell, 2019).

Shalka's (2019b) grounded theory research on the conceptualization of traumatic experiences on college student identity development revealed how social identities and social discourse, or external messaging, contributed to how participants developed part of their sense of self and their psychophysical, relational, and negotiated identities. Social identities such as race, gender identity, sexual orientation, religion, and socio-economic status inform how traumatic experiences can be processed. For example, stereotypes of social identities impacted the approach of how trauma is processed. On perceived social discourse, trauma survivors refrained from speaking about their experience as they did not want to upset others or could be seen as wanting attention. Identity development through interactions with others as a trauma survivor was critical for clarifying their identity post-trauma. Participants reported anticipating alienation and not being understood by those in their support system; this feeling of separation and noted difference from others contributed to questioning their identity. Other participants noted a general feeling of connection to others that lived through trauma. Shalka (2019b) concluded that trauma had shaped self-understanding, with positive outcomes such as being comfortable with unpredictability and learning about themselves, and negative outcomes like being less trusting of others.

Matching the aforementioned finding of Frazier et al. (2009) that 85% of college students have experienced trauma with the prevalence of peoples' exposure to more than one instance of trauma beckons a consideration of retraumatization. The rates of retraumatization vary. However, even when "stringent criteria" are used, the American Psychological Association claims 34.2% of men and 24.9% of women experienced more than one traumatic event (Fiorillo & Follette, 2012, p. 188). Other rates for child sexual abuse survivors, for example, show anywhere from 16% and 72%, and rates for child physical abuse at 50% for revictimization (Fiorillo & Follette, 2012).

Retraumatization, the experience of experiencing multiple traumas, is also known as revictimization, repeated trauma, multiple traumatization, and continuous trauma. Key to this phenomenon is the reactivation of the trauma-related distress and an increase or exacerbation of the stress. Thus, the nature of retraumatization appears to be almost unavoidable: "One of the greatest risk factors for future trauma is previous exposure" (Lesher et al., p. 573).

Keller-Dupree (2013) outlines a number of practices for educators to prevent retraumatization. While recommending these for the K-12 context, she asserts that trauma reactions share similarities across the developmental spectrum, including for high school students and adults. Carello and Butler (2015) expand their treatment of TIC to consider college-aged students and advocate for principles and practices to avert more trauma. These two approaches highlight student self-care, and instructional consistency and emotional safety in the classroom. Additionally, they call for the instructor to establish a trauma-sensitive attitude that does not insist that traumatic events must be extreme to prompt retraumatization. Here, the example at the beginning of this chapter illustrates how the simplicity of a professor's ignorant rant could, in fact, retraumatize a seemingly calm, trauma-healed student.

3.1   *Systems of Support*

For a number of students, the transition to college can also mean a transition or adjustment of support systems. Whether students commute or move away from home to attend college, they will need to adjust to a new environment. Family and friends from home can continue to serve as a social support system (Banyard & Cantor, 2004). Academic, social, and personal support allows students to feel connected (Tinto, 2006). In consideration of Generation Z college students, their college experience can be made more meaningful if they find their experiences to be relevant and receive directed communication.

Within classroom settings, faculty can observe how stress and trauma can manifest within a student's academic performance. Students may withdraw from others, have variable attendance, submit late or miss coursework, avoid work, and have decreased well-being (Bohannon et al., 2019; Gutierrez & Gutierrez, 2019). Bohannon et al. (2019) caution that these behaviors can be misinterpreted as apathy and suggest that introducing a reflective, open-ended writing piece that allows students to communicate openly about themselves can at least help with establishing a supportive environment among the students and faculty member. This particular approach may work well in some types of courses more so than others. They also suggest that providing specific verbal encouragement and identifying the strengths can help students focus on mastering skills to develop stronger self-efficacy and resiliency (Bohannon et al., 2019).

Further, some topics may prove to be difficult for group discussions. Gutierrez and Gutierrez (2019) advise faculty to establish a safe environment and consider how some students might not be willing to engage in open dialogue about challenging subjects such as sexual abuse, domestic violence, and substance abuse.

Specifically, for students that reside on campus, Resident Assistants (RA) are an important student resource. RAs are able to establish relationships and tend to be a primary encounter for residential students that need guidance and support (Canto et al., 2017). Though RAs are an important peer resource, campus counseling centers are considered a primary resource for students, followed by the campus medical center, Dean of Students staff, and campus safety and security (Canto et al., 2017). Counseling centers have been cited as critical support resources for college students (Banyard & Cantor, 2004; Frazier et al., 2009; Yoshimura & Campbell, 2016)

Researchers have noted the importance of counseling staff in their role to identify different strategies to support the challenges that trauma survivors face (Banyard & Cantor, 2004; Frazier et al., 2009; Yoshimura & Campbell, 2016). Banyard and Cantor (2004) advise that in addition to assessing a student's areas of distress, counselors should also determine how certain protective factors can encourage resilience. Frazier et al. (2009) also recommends assessing trauma exposure of students during an intake session so that counselors can generate understanding of possible continuing effects on a student's past trauma exposure and possible exposure during college.

Further, counselors can work on how to strategically plan specific outreach efforts based on most common traumatic experiences and populations that are unlikely to seek support. An example of an outreach effort is providing counseling services for sexual assault survivors. Yoshimura and Campbell (2016) advise that counselors should emphasize the physical, psychological, and emotional well-being of those that receive care. This approach encourages providers to speak with empathy and respect in order for students to feel supported and have a mutual understanding and positive intent with the counselor. Artime et al. (2018) also note the high utilization rates of counseling for students that have experienced sexual and physical assault. However, they also note that populations that tended to be younger and male underutilized counseling as a resource; therefore, special attention should be made for how to reach out to populations that underutilize counseling services.

4   Community-Based Collaboration and Response

As college student success and engagement not only includes the quality of classroom experience but also experiences outside of the classroom and within the campus community, it is critical for faculty and administrators to consider their role in creating and maintaining an environment that is meant to empower students and allow them to develop their sense of control and self-efficacy (Baier et al., 2019; Banyard & Cantor, 2004; Bohannon et al., 2019; Gutierrez & Gutierrez, 2019). Trauma survivors may come forward to faculty or student affairs professionals, especially when faced with dealing with their trauma histories and are in a new environment on their own after they leave home, even if family and friends from home can continue to serve as a social support system (Banyard & Cantor, 2004). However, some of these students may not seek assistance for a variety of reasons. As such, faculty and administrators are called to pay attention to changes in student behavior and performance and know when and how to refer a student.

In addition to recommending training for faculty and administrators to learn how to effectively respond to students who come forward and self-disclose difficult experiences, the authors also recommend collaborative efforts between faculty and student affairs administrators in the form of behavioral intervention teams (Banyard & Cantor, 2004; National Behavioral Intervention Team Association, 2018). A behavioral intervention team (BIT) is a group that can have a combination of faculty and administrative representatives for the purpose of providing early intervention for an individual that exhibits concerning behavior and may be struggling academically, emotionally, or psychologically (NaBITA, 2018). This group can direct student interventions by using a reporting system that can monitor student referrals, alerts, engagement, and wellness (Bohannon et al., 2019).

5   Method

Researchers performed a content analysis of websites from five colleges and universities. These institutions were selected through a search engine using terms such as 'BIT team' or 'CARE team.' Information that the researchers found were offices that were represented on the BIT/CARE teams, how potential reporters

TABLE 8.1 Institution profiles

Institution	Institution size	Type	Description	Region of US
S1	Very large	Public, four year, primarily non residential	Doctoral University: Very High Research Activity	Southeast
S2	Very large	Private, not for profit, four year, primarily residential	Doctoral University: Very High Research Activity	Midwest
S3	Very large	Public, four year, primarily residential	Doctoral University: Very High Research Activity	Northeast
S4	Very large	Public, four year, primarily residential	Doctoral University: Very High Research Activity	Midwest
S5	Medium	Private, not for profit, four year, highly residential	Doctoral/ Professional University	Southeast

were prompted on how to fill out a referral form and information needed, and overall messaging and themes from the websites. Table 8.1 provides institutional information of the websites reviewed (Carnegie Classifications, 2017).

Upon review, researchers identified notable words or phrases that were present throughout the websites. After these words or phrases were identified, researchers determined themes from open coding approach that were present within the website and across all the websites (Corbin & Strauss, 1990).

6 Findings

6.1 *Office Representation*

As Table 8.2 illustrates, the top five offices represented on a BIT/CARE team are the Dean of Students, Counseling Center, Campus Safety/Police Department, Student Conduct, and Housing and Residential Life. These offices likely

TABLE 8.2 Offices represented on BIT/CARE teams at five institutions

Offices represented	S1	S2	S3	S4	S5
Dean of Students	x	x	x	x	x
Counseling Center	x	x	x	x	x
Campus Safety/Police Department	x	x		x	x
Student Conduct	x	x	x		x
Housing and Residential Life	x	x	x	x	
Health Services	x	x			x
Disability Services	x	x	x		
Athletics		x	x		
Academic Services		x	x		
International Programs		x		x	
Provost		x		x	
Title IX		x	x		
Campus Ministry		x			x
Veteran Services	x				
Victim Advocacy	x				
Human Resources		x			
General Counsel		x			
Enrollment and Financial Services				x	
Diversity and Inclusion			x		

have high student contact, with staff members from offices such as Campus Safety/Police Department and Housing and Residential Life having to be first responders to student emergencies.

6.2 *Referral Forms*

All of the websites from the five institutions provided an online referral form. The referral form provides information that is sent to the BIT or CARE team for review. All five referral forms contained the prompts:
– Name of reporter and contact information
– Name of student of concern and contact information
– Time, date, location of witnessed incident
– Description of incident
– Uploading additional documentation (video, screenshots)

Three of the five institutions, S2, S4, and S5, had a section on the form where the reporter can indicate the type of concern. S2 listed concerns such as alcohol use, disruptive behavior, death, eating disorder, economic/financial, family issues, grief/loss, behavioral health concern, self-harm. S4 featured three categories of concern: academic, physical, and emotional. Finally, S5 featured two categories of concern, academic and behavioral.

6.3 Themes

Two themes emerged from the review of the five websites: communication and care. Within the referrals, reporters were prompted to describe behaviors in detail, examples, and use descriptive or objective language. Communication was operationalized through the emphasis on language and description of incidents. Care was operationalized through promoting the safety and wellness of the student of concern, providing support, and the BIT/CARE team follow up with the student of concern.

7 Discussion of Findings

Within the scope of this review, all five of the institutions reviewed provide a guide on examples of concerning behaviors that should be referred to the BIT or CARE teams. However, only one out of the five institutions offer trainings to campus stakeholders on how to identify concerning behaviors and provide referrals. As the review of literature noted, trainings are an area of further development that are necessary for faculty and administrators to develop a trauma-informed perspective.

The BIT and CARE team information reviewed showed that many of the representatives on the team tended to be from student affairs. This is not to suggest that there should be more academic or faculty representation on these teams, but depending on the organizational structure and complexities of a college or university, additional academic representation may be necessary, especially when there is concern over a student's continued persistence or retention at the institution. Notably, S2 listed representatives from undergraduate and graduate schools as being on the team, though these representatives would be called in on a case by case basis.

8 Recommendations

8.1 Training

With national trends showing declines in mental and emotional wellness and studies on prevalence of trauma survivors entering college, it is essential for faculty and administrators to develop a trauma-informed understanding and approach to foster an environment that allows students to develop resiliency (Banyard & Cantor, 2004; Shalka, 2019b). For this to occur, faculty and administrators need to understand how students endure trauma to respond appropriately (Frazier et al., 2009; Shalka, 2019b).

Training opportunities for faculty and administrators should extend beyond being able to identify concerning behaviors (Gutierrez & Gutierrez, 2019). Specifically related to the two themes, communication and care, faculty and administrators should be trained on how to establish a caring, student-centered environment, write a referral report, and have a working knowledge of on and off campus resources. Staff from Dean of Students office, campus safety, and counseling and health services can conduct trainings on writing referral reports and provide information on services offered to students, especially those who are trauma survivors. Baier et al. (2019) state that faculty and staff that receive training on building caring environments can help promote "self-efficacy and belonging for students" (p. 7). Finally, additional consideration should be made for students from underrepresented or marginalized social identities that may have experienced traumatic structural oppression. For instance, cultural competency training can inform how racial oppression and exclusion can be traumatic and impact students' ability to learn and establish relationships with peers and teachers (Blitz et al., 2020). Shalka (2019b) indicated how social identities can shape how students processed trauma exposure.

While BIT and CARE teams have representatives from counseling and health services that likely have the most experience in handling trauma survivors and providing TIC, we recommend that counseling professionals, internal or external, provide training for faculty and administrators on what it means to be trauma-informed when interacting with students and developing curriculum that may feature difficult topics. How students experience and process traumatic events are unique; therefore, interactions and interventions for trauma survivors should be carefully considered.

8.2 Theoretical Model for Trauma Informed Understanding

An adaptation of the Sanctuary Model in school settings offers a perspective to allow faculty and administrators to make sense of how trauma impacts school climate (Blitz et al., 2020). Originated by Bloom (1997), the Sanctuary Model emphasizes commitments to non-violence, emotional intelligence, open communication, social learning, democracy, social responsibility, and growth and change (Esaki et al., 2013). Blitz et al. (2020) state that Sanctuary can be adapted to focus on domains such as safety, emotions, learning, and family and guide practice for teaching, learning, and discipline to support students in their emotional and cognitive development.

8.3 *Programs to Be Adapted for Trauma Survivors in College*

As noted earlier in the chapter, transition to college can be fraught with challenges for someone not impacted by trauma. For a student carrying trauma, the challenges will likely increase. Research on high-school-based programs to aid, in particular, trauma-affected students' transition to college is minimal. However, a consideration of the values of three programs to help at-risk college students succeed and persist in college merits consideration for college administrators to reflect on how to apply them at their own institution.

First, the U.S. Department of Education's TRIO initiatives, born from President Johnson's War on Poverty and the Economic Opportunity Act of 1964, are a collection of three programs, two targeted to high school and the other to college, respectively: Educational Talent Search, Upward Bound, and Student Support Services. Designed to bring more students who are poor or members of racial and ethnic groups who were not attending college, these initiatives have helped to reverse the trends that prompted their conception. While different in nature, their common focus is academic remediation. However, accompanying the remediation are workshops on self-esteem, goal setting, and decision making facilitated by caring adults whose relationships with vulnerable students increase their motivation (Cowan Pitre & Pitre, 2009).

As mentioned, trauma-impacted students may experience reduced social support, which can be reversed in settings that prepare students for college including opportunities to meet and connect with peers and developing relationships with trusted adults that heal and redress earlier trauma. Additionally, as these peer and appropriate power relationships are developed, students who have been reluctant to discuss their trauma may be moved to disclose and begin some necessary healing.

Second, summer bridge programs at colleges and universities seek to resource rising freshmen with the necessary academic and support skills during the weeks prior to initial classes. A natural byproduct is the orientation to the physical space of the student's new campus home before large numbers of future classmates arrive.

A program at the University of North Carolina (UNC) focused on academic remediation and nonacademic factors that can impact student success and persistence. UNC hosted formal classes in math and English and various activities and services, including social bonding opportunities, counseling, mentoring, support labs (Wachen, Pretlow, & Dixon, 2018). As the TRIO practices that led to increasing enrollment rates of poor and underrepresented ethnic and minority groups could be adapted to aid trauma-impacted students, these summer bridge experiences could be planned for students vulnerable from trauma.

Third, the University of Washington's DO-IT Center has been developing programs since 1992 for people with disabilities. An acronym for disabilities, opportunities, internetworking, and technology, DO-IT's program was originally designed like the TRIO and summer bridge programs, with an emphasis on those who were differently abled. Three foci addressed preparing for college while in high school, staying in college, and preparing for life beyond it. In addition to the traditional support services and study skills, self-advocacy and self-management skills were taught to the students once enrolled (National Science Foundation, 1996). In particular, these two last sets of skills could aid trauma-impacted students in their work towards resiliency (Banyard & Cantor, 2004; Blitz et al., 2020; Shalka, 2019b). Colleges may find it beneficial to integrate these into their trauma-informed initiatives (National Science Foundation, 1996).

8.4 *Establishing BIT or CARE Team*

For institutions that are considering establishing a BIT or CARE team, institutions should consider the makeup of teams and resources needed (NaBITA, 2018). A SWOT (strengths, weaknesses, opportunities, and threats) analysis can identify strengths and gaps in services. Once this analysis is completed, institutions determine how to form their BIT or CARE teams with the following questions and considerations (NaBITA, 2018):

– What is the mission and vision of the team? How do the team goals fulfill the mission and vision?
– Who are the college/university members who will be on the team?
– What types of backgrounds and expertise will be needed? Some suggestions: mental wellness, student affairs, campus safety, student conduct, human resources, academics, athletics, international student services, spiritual counseling, art therapy, and veteran affairs.
– What are the responsibilities of each team member?
– How does the team establish themselves with one another and with campus constituents to build rapport and trust?
– How does the team define concerning behavior?
– What kind of rubric will be used to assess behaviors and determine interventions?
– What data system management will track interventions and assignments?
– How can the team promote education and training to campus community on supportive resources to help students with academics and wellness?

9   Limitations

The content analysis of these websites provide insight as to what exists at the time of retrieval and review of information. As this information was publicly available, this information can be readily accessed and reviewed with ease. Disadvantages of content analysis are that information may be or become out of date, the documents were not created for research purposes, and any themes gathered are limited to the institution websites that were reviewed (Berg & Lune, 2012).

References

Aarstad-Martin, S., & Boyraz, G. (2017). Posttraumatic stress, risky drinking, and prescription drug misuse in trauma-exposed college students. *Journal of Loss and Trauma*, 22(7), 599–612.

Anotale, E. (2013, May 28). Generation Z: Rebels with a cause. *Forbes*. http://www.forbes.com/sites/onmarketing/2013/05/28/generation-z-rebels-with-a-cause/#31f097ba6aa1

Artime, T. A., Buchholz, K. R., & Jakupcak, M. (2019). Mental health symptoms and treatment utilization among trauma-exposed college students. *Psychological Trauma: Theory, Research, and Policy*, 11(3), 274–282.

Baier, S. T., Gonzales, S. M., & Sawilowsky, S. S. (2019). Classroom learning communities' impact on students in developmental courses. *Journal of Developmental Education*, 42(3), 2–28.

Banyard, V. L., & Cantor, E. N. (2004). Adjustment to college among trauma survivors: An exploratory study of resilience. *Journal of College Student Development*, 4(2), 207–221.

Berg, B. L., & Lune, H. (2012). *Qualitative research methods for the social sciences* (8th ed.). Allyn and Bacon.

Blitz, L. V., Yull, D., & Clauhs, M. (2020). Brining sanctuary to school: Assessing school climate as a foundation for culturally responsive trauma-informed approaches for urban schools. *Urban Education*, 55(1), 95–124.

Bloom, S. L. (1997). *Creating sanctuary: Toward the evolution of sane societies*. Routledge.

Bohannon, L., Clapsaddle, S., & McCollum, D. (2019). Responding to college students who exhibit adverse manifestations of stress and trauma in the college classroom. *FIRE: Forum for International Research in Education*, 5(2), 66–78.

Boylan, H. R. (1999). Exploring alternatives to remediation. *Journal of Developmental Education*, 22(3), 2–11.

Boyraz, G., & Waits, J. B. (2018). Interpersonal trauma and physical health symptoms in college students: Mediating effects of substance use and self-blame. *Journal of Loss and Trauma, 23*(1), 70–87.

Canto, A. I., Swanbrow Becker, M., Cox, B. E., Hayden, S., & Osborn, D. (2017). College students in crisis: Prevention, identification, and response options for campus housing professionals, *Journal of College and University Student Housing, 43*(2), 44–57.

Carello, J., & Butler, L. D. (2014). Potentially perilous pedagogies: Teaching trauma is not the same as trauma-informed teaching. *Journal of Trauma & Dissociation, 15*(2), 153–168.

Carello, J., & Butler, L. D. (2015). Practicing what we teach: Trauma-informed educational practice. *Journal of Teaching in Social Work, 35*(3), 262–278.

Carnegie Classification. (2017). *Size & setting classification description.* The Carnegie Classification of Institutions of Higher Education. https://carnegieclassifications.iu.edu/classification_descriptions/size_setting.php

Corbin, J., & Strauss, A. (1990). Grounded theory research: Procedures, canons, and evaluative criteria. *Qualitative Sociology, 13*(1), 3–21.

Cowan Pitre, C., & Pitre, P. (2009). Increasing underrepresented high school students' college transitions and achievements: TRIO opportunities. *NASSP Bulletin, 93*(2), 96–110.

Dupont, S. (2015, May 1). *Move over millennials, here comes Generation Z: Understanding the new realists who are building the future.* Public Relations Tactics. https://www.prsa.org/Intelligence/Tactics/Articles/ view/11057/1110Move_Over_Millennials_Here_Comes_Generation_Z_Unde#.Xlf6tRNKjMl

Eagan, K., Stolzenberg, E. B., Bates, A. K., Aragon, M. C., Suchard, M. R., & Rios-Aguilar, C. (2015). *The American freshman: National norms fall 2015.* Higher Education Research Institute, UCLA.

Eagan, K., Stolzenberg, E. B., Zimmerman, H. B., Aragon, M. C., Sayson, H. W., & Rios-Aguilar, C. (2017). *The American freshman: National norms fall 2016.* Higher Education Research Institute, UCLA.

Esaki, N., Benamati, J., Yanosy, S., Middleton, J. S., Hopson, L. M., Hummer, V. L., & Bloom, S. L. (2013). The sanctuary model: Theoretical framework. *Families in Society: The Journal of Contemporary Social Services, 94*(2), 87–95. doi:10.1606/1044-3894.4287

Fiorillo, D., & Follette, V. M. (2012). Cumulative trauma. In C. Figely (Ed.), *Encyclopedia of trauma: An interdisciplinary guide* (pp. 187–189). Sage.

Ford, J. D., Fallot, R., & Harris, M. (2009). Group therapy. In *Treating complex traumatic stress disorders: An evidence-based guide* (pp. 415–440). Guilford Press.

Frazier, P., Anders, S., Perera, S., Tomich, P., Tennen, H., Park, C., & Tashiro, T. (2009). Traumatic events among undergraduate students: Prevalence and associated symptoms. *Journal of Counseling Psychology, 56*(3), 450.

Galatzer-Levy, I. R., Burton, C. L., & Bonanno, G. A. (2012). Coping flexibility, potentially traumatic life events, and resilience: A prospective study of college student adjustment. *Journal of Social and Clinical Psychology, 31*(6), 542–567.

Gubi, A. A., Strait, J., Wycoff, K., Vega, V., Brauser, B., & Osman, Y. (2019). Trauma-informed knowledge and practices in school psychology: A pilot study and review. *Journal of Applied School Psychology, 35*(2), 176–199.

Gutierrez, D., & Gutierrez, A. (2019). Developing a trauma-informed lens in the college classroom and empowering students through building positive relationships. *Contemporary Issues in Education Research, 12*(1), 11–18.

Han, S., Dean, M., & Okoroji, C. (2018). Minority student experiences in a living and learning community on a predominantly white college campus. *Journal of Ethnographic & Qualitative Research, 13*(2), 107–121.

Keller-Dupree, E. A. (2013). Understanding childhood trauma: Ten reminders for preventing retraumatization. *The Practitioner Scholar: Journal of Counseling and Professional Psychology, 2*(1), 1–11.

Kuhl, M., & Boyraz, G. (2017). Mindfulness, general trust, and social support among trauma-exposed college students. *Journal of Loss and Trauma 22*(2), 150–162.

Lenning, O. T., & Ebbers, L. H. (1999). The powerful potential of learning communities: Improving education for the future. *ASHE-ERIC Higher Education Report, 26*(6), 3–173.

Lesher, A. F., Kelly, C. M., Schutz, K. E., & Foy, D. W. (2012). In C. Figely (Ed.), *Encyclopedia of trauma: An interdisciplinary guide* (pp. 570–573). Sage.

National Behavioral Intervention Team Association (NaBITA). (2018). *NaBITA standards for behavioral intervention teams*. https://cdn.nabita.org/website-media/nabita.org/wordpress/wp-content/uploads/2018/08/NaBITA-Standards-FINAL-2.pdf

National Science Foundation. (1996). *College: You can do it!* DO-IT Program.

Nicholls, J. (2017, May 15). 6 reasons your teen's life is more stressful than your own. *The Washington Post*. https://www.washingtonpost.com/news/parenting/wp/2017/05/15/6-reasons-your-teens-life-is-more-stressful-than-your-own/?noredirect=on&utm_term=.17f6c4f9d034

Read, J. P., Ouimette, P., White, J., Colder, C., & Farrow, S. (2011). Rates of DSM–IV–TR trauma exposure and posttraumatic stress disorder among newly matriculated college students. *Psychological Trauma: Theory, Research, Practice, and Policy, 3*(2), 148–156. http://dx.doi.org/10.1037/a0021260

Seemiller, C., & Grace, M. (2019). *Generation Z: A century in the making*. Sage Publications.

Shalka, T. R. (2019a). Mapping the intersections of gender and college trauma. *International Journal of Qualitative Studies in Education, 32*(6), 560–575. https://doi.org/10.1080/09518398.2019.1597207

Shalka, T. R. (2019b). Saplings in the hurricane: A grounded theory of college trauma and identity development. *The Review of Higher Education, 42*(2), 739–764.

Siegel, E. (2016). Generation Z goes to college: An interview with the author. *Learn Forward*. http://learnforwardblog.orgsync.com/generation-z-goes-to-college-interview-with-the-author/

Slaninova, G., & Stainerova, M. (2015). Trauma as a component of the self-concept of undergraduates. *Procedia – Social and Behavioral Sciences, 171*, 465–471. https://doi:10.1016/j.sbspro.2015.01.148

Stolzenberg, E. B. (2018, September 6). *The mental and physical well-being of incoming freshmen: Three decades of research*. https://www.higheredtoday.org/2018/09/06/mental-physical-well-incoming-freshmen-three-decades-research/

Stolzenberg, E. B., Eagan, M. K., Zimmerman, H. B., Berdan Lozano, J., Cesar-Davis, N. M., Aragon, M. C., & Rios-Aguilar, C. (2019). *Undergraduate teaching faculty: The HERI faculty survey 2016–2017*. Higher Education Research Institute (HERI), UCLA.

Tinto, V. (2006). Research and practice of student retention: What next? *Journal of College Student Retention: Research, Theory & Practice, 8*(1), 1–19. https://doi.org/10.2190/4YNU-4TMB-22DJ-AN4W

Twenge, J. M. (2017). Have smartphones destroyed a generation? *The Atlantic*. https://www.theatlanic.com/magazine/archive/2017/09/has-thesmartphone-destroyed-a-generation/534198/

Vrana, S., & Lauterbach, D. (1994). Prevalence of trauma events and post-traumatic psychological symptoms in a nonclinical sample of college students. *Journal of Traumatic Stress, 7*(2), 289–302. https://doi.org/10.1007/BF02102949

Wachen, J., Pretlow, J., & Dixon, K. G. (2018). Building college readiness: Exploring the effectiveness of the UNC academic bridge summer program. *Journal of Student Retention: Research, Theory & Practice, 20*(1), 116–138. https://doi.org/10.1177/1521025116649739

Wiedmer, T. (2015). Generations do differ: Best practices in leading traditionalists, boomers, and Generations X, Y, Z. *The Delta Kappa Gamma Bulletin: International Journal for Professional Educators, 82*(1), 51–58.

Yoshimura, C. G., & Campbell, K. B. (2016). Interpersonal violence and sexual assault: Trauma-informed communication approaches in university counseling centers. *Journal of College Student Psychotherapy, 30*(4), 300–312. https://doi.org/10.1080/87568225.2016.1221720

Zhao, C. M., & Kuh, G. D. (2004). Adding value: Learning communities and student engagement. *Research in higher education, 45*(2), 115–138.

CHAPTER 9

Trauma-Informed Classrooms
An Empathic Approach

Vanessa Smith-Washington and Edna Aurelus

Abstract

A traumatic event can have a long-lasting effect on an individual's overall growth and development. Because individuals exposed to trauma may be impacted in different ways, and trauma may manifest in different forms, there is a continuous need to learn from professionals from different fields and with an array of experiences related to trauma.

This chapter highlights the individual perspectives of two professors training professionals working in fields exposed to individuals that have experienced or are currently exposed too or experiencing trauma in their lives. The overall goal of the chapter is to consider how these personal insights and reflections can help readers consider how different perspectives and lenses may inform overall practice. Empathy, a common link between both professionals, is also discussed.

The chapter calls upon readers to consider their own personal insights and reflections in order to reflect upon different lenses that can inform decisions of practice.

Keywords

empathy – psychological safety – novice special education – pre-service teachers – in-service teachers – teacher preparation – inclusion – diversity – professional development – behavior – mentoring

1   Empathy and Teachers' Readiness: Reflections of an Education Professor

Students will always remember how a teacher made them feel. Ways in which teachers connect and support students exposed to daily trauma and stressors can make a difference in students' overall social-emotional and academic growth. Feelings of insecurity, not feeling cared for, and lack of trust for adults are barriers that prevent students from learning and feeling comfortable enough to accept outside help. Understanding students' narratives can provide teachers with important insights on ways to address the individual needs of students exposed to trauma. When teachers are empathetic to students' experiences, they are mindful that students are experiencing "something meaningful" (Moring, n.d., #5).

Empathy has been defined in many ways. One way in particular that captures my best understanding of empathy is to *"walk in someone's shoes"* and understand what that person is going through. In discussing how empathy can be expressed by others, Makoelle (2019) identifies two forms: *emotional* (or affective) empathy, or the sharing of the emotions experienced, and *cognitive empathy, or* the ability to understand a situation, experience, or emotion from the point of view of another person. Many teachers use emotional and cognitive empathy to help students with diverse backgrounds, emotional difficulties, and learning difficulties (p. 2). Teachers who understand the cultural, environmental, and psychological needs of their students are able to make a difference in the students' lives. This understanding enables pre-service and in-service teachers who have been reluctant or do not know how to work with students exposed to trauma to deepen their relationship with their students and make connections.

Makoelle (2019) points out how empathy is often regarded as a social skill, and how teachers have the ability to imagine and understand what their students are going through. When teachers demonstrate skills such as becoming good listeners, showing interest and enthusiasm, and engaging in positive interaction with their students, eventually misbehavior will gradually change (p. 3). Morin (n.d.) adds that empathy can be viewed as … "a way of connecting with other people that shows you understand that they're experiencing something meaningful, even though you may not understand exactly how it feels for them" (#6), and emphasizes that developing empathy for students' experiences requires educators to consider the "four parts of empathy: perspective taking, putting aside judgment, trying to understand the students' feelings, and communicating that you understand" (#12).

McDonald and Messinger (2011) discuss how when individuals are able to "feel or imagine another person's emotional experience" it becomes a growth in "social and emotional development" (p. 2). The relationship can develop if the teacher and the student are willing. Students suffering from trauma have difficulty forming positive relationships and adjusting to the classroom environment. Accordingly, it is essential for teachers to create a safe and supportive environment for all students to succeed. The teacher, classmates, and the classroom become a safe haven. Students suffering from trauma need teachers who care and want the best for their students, take the time to listen and put themselves in the students' shoes to find solutions. Empathy is the heart of a great classroom (Owen, 2015).

The need for teachers to work collaboratively with students and families, school support teams, outside community programs and to help students cope with the crisis in their lives, is imperative. Based on the experiences of the author, most families are often appreciative when ongoing collaboration and resources are provided to target a specific need of a student. Ways in which "action plans" with families are developed can help target short and long-term goals more effectively. A teacher's role in shaping a student's behavior and providing a sense of security in the classroom is critical to a student's socio-emotional and academic success. Many pre-service and in-service special education and general education teachers in diverse and inclusive classrooms are not fully knowledgeable about how to focus on the various emotional, cognitive and behavioral challenges students bring to school. This is where empathetic thinking comes into play. Empathy is a useful skill to help teachers understand how to handle students' misbehaviors, such as outbursts or physical aggression in the classroom. Teachers' understanding of students' feelings and ability to be empathetic increases the likelihood that they will be calm and able to handle the situations and resume routines.

Studies on teachers' attitudes towards students with challenging behaviors revealed that teachers are less willing to accommodate students with intellectual delays and severe behavior problems into their inclusive classroom, and that they expressed negative attitudes towards students with emotional or behavioral difficulties (Krischler & Pit-ten Cate, 2019). Furthermore, research highlighting pre-service and in-service teachers revealed that teachers were more likely to accept students with learning disabilities and physical challenges in their classrooms and veteran teachers were described as less likely to be accepting of students with challenges related to behavior. This alarming information suggests that some teachers are unsympathetic towards students who have traumatic lives (Meyers et al., 2019). Learner's First (2016), examined novice special education and general education teachers in diverse and inclusive settings and pointed out how teachers often struggle with finding ways to engage students with severe social-emotional and cognitive delays. This suggests that inexperience and a lack of training limits novice teachers' ability to understand how trauma can impact a student's learning.

In each of the above studies, teachers in inclusive and diverse classroom settings with limited experience often found it difficult to understand the social emotional struggles of students dealing with trauma. Schools often target empathy training for pre-service and in-service special education and general education teachers in the hope that teachers will learn new ways to help students become better citizens, learn from others, and share experiences. Whichever training method is used, teachers, school-based administrators, and district leaders recognize the importance of empathy training as a method that can be used to change students' behavior.

Teaching preK-12 students about empathy has been extremely successful in helping develop students' socio-emotional skills. This can lead to reducing bullying, and allow students in diverse and inclusive classrooms to learn how to create positive and productive changes in their lives. Through a series of ongoing professional development activities throughout the school year, in-service teachers' knowledge about empathy in a trauma-informed classroom becomes an important part of their pedagogical repertoire. School leaders and other staff play a major role in supporting, creating, and implementing professional development training.

Parchomiuk (2019) describes empathy as a personality attribute involving the capacity to respond emotionally, cognitively, and communicatively to other persons without loss of objectivity. Trauma-informed teaching is not a curriculum, set of prescribed strategies, or something that needs to be added to a checklist. However, it is the awareness of knowing your students' emotions and allowing them to freely express themselves and feel a sense of safety in the classroom.

Pre-service teachers, novice in-service special education teachers, and general education teachers can use a variety of social emotional strategies to provide students with a feeling of safety. Social emotional strategies can be developed through the use of art, mindfulness practice, role-playing, gestalt techniques, and imitative play, students can learn about empathy for themselves and others in order to focus on perspective taking and emotional self-regulatory behaviors (Gerdes et al., 2013).

Empathy training does not typically exist as a separate course in teacher preparation programs, typically embedded within course discussions. Many teachers are skilled at finding books and other resources related to the various ways to teach about empathy and it is not uncommon for teachers to focus on serving as role models to support specific behaviors. When training related to empathy is specifically provided to educators, the focus has generally been on specific strategies and techniques to support students (Croft, Coggshall, Powera, & Killion, 2010), but not necessarily on teachers' development of their own empathetic efficacy. Today's teachers are aware that they play a major role in influencing their students and are seeking positive ways to help their students by targeting their own knowledge, skills, and overall efficacy related to the topic.

There are many effective ways in which teachers can learn about empathy. During school-based professional development, teachers can be provided with opportunities to learn from experts and learn along with and from their peers about empathy. These best practices can be used to teach teachers how to show students that they care and value them both in their role as students and, in general, as people. Working with teachers in teams during professional development is another best practice that can be used to teach teachers about empathy. Research suggests that working with teams is one effective way to collaborate with other teachers. Glaze (2014) notes that it is important for teachers to work together. Teachers have a stressful and challenging job. At times, their stress and anxiety can be reduced when they are engaged in activities that allow them the opportunity to share their ideas and collaborate with others. However, professional development can look differently in each school. Schools might consider exploring a variety of ways that will help to find the best type of professional development training to fit the needs of special education teachers and in-service general education teachers.

There are many best practices that can help build empathy in teachers and students. For example, another effective method known as SEL: Social Emotional Learning is a commercially developed program. SEL was designed by two organizations known as the Empathy Fellowship. The program is "a time-bound learning experience that engages cohorts of educators in professional development and is designed to teach teachers, students and school personnel how to build empathy in the classrooms and the entire school" (Otto, 2019, #4). There are several interesting components of SEL. These program components include a virtual program that can be used by both teachers and school personnel. Also, SEL engages cohorts of educators in professional development blended or online for three months around a virtual exchange. The objective of the SEL program is to increase teachers' abilities to build empathy in their classrooms and outside the classroom.

SEL gives teachers an opportunity to collaborate. SEL is a commercially made program and teachers can receive professional development training at their schools and they do not have to travel to a different location. As teachers work in teams, teachers and students learn to identify and to focus on their needs and to share ideas with others. Teachers find the SEL program appealing because they can work with many teachers in teams to brainstorm, foster new ideas and increase creativity. Another appealing feature in the SEL program allows teachers the opportunity to receive training from familiar faculty members, school administrators or district level staff developers during the workday. SEL also has benefits for school district leaders, as well. It allows teachers an opportunity to connect to many other teachers globally, discuss and learn about empathy. The SEL program has many components that are beneficial to school and district staff to develop faculty and students' understanding about empathy.

Training teachers about empathy may seem challenging to some but it is necessary. Teachers are routinely faced with student crises and do their best to help their students. Teachers rarely have much time, but they do receive training in their schools through professional development and college courses on how to address and identify when their students are faced with trauma. These courses and training opportunities must embed opportunities to consider how empathy must serve as a foundation to pedagogy.

2 Health Care Training and Empathy: Reflections from a Nursing Professor[1]

Empathy is an important attribute that needs to be made mandatory in healthcare training programs. Training for healthcare providers focuses on exhibiting skills that are important factors of empathy. Skills like non-judgmental approach, self-awareness and mutual respect are all important factors required when applying empathy. College students who receive healthcare training with the integration of empathy are likely to provide quality care to all patients without any judgment or biases. Empathy can help prevent social biases and help with the promotion of others' integrity and respect. When empathy is applied during the delivery of care, patients seem to feel safer and display more trust toward their providers.

Implication of empathy in healthcare training is not new to the healthcare system. For a psychiatric mental health provider, empathy is required to be part of the treatment plan. Every psychiatric mental health student is mandated to learn about empathy. Teachers are aware of incorporating empathy in the course curriculum in order to assure that students are well educated and skilled about the concept. Empathy in healthcare training is a guarantee that the public will receive quality care and build excellent relationships and rapport with their healthcare providers.

3 A Psychological Safety Approach

Psychological safety, according to Khan William (1990), is the ability to show and employ one's self without fear of negative consequences of self-image, status or career. Five decades ago, the term psychological safety was first mentioned to express how people interact with each other in difficult environments. Psychological safety today is seen as especially important for enabling learning and change in contexts characterized by high stakes, complexity, and essential human interactions, such as hospital operating rooms (Edmondson, Bohmer, & Pisano, 2001). Although it would make sense why psychological safety would be important in settings like a hospital operating rooms, where critical human thinking is extremely mandated, classrooms require a similar approach. Therefore, psychological safety is not only beneficial in healthcare settings, but also within the academic settings such as the classrooms, or any setting where human interaction is in process.

For learners in healthcare settings, ability to speak freely among peers about challenging concepts as well as about interactions with patients, peers, and various healthcare professionals is crucial for the development of essential knowledge, skills, and appropriate interactions. Particularly in instances when traumatic situations have been part of an experience under discussion, the maintenance of an environment of psychological safety aids in promoting interactions. Principles of psychological safety are integrated into the second author's own college classroom. College students are aware that they have the freedom to express themselves without the fear or feeling that other students will ridicule them. Psychological safety allows all students to feel confident and valued. This is evident in students' comments during our conversations. They feel less stressed in classroom discussions and their assignment results effectively reveal that under less stress and anxiety, they definitely retain the information. As shown in numerous studies, psychological safety, defined as the degree to which people view the environment as conducive to interpersonally risky behaviors like speaking up or asking for help, is a salient variable in work environments in which learning matters (Edmondson & Lei, 2014).

4   The Importance of Inclusion and Diversity

Psychological safety is particularly relevant in classroom environments that are diverse and inclusive. When students understand the notion that each individual has a set of unique traits and diverse characteristics, it becomes easier to accept behaviors and social norms that are different from their own. When students participate in settings predicated on principles of empathy and psychological safety, the notion of inclusion and diversity become embedded in the environment and, accordingly, is easier to understand and put into practice. Psychological safety is relevant to settings beyond classrooms. As students in healthcare professions participate in clinical, internship, or preceptorship rotation, they constantly interact with a diverse group of people in a variety of settings. Their knowledge of psychological safety is likely to be key to successful interactions and can positively impact others in diverse and inclusive contexts.

With the proliferation of information technology, humans are condemned to live closer to each other. That type of cohabitation gives rise to the obligation to understand and learn from each other. Learning about and understanding each other's upbringing and background provides one the resources to avoid peer biases. It is important and fair to understand that when debating about inclusion and diversity one will be faced with a lot of push back resistance. For example, a department within a large institution may complain of not having enough budget to accommodate extra supplies for a student who is a nursing mother. Therefore, the student may feel rejected and not valued as a human being because of her current situation.

Humans tend to feel comfortable with routine behavior, and when they are forced to adapt to a potential change, retaliations are often the results. Some of the vivid memories of my elementary school were not so pleasant. Students who could not learn at a faster pace with the rest of the class were marginalized. They were placed in the back row as a statement that they were less competent than the rest of the class. Those students at times could be seen in the schoolyard, isolated because they felt different than the rest. The amount of trauma that those students potentially will have to face during their adulthood is unknown. It was a failure on the educator's part to purposely create such a hostile environment for those students. The world is evolving at a high speed and we must dynamically conform to the ethical changes or we will be left behind with the traditional views that were oftentimes homogeneous.

These changes bring forth hope that people's mindset is evolving; therefore society as a whole can also be changed. Inclusion and diversity approaches allowed both the instructor and students to be more tolerant and sensitive as human beings. It is okay to ask questions if one is not familiar with a certain population or behavior. It is better to ask questions than to assume and treat someone poorly. If a student's behavior is different from the norm, it is permissible to approach the student in a non-judgmental way in order to prevent any expression of refusal or emotional pain. The importance of inclusion and diversity stems back to the antidiscrimination movement in employment in the United States in the 1940s. However, in the 1990's the American Disabilities Act (ADA) was enacted as the first law to endorse the right of individuals with disabilities and those who decided to seek employment. It is a relief to know that there is a legal requirement for something as important as inclusion and diversity. The ADA can also be applied in the classroom. However, supporting the development of a healthy relationship between people with and without disabilities and a more inclusive culture requires the ability and effort to engage them in a mind-change process (Shady & Larson, 2010). Concluding that we are all different from each other will exhibit mutual respect that eventually will result in an inclusion and diversity mindset in the classroom.

5   Exploring Students' Outcomes

How can a disposition as important as empathetic thinking and response be measured in classrooms? We can teach someone how to be empathetic, however the act of applying what is learned is personal and individual. While we are aware that measuring students' outcome can be a challenge, it is important to know that personal observation made in the classrooms can be used to determine whether or not students' behavior have been respectful and positive reciprocally. Anecdotal evidence has proven that students' comfort level has grown from the first day they attend class. In classroom discussion, they verbalize how they feel confident and how they look forward to the next class. As a health professional, teaching in the classroom, an assessment tool used in the classroom to evaluate if empathy in the classroom is effective is a pre-and-post reflective paper asking students to explain their anticipated experience in the classroom. Many students often express a fear of not being familiar with the subject and fear of feeling intimidated to express themselves among other peers. At the end of the course, the same paper is given to students asking them to express their experience in the classroom and a common theme is that they felt very understood and free to express their concerns without any fears. Hence, the goal of an empathic approach was realized. The goal is to make students feel empowered, while guiding them on the right track. Empathy in the classrooms is extremely important to decrease fear and anxiety in students. The more confident students feel in the classroom, the better the success rate will be. As educators with a healthcare background, students often refer to the profession as a dignified profession, therefore it is our responsibility to exemplify ethical and empathetic approach to all students. Adapting to psychological safety allows our students to become more empathetic towards each other.

The empathy, psychological safety, inclusion, and diversity topics are often reiterated in the classrooms to assure that all students have the same right to participate in class discussions without any fear that someone will ridicule them because of their differences. Aside from their positive verbal feedback, students' evaluations often reflect their satisfaction with the positive atmosphere in the classroom. Goroshit and Hen (2016) indicated that empathetic teachers were found to possess a higher level of morality and the ability to communicate more successfully with their students. An individual who is not limited in learning about others' backgrounds is more likely to be empathetic to other people. However, those who choose to be conservative in their ideology of homogeneity often do not respond well to the idea of empathy beyond their own environment.

6   The Importance of a Non-judgmental Approach

Training a person to be non-judgmental requires constant self-reflection. It is a conscious technique that needs to be adapted in order to prevent biased opinion towards someone else. Empathy requires a broad understanding of the other parties in question. Approaching students in a non-judgmental manner has nothing to do with being less productive as a professional. Rather, it is an approach that facilitates and triggers confidence in a person. Students can be redirected or instructed in an understanding manner that allows them to feel that they are understood and valued by their instructors. An observation made from the classroom is that students' participation increases once they learn that they will not be judged on the questions asked. A non-judgmental environment undoubtedly promotes students' confidence and increases class participation. For example, if a student constantly pulls her hair while taking an exam, before asking the student to stop the behavior, the best approach would be to understand the reason why she repeatedly pulls her hair. If the student indicates that pulling her hair makes her feel less anxious during the exam, acknowledging understanding of the behavior will put the student at ease to be more productive during the exam. An important concept one needs to understand in a daily routine is that we have more similarities than differences with the simple fact that we are all human beings. The non-judgmental approach helps teachers and health professionals to self-reflect, a mechanism of the empathic approach used prior to direct conscious judgment. Our goal as educators and health providers is to provide quality services to all without any reserve.

A judgmental approach can incite a traumatic experience. For example, if a student attempts to ask a question and the instructor insinuates that the question is an "irrelevant question," that can create an atmosphere where the student can be ridiculed by peers or simply can embarrass the student. Therefore, using this approach is a mechanism of action for psychological safety, which in turn will impact greatly empathy. The implication of psychological safety while using empathy can result in preventing emotional trauma in the classrooms. More awareness of this concept needs to be promoted to bring about its positive outcome.

7 Conclusion

From the educator's perspective, empathy creates much needed trust between teachers and students and opportunities for dialogue. The use of an empathetic approach, instead of a punitive approach to help students, is beneficial for reducing classroom bullying and promoting a safe environment for both the teachers and students.

Like the educator, the health professional found that the use of empathy in the classroom has positive results. In the health professional's perspective, empathy triggers psychological safety in the classroom, allowing students to feel comfortable and confident in their discussion participation. Such an outcome is mutually beneficial for the students and the teacher in the classroom environment. The result of an empathetic teaching technique, per the health professional, assures the public that those students once graduated will have a non-judgmental approach towards other people. Additionally, these health professionals will provide quality care to all without biases.

Note

1   The author's use of students refers to healthcare students in the professor's college course, not preK-12 students.

References

American Psychological Association. (2008). *Children and trauma: Update for mental health professionals.* https://www.apa.org/pi/families/resources/children-trauma-update

Armstrong, A. C., Armstrong, D., & Spandagou, I. (2011). Inclusion by choice or by chance? *International Journal of Inclusive Education, 15*(1), 29–39. https://doi.org/10.1080/13603116.2010.496192

Badar, J., & Kauffman, J. M. (2014). Inclusion should be the central issue in special education: An alternative view from the USA. *Journal of International Special Needs Education*, *17*(1), 13–20.

Barr, J. (2013). Student-teachers' attitudes toward students with disabilities: Associations with contact and empathy. *International Journal of Education and Practice*, *1*(8), 87–100.

Berardi, A., & Morton, B. M. (2019). *Trauma-informed school practices: Building expertise to transform schools*. George Fox University Library.

Bouton, B. (2016). Empathy research and teacher preparation: Benefits and obstacles. *Southeastern Regional Association of Teacher Educators Journal*, *5*(2), 16–25.

Brooks, R. (2016, June 15). *Improving teacher empathy to improve student behavior*. http://www.drrobertbrooks.com/improving-teacher-empathy-improve-student-behavior/

Brotherson, M. J., Peck, N. F., & Maude, S. P. (2015). Understanding preschool teachers' perspectives on empathy: A qualitative inquiry. *Early Childhood Education Journal*, *43*, 169–173. https://doi.org/10.1007/s10643-014-0648-3

Cherry, K., & Morin, A. (2020, May 2). *What is empathy?* Very well mind. https://www.verywellmind.com/what-is-empathy-2795562

Croft, A., Coggshall, J. G., Dolan, M., Powers, E., & Killion, J. (2010, April). *Job embedded professional development: What it is, who is responsible, and how to get it done well* [Issue Brief]. National Comprehensive Center for Teacher Quality. https://files.eric.ed.gov/fulltext/ED520830.pdf

Crowley, B., & Saide, B. (2016, January 20). Building empathy in classrooms and schools. *Education Week*. https://www.edweek.org/leadership/opinion-building-empathy-in-classrooms-and-schools/2016/01

Edmondson, A. C., Bohmer, R. M., & Pisano, G. P. (2001). Disrupted routines: Team learning new technology implementation in hospitals. *Sage Journals*, *46*(4), 685–716. https://doi.org/:10.2307/3094828

Edmondson, A. C., Higgins, M., Singer, S., & Weiner, J. (2016). Understanding psychological safety in health care and education organizations: A comparative perspective. *Research in Human Development*, *13*(1), 65–83. https://doi:10.1080/15427609.2016.1141280

Edmondson, A. C., & Lei, Z. (2014). Psychological safety: The history, renaissance, and future of an interpersonal construct. *Annual Review of Organizational Psychology and Organizational Behavior*, *1*, 23–43.

For Educators: How to build empathy and strengthen your school. (2018, November 1). *Making caring common*. The President and Fellows of Harvard College. https://www.mcc.gse.harvard.edu

Gerdes, K., Segal, E. A., Jackson, K. F., & Mullins, J. L. (2013). Teaching empathy: A framework rooted in social cognitive neuroscience and social justice. *Journal of Social Work Education, 47*(1), 109–131.

Glaze, S. (2014, May 16). *For effective schools, teamwork is not optional.* Edutopia. https://www.edutopia.org/blog/effective-schools-teamwork-not-optional-sean-glaze

Goroshit, M., & Hen, M. (2016). Teachers' empathy: Can it be predicted by self-efficacy? *Teachers and Teaching, 22*(7), 805–818. https://doi:org/10.1080/13540602.2016.1185818

Ha, D., & Park, W. (2014). The relationship among teachers' empathy, communication style and coping type for students with attention deficit hyperactivity disorder. *Journal of Korean Academy of Psychiatric and Mental Health Nursing, 23*(2), 103–112.

Johnson, S. (2019, February 19). *The science of empathy: What researchers want teachers to know.* EdSurge. https://www.edsurge.com/news/2019-02-19-the-science-of-empathy-what-researchers-want-teachers-to-know

Khan, W. A. (1990). Psychological conditions of personal engagement and disengagement at work. *The Academy of Management Journal, 33*(4), 692–724.

Krischkler, M. (2019). Pre-and-inservice teachers' attitudes towards students with learning difficulties and changing behavior. *Frontiers Psychology, 10,* 327. https://doi.org/10.3389/fpsyg.2019.00327

Learner's First. (2016). *For educators: How to build empathy and strengthen your school.* www.mcc.gse.harvard.edu

Making and Caring Commons. (2020). *Raising kids who care about others and the common good.* https://mcc.gse.harvard.edu/about/mission

Makoelle, T. M. (2019). Teacher empathy: A prerequisite for an inclusive Classroom. In M. Peters (Ed.), *Encyclopedia of teacher education.* Springer. https://doi.org/10.1007/978-981-13-1179-6_43-1

McDonald, N. M., & Messenger, D. S. (2011). *The development of empathy: How, when, and why.* http://local.psy.miami.edu/faculty/dmessinger/c_c/rsrcs/rdgs/emot/McDonald-Messinger_Empathy%20Development.pdf

Meyers, S., Rowel, K., Wells, M., & Smith, B. C. (2019). Teacher empathy: A model of empathy for teaching for student success. *College Teaching, 67,* 3. https://doi:10.1080/87567555.2019.1579699

Middle Level Education Research Special Interest Group. (2016). *The MLER SIG research agenda.* https://mlersig.net/research/mler-sig-research-agenda

Miller, S. R. (2013). A curriculum focused on informed empathy improves attitudes toward persons with disabilities. *Perspectives on Medical Education, 2*(3), 114–125. https://doi:10.1007/s40037-013-0046-3

Mizel, H. (2010). *Why professional development matters.* Learning Forward. www.learningforward.org/advancing/whypdmatters.cfm

Morin, A. (n.d.). *Teaching with empathy: Why it is important.* Understood. https://www.understood.org/en/school-learning/for-educators/empathy/teaching-with-empathy-why-its-important

Otter, M. (2019, August 12). *Designing empathy based professional development that teachers will use.* EdSurge. https://www.edsurge.com/news/2019-08-12-designing-empathy-based-professional-development-that-teachers-will-use

Owen, L. (2015, February 10). *Empathy in the classroom: Why should I care?* https://www.edutopia.org/blog/empathy-classroom-why-should-i-care-lauren-owen

Parchomiuk, M. (2019). Teacher empathy and attitudes towards individuals with disabilities. *International Journal of Disability, Development and Education, 66*(1), 56–69. https://doi:10.1080/1034912X.2018.1460654

Shady, S. L. H., & Larson, M. (2010). Tolerance, empathy, or inclusion? Insights from Martin Buber. *Educational Theory, 60*(1), 81–96. https://doi.org/10.1111/j.1741-5446.2010.00347.x

The Educational Team. (2020, March 26). *Trauma-informed strategies to use in your classroom.* https://resillenteducator.com/

Index

acute trauma   2
adverse childhood experiences   2–4, 8, 11, 12, 14, 15, 95, 169, 170, 173, 176–178, 182
art-based   43, 125, 126, 130, 140

behavioral intervention team   207, 215–219, 221

children's literature   67–76, 81
chronic trauma   2, 3, 12
collaboration   52, 119, 125, 126, 130, 139, 146, 151, 154, 159, 169, 180–183, 185–190, 193–197, 207, 215, 228
commitment   79, 127, 130, 145, 155, 165, 219
complex trauma   2, 3, 7, 9, 12
cross cultural differences   50
cultural competence   18
culturally responsive   VII, 6

death   2–4, 26, 27, 29–36, 38–42, 44–46, 48, 50, 52, 53, 68, 170, 210, 212, 218
dispositions   VIII, 59, 60, 82, 83, 90, 119, 123, 129, 130, 139, 145, 155, 157, 158, 159, 163, 165, 234

empathetic thinking   228, 234
empathy   XII, 15, 63, 70, 71, 76, 83, 85, 127, 211, 214, 226–232, 234–236

families   VII, VIII, XX, XXII, 18, 41, 45–47, 49–52, 60, 62, 65, 68, 76–78, 84, 85, 88, 117, 150, 156, 171–173, 181, 182, 188, 207, 228
fixed mindset   78

Generation Z   XI, 205–207, 213
grief   VII, 26–29, 33–43, 45–53, 218
grieve   X, 26, 27, 35, 36, 47, 50, 52, 53, 151
grit   80, 90
group dynamics   150, 151, 156
growth mindset   65, 66, 77–84, 87–90, 106
guided meditation   65, 66, 82, 85, 109, 110

health care professionals   180, 181, 232
healthcare   18, 180, 181, 231, 232, 234, 236
higher education   VII, 62, 65, 129, 132, 142, 143, 207, 210, 211

inclusion   VIII, 73, 144, 151, 156, 163, 217, 232–234
inclusive   29, 69, 77, 228, 229, 232–234
in-service   227–230
intercultural   VII
intercultural communication   206

macro-traumatic   206
meditation   65, 66, 69–77, 82, 84, 85, 87, 96, 97, 100, 103–106, 108–112
mental health   VII, 2, 3, 8, 9, 11, 12, 15, 37–39, 42–44, 53, 60, 62, 64, 78, 87, 88, 106, 127, 128, 170, 171, 175–177, 180, 183–187, 189, 208, 231
mentoring   152, 153, 156, 157, 160, 220
micro-traumatic   206
mindfulness   X, 13, 16, 63–66, 69–77, 81–85, 88–90, 94, 97, 100–106, 109, 211, 229

novice   228, 229

pandemic   XX–XV, 60–62, 76
pedagogy   XI, 84, 122, 131, 138, 231
post-traumatic stress disorder   40, 177, 210, 212
pre-service   227–229

reflection   VIII, XX, XXIV, 18, 48, 64, 66, 77, 78, 82, 85–87, 109, 130, 136, 137, 145, 156, 157, 164, 166, 212, 226, 231
resilience   X, XI, 1, 5, 65, 69, 76, 81, 87, 89, 90, 101, 172, 179, 211, 214
retraumatization   9, 10, 13, 19, 213

secondary traumatic stress   13–18
self-efficacy   131, 134, 138, 139, 208, 214, 215, 219
self-regulation   9, 12, 62, 64, 78, 86, 102, 107
social and emotional learning   XXII, 17, 101, 102, 108, 109, 230
social-emotional   VII, 9, 62, 67, 86, 102, 108, 119, 120, 160, 182, 184, 226, 228
Solution-Focused Brief Therapy (SFBT)   212
stressors   VII, VIII, 3, 14, 15, 38, 42, 45, 61, 62, 65, 68, 80, 84–86, 89, 95, 99, 150, 157, 170, 173, 175, 208, 226

supports x, 39, 51, 52, 60–66, 69, 77, 80, 83–86, 89, 100, 118, 146, 153, 175, 177, 190, 210

teachers VIII, X, XI, XX–XXV, 6–19, 27, 28, 38, 45–51, 60–66, 68, 69, 76, 78–80, 83–85, 87–89, 96, 97, 101, 102, 104–110, 117–145, 149–167, 172, 177, 178, 186–188, 192, 219, 226–236

trauma VII, X, XI, 1–5, 7–19, 40, 43, 59–61, 63, 67–69, 76–77, 83, 86–90, 94, 96, 107–109, 118, 124, 127, 171–181, 191, 205–208, 210–215, 217–221, 226–229, 231, 233, 236

trauma-informed VII, XII, 1, 11–13, 17–19, 60, 63, 86, 89, 108, 109, 118, 177, 178, 181, 205–208, 210, 212, 218, 219, 221, 226, 229

trauma-sensitive 5, 19, 59–61, 67, 69, 77, 88–90, 206, 213

vicarious trauma 206
virtual XX–XXIV, 230

yoga XI, 16, 65, 66, 75, 82, 85, 87, 94, 96–110, 112